The Naturalist Drama in Germany

To Janet Osborne

John Osborne

The Naturalist Drama
in Germany

Manchester University Press
Rowman and Littlefield, Inc.

© 1971 John Osborne

All rights reserved

Published by
Manchester University Press
316–324 Oxford Road
Manchester MI3 9NR

ISBN 0 7190 0459 4 (U.K.)

U.S.A.
Rowman & Littlefield, Inc.
81 Adams Drive, Totowa
New Jersey, 07512

ISBN 0–87471–027–8 (U.S.A.)

Printed in Great Britain
by W & J Mackay & Co Ltd
Chatham

Contents

Preface

My thanks are due to the editors of *The Modern Language Review*, *Forum for Modern Language Studies*, and *Arcadia*. *Zeitschrift für vergleichende Literaturwissenschaft*, for permission to use material which originally appeared in their pages; and to Hamish Hamilton for permission to quote an extract from Raymond Chandler's novel, *The Lady in the Lake*.

In most of my references to literary works I have found it preferable to quote in German. Where the sense of the German is not evident from the context, I have provided translations. When referring to the work of Gerhart Hauptmann I have, where possible, used the centenary edition: *Sämtliche Werke*, ed. H.-E. Haß, Frankfurt a.M., 1962– . References to this edition take the form of volume and page numbers only.

In writing this book I have profited from the generous help of many colleagues and friends. I owe a very substantial debt to Dr J. P. Stern, whose patient guidance from the earliest stages of the work has been invaluable. I am particularly grateful to Professor J. W. McFarlane and Dr F. J. Stopp for their most helpful criticism of the doctoral thesis out of which this study has emerged. I am also much indebted to Professor Ronald Taylor for his advice, encouragement, and unfailing interest; and to Dr Laci Löb for many constructive comments.

Finally I wish to thank my wife for her assistance in countless ways.

Introduction

The Naturalist period in German literature extends over the last two decades of the nineteenth century, and consists of the work of a body of writers who grew up in Bismarck's Germany. As a literary movement it petered out some time in the 1890s, but its only major dramatist, Gerhart Hauptmann, continued, intermittently, to write in his Naturalist vein beyond the turn of the century. Initially this is all I have to offer by way of a definition. I do not wish to include any writers whom the consensus would exclude, such as Wedekind or Schnitzler; nor do I wish to make yet another special-plea for the exclusion of Gerhart Hauptmann. This study itself is intended as a definition, or rather a description, of what the German Naturalist movement—more particularly the German Naturalist drama—really was. Acceptance of the term Naturalism as the name of this literary movement is to accept a fact of literary history, and has no further implications.

It is rapidly becoming a truism that literature needs to be seen in relation to its social and political background, and it is indeed part of the aim of this study to do just that. The opening chapter is a survey of the reaction of the Naturalists to the preceding generation over a broad front, and it concludes with an examination of the confrontation between fathers and sons over the challenge presented by the work of Zola. The subsequent chapters consider the further development of the Naturalists in three important fields: in the theatre, in the study, and in society. Chapter 2 is concerned primarily with the achievement of the great critic and theatre-director, Otto Brahm, whose importance as one of the founders of the modern European theatre has not been fully acknowledged. Chapter 3 consists of an examination of Naturalist literary theory, concentrating on the theory of Arno Holz, but without too much regard for the many pre-conceptions which can easily cloud our judgement of this theory. Chapter 4 considers the development of the political attitudes of the German Naturalists, particularly their relationship with the Social Democrat movement of their own day. This is an important and neglected aspect of the Naturalist movement, and it contains, in the *Volksbühnen*, a substantial achievement; but, on the whole, it is a story of misunderstanding, distrust, and failure. It is doubly interesting, for it not only throws light on the Naturalist drama, but also on the start of Gustav Landauer's political career; it is here that the historians of the ill-fated Munich Republic of 1919 need to begin.

In our current preoccupation with the background behind literature it is easy to forget that works of literature can be treated as primary phenomena, and are susceptible to evaluation without reference to their origins. While I do not wish to make a stand for purely literary values—and no one who did would choose the German Naturalist drama as the ground on which to make his stand—I do wish to align myself with Karl Jaspers, whose examination of the artistic work of four great schizophrenics contains the warning: 'Geistige Werke existieren zunächst an sich, sind, ohne daß ihre Genese betrachtet wird, in reiner qualitativer Anschauung zugänglich, verstehbar, wertbar.'[1] The second part of this study therefore moves in the opposite direction from the first, starting with the literary works rather than the situation in which they were produced. The basis of this section is provided by the dramas of Gerhart Hauptmann, the only dramatist of the period whose works are substantial enough to warrant intensive critical analysis.

I make no apology for placing Hauptmann so firmly at the centre of this study of German Naturalism, although many of his admirers—and probably Hauptmann himself—would not have wished to see him there; as far as I am concerned this is a private dispute among those critics who regard 'naturalism' as a term of abuse.[2] It may even be true, as Hauptmann's friend, F. A. Voigt, has insisted, that the young Hauptmann was not the 'real' Hauptmann;[3] but this will, perhaps, not mitigate our regret that the 'real' Hauptmann took over, abandoning the restraint of his Naturalist works for the self-indulgence of his lesser-known 'poetic' works.

Notes to the Introduction

[1] Karl Jaspers, *Strindberg und van Gogh: Versuch einer pathographischen Analyse unter vergleichender Heranziehung von Swedenborg und Hölderlin*, Berlin, 1926, p. 85.

[2] Cf. J. W. McFarlane, 'Hauptmann, Ibsen and the concept of Naturalism', *Hauptmann. Centenary Lectures*, ed. K. G. Knight and F. Norman, London, 1964, pp. 31–35.

[3] 'Grundfragen der Gerhart-Hauptmann-Forschung', *Germanisch-Romanische Monatsschrift*, XXVII (1939), pp. 276 f.

PART ONE
Theory and background

I

The first steps to Naturalism

The Naturalist movement in German literature might reasonably be said to have begun in the year 1878. This year saw the appearance of the first of the many literary journals associated with those indefatigable brothers, Heinrich and Julius Hart, the *Deutsche Monatsblätter*. It also saw—and in the long run this was to be of greater significance—the first German performance of Ibsen's social drama, *Pillars of Society*. It would, nevertheless, be wrong to assume a close connection between these two events, and regard this as the beginning of Ibsen's break-through in Germany. It was some time before Ibsen came to be recognized by the German Naturalists as an ideological ally, and some time before they came to regard his dramas of social realism as their model. It is true that in certain quarters (the Harts', for instance) the drama was very soon recognized as the ultimate citadel, but in the early years the aspirations of the Naturalists found more ready expression in the form of criticism and theory, novel and lyric. Despite achieving fairly considerable public success with *Pillars of Society* and *A Doll's House* (which was known in Germany as *Nora*), Ibsen was, until 1887, a neglected dramatist, and the German Naturalists' great foreign model was Zola.

The ten or so years which preceded the real breakthrough of Ibsen (with *Ghosts* in 1887) and Gerhart Hauptmann (with *Vor Sonnenaufgang* in 1889) are a very confused decade. Ten years is probably too long a period for any but the smallest and tightest literary circle to preserve its identity, and the term Naturalism, in the context of German literature, describes a very loose coalition over which no single figure ruled in the manner of a Stefan George. It is only in the early years of the movement, when the principal task is a negative one, that there is any very wide degree of agreement between the factions which went to make up the coalition. Their first task was the overthrow of contemporary idols, and the Harts took this up with the zeal of pioneers, and some polemical skill. Soon they had the support of Otto Brahm, the most perceptive of the Naturalist critics, and the strident chorus of Alberti, Bleibtreu, Conrad, and others. The achievement of these writers is mixed. With the exception of Brahm, their positive contribution to the future of German literature was insignificant. They undoubtedly contributed to, and expressed, a growth of confidence among the younger generation, and, in certain instances they cleared the ground of over-esteemed minor figures—this is especially true of the Hart brothers—but it is easy to be misled by the sound and fury of their polemic into regarding them as genuine revolutionaries. The theory that since the eighteenth century German literature has, very conveniently, behaved like a pendulum, swinging between *Aufklärung* and *Sturm und Drang*, Classicism and Romanticism, is a very misleading, but very tenacious one; and the belief that Naturalism fits into such a pattern (at either end of its life) is in need of considerable qualification.

The period immediately preceding the Naturalist era, the *Gründerzeit*, is a period whose distinct character is now becoming more widely understood. Jost Hermand has quite convincingly demonstrated that there is indeed a certain unity underlying the work of such apparently diverse writers as Nietzsche, Meyer, Heyse, Storm, Anzengruber, Wildenbruch, Spitteler, Wilhelm Jordan, Felix Dahn, Hermann Lingg, Adolf Wilbrandt, Arthur Fitger, Albert Lindner, Franz Nissel, Georg Ebers, Heinrich Kruse, Julius Wolff, Ernst Eckstein, Heinrich Leuthold, Richard Voß, Willhem Jensen, Robert Hamerling, Eduard Grisebach, Graf Schack, and Martin Greif.[1] And I give Hermand's list in full, because—as will emerge from my discussion—this is a curious mixture of writers who were singled out for special praise or special obloquy by one or other of the pioneers of the German Naturalist movement; it is difficult to define German Naturalism in terms of its attitude to its predecessors. The fact that many of the writers named above wrote in a decidedly nationalistic manner, and that some of them *were* subsequently attacked by the self-styled revolutionaries of the next generation, has lent weight to the assumption that they represented a kind of literary establishment in this period. In many respects their work can indeed be seen as a frenetic attempt at self-justification by the new German *Reich*; but behind the great figures who stride through the dramas, epics, and *Novellen* of the *Gründerzeit* there lurks an ill-concealed resentment of the political reality of Bismarck's state, and the place of the artist in it. The typical heroes of this literature are, as Hermand so nicely puts it, 'die großen Einzelnen, die ihren "einsamen Weg" mit "innerer Größe" bis zum "bitteren Ende" gehen';[2] in the face of an increasingly prosperous and increasingly materialistic bourgeoisie, the politically impotent artist finds self-expression in wish-fulfilment, in the fanciful flight into a Utopia, in which the great creative individual grandly asserts himself, with a supreme unconcern for base social reality.

The socialism and the socialist attitudes with which the German Naturalist movement is more usually associated should not blind us to the fact that many of the seemingly incompatible views held by the preceding generation were not jettisoned by the Naturalists; among these were the belief that the artist belongs to an élite, an *Aristokratie des Geistes*, and a certain distaste for political realities and political action. The socialism of the Naturalist writers is itself something which is not fully understood. In fact the Naturalists were never able to find a real home for their political aspirations, and they eventually withdrew from the political scene, muttering the same sort of slogans as the generation of writers they had once criticized.

There is in the literary memoirs of Heinrich Hart considerable evidence of sympathy for the kind of *Gründerzeit* attitudes diagnosed by Hermand. Heinrich Hart claims to have perceived an upsurge of optimism and idealism in German literature around 1870, which was, he says, soon replaced by disappointment, as economic and material interests were seen to be playing a predominant role in the politics of the age.[3] He describes the theatre of this period as particularly empty and imitative, particularly conscious of the box-office; but in other fields of literature he notes the following 'outstanding' works: Wilhelm Jordan's *Nibelungen*, Robert Hamerling's *Ahasver in Rom*, and Heyse's *Kinder der Welt*. The figure whom Heinrich Hart singles out for special criticism, both here and in the earlier *Kritische Waffengänge*, is the Berlin critic and dramatist, Paul Lindau, who remained the Naturalists' principal whipping-boy for some years. Gerhart Hauptmann writes of an encounter with Lindau in 1889 as follows:

Paul Lindau als Novellist, Dramatiker und auch Kritiker war damals wohl der meistgenannte Name in Berlin und der einflußreichste unter den Schriftstellern. Bei uns Jungen—Gott mag wissen warum—war er zugleich der meistgehaßte. Er war, ich habe es später erfahren, durch und durch Liebenswürdigkeit. Er kam bei diesem Diner auf mich zu, schenkte mir laute und herzliche Worte, wünschte Hals- und Beinbruch für meine kommende Aufführung und sagte, er werde die Daumen halten. Wird man es glauben, daß ich, der junge Neuling, dem alten Herrn mit frostigem Hochmut antwortete und gleichsam wie einen begossenen Pudel fortschickte?[4]

Paul Lindau, the writer of *Novellen*, dramas, and criticism, was at that time the most famous name in Berlin, and the most influential man of letters. Among us young men—God alone knows why—he was the most detested. He was, as I discovered later, a thoroughly charming person. He came up to me at this dinner, addressed me cordially, wished me the best of luck for the coming performance of my play, and said he would be keeping his fingers crossed. Is it credible that I, the young novice, answered the respected old man with chilly pride, and sent him away like a naughty schoolboy?

Along with writers like L'Arronge, Lubliner, and Blumenthal, Paul Lindau was the leading exponent of a style of drama which dominated the Berlin theatres from about 1870 onwards; he was seen as the leader of a group of writers whose hold had to be broken before the younger generation could penetrate the theatre. The style these writers cultivated was a moderate social realism; they wrote *pièces à thèse* in the manner of the French dramatists, Dumas *fils*, Augier, and

Scribe, and the young Naturalists had no hesitation in appealing to nationalistic sentiments in their criticism of this foreign influence. The principal feature in the works of these writers was a tendentiousness which sought the causes of personal misery in social conditions and conventions. Lindau explained that in his play *Marion* he wanted to show

wie die vorhandenen Zustände allein genügen, um diesen Untergang herbeizuführen, daß die beiden entscheidenden Faktoren im menschlichen Leben: die Erziehung und die Art und Weise, wie die Ehe geschlossen und die Familie begründet wird, . . . die Lockerung der Familienbande, den sittlichen und auch physischen Untergang des Individuums zur notwendigen Folge haben.[5]

how prevailing conditions alone are enough to bring about this tragedy, that the two decisive factors in human life, education and the way in which marriage is entered into and the family established . . . lead inevitably to the weakening of the family and the moral and physical destruction of the individual.

These works were, it would seem, intended to display that same belief in social determinism which is such a dominant factor in the Naturalists' own writings. What, then, were the young Naturalists' objections?

If, for the moment, we overlook the fact that the Naturalists were by no means uniformly fervent in their adherence to a creed of scientific determinism—and Heinrich Hart, for one, praises Goethe for tempering the modernity of his outlook with what he calls a 'germanisches Urempfinden'—then there remain certain other significant differences between Lindau, Dumas, and the rest, on the one hand, and their Naturalist successors, on the other. The earlier dramatists are decidedly bourgeois dramatists, and the restricted scope of their work seems to imply a conviction that bourgeois conventions and prejudices are indeed the most serious problems in human life. Furthermore, the authenticity of the moral purpose proclaimed by these writers is called into question by their evident reluctance to treat social problems which are less attractive, in a superficially theatrical sense, than that of the 'fallen woman'. Looking back in 1893, Julius Hart wrote:

aus den glänzenden Salons und parfümierten Boudoirs, in denen unsere Alten vor ein und zwei Jahrzehnten daheim waren, flüchtete die Kunst, wie von einem jähen Ekel ergriffen vor der tanzenden, lachenden und soupierenden Welt des 'ancien regime', um in den Hütten der Armen und Unterdrückten einzukehren.[6]

art fled from the elegant salons and perfumed boudoirs, in which our elders were at home ten or twenty years ago, as if seized with a violent disgust for the dancing, laughing, dining-and-wining world of the 'ancien régime', in order to enter the homes of the poor and the oppressed.

When faced as a critic with the working-class drama, *Vater Brahm*, by Heinrich Schaufert, Lindau concedes the gravity of the social problem being treated, but argues that such problems are not the concern of the dramatist. He is satisfied that the minds of the specialists, 'die vornehmsten Geister aller Länder', are being applied to the subject, and is content to leave it to them to find a solution. Such a play, he concludes, is only likely to encourage discontent, and increase class hatred.[7]

This desire to avoid material which might be politically or morally offensive to a theatre-going public in search of undemanding and undisturbing entertainment is an aesthetic principle for which the critic, Lindau, is severely taken to task by Julius Hart in the *Kritische Waffengänge*. Views like these, of course, made Lindau one of Zola's most hostile German critics in the 1880s; and because such views were widely shared by Lindau's generation, they gave rise to a running fight on the subject of art and morality which lasted throughout the Naturalist period.

When, in 1880, the Hart brothers left their native Westphalia to settle in Berlin, they immediately saw themselves in direct confrontation with Lindau. Among the Naturalists they were most consistent in their rejection of Lindau's type of drama, the *pièce à thèse*. Others were less doctrinaire; on occasion Otto Brahm was prepared to praise the skill with which the dramatist presented his thesis, even if he happened to disagree with this; and one German exponent of the form, Richard Voß, was highly regarded by the Munich circle of Naturalists. The form itself was taken over, with little modification, by such Naturalist dramatists as Sudermann and Ludwig Fulda. Although Ibsen's social dramas are immeasurably more original and more powerful, a distinct formal debt to the French salon-drama is still recognizable. In this context it is interesting to note that Lindau, and the social novelist, Friedrich Spielhagen (another writer severely criticized in the *Kritische Waffengänge*), were among the earliest German admirers of *Pillars of Society* and *A Doll's House*, at a time when Otto Brahm was still criticizing Ibsen for his tendentiousness, and the Harts' praises were directed towards the Ibsen of *Brand* and *Peer Gynt*.[8] All of which serves to illustrate my point that there is a modest degree of continuity between the work of the Naturalists and one of the trends they were consciously seeking to displace; it is also a typical illustration of the confusion of the whole period.

After Berlin, the great German literary centre in this period was Munich, and here too the Naturalists made a bid for power, under the leadership of Michael Georg Conrad. In 1885 Conrad founded the literary periodical, *Die Gesellschaft*, which remained the Naturalists' leading organ until the launching of the *Freie Bühne für modernes Leben* in Berlin in 1890. In the Munich of this time the literary tone was set by the *Münchener Dichterschule*, patronized by Maximilian II, and

led by Emanuel Geibel and (after his death) Paul Heyse. Munich was emphatic-
ally the home of the grand style in literature and the theatre; the historical drama
and the historical epic were the genres especially favoured. Now in this context
historical drama does not mean the drama of Hebbel, nor does historical epic
mean something which resembles Freytag's *Bilder aus der deutschen Vergangen-
heit* or Riehl's *Die deutsche Arbeit*. Hebbel's historical dramas, particularly
Agnes Bernauer, may be said to correspond to the historiography of the Hegel-
Ranke school, in that they are concerned predominantly with the state, or the
great individual as the embodiment of the state. The withdrawal of a disillusioned
bourgeoisie from political activity in the years after 1848 was accompanied by a
decline of interest in ideological history, and this is at least one probable reason
for the neglect of Hebbel's work during his own lifetime. In the first instance
ideological history is replaced by the 'non-political', cultural history, as the
middle classes seek some consolation for political failure; in the words of Riehl:
'in den 50er Jahren waren Volkstudien sehr beliebt und begünstigt, weil das
staatliche Leben so matt und müde und die politische Erörterung so aussichtslos
war. Man tröstete sich mit dem Volke, um für den Staat die Hoffnung nicht zu
verlieren.'[9] Romantic, conservative, and selective they may be, but Freytag and
Riehl are concerned to depict a definite social reality, in fairly considerable detail.
This is not true of the historical literature of the *Gründerzeit*; the great heroes do
not face political dilemmas, and they are not placed in any real historical context;
they strike the sublime attitude of truth to their own inner selves in a world
chosen primarily for its spectacular quality.[10] Thus Lindau criticizes *Die Nibelungen* precisely because Hebbel's figures aspire to representative (i.e. political)
grandeur, contrasting it unfavourably with Geibel's *Brunhild*, in which the
historical-political dimension is submerged in a story of love and jealousy; and
Heinrich Laube, the director of the *Burgtheater*, attributes Hebbel's failure to a
lack of visual splendour, for this was an age which liked to see its history presented
as in the paintings of Piloty, 'großzügig, dekorativ, stark aufgetragen und effekt-
voll'.[11]

The weakness of the *Gründerzeit* for the superficially decorative, for painters
such as Makart, Piloty, and Kaulbach, was nowhere more evident than in the
field of theatrical production. The Meiningen Court Theatre, of which I shall
have more to say, owed much of its popularity to this weakness. This was a period
which saw and encouraged rapid advances in the skills and techniques of theatrical
decoration; much was imported into Germany from London's Princess Theatre,
where Charles Kean had been the director. Theodor Fontane, who as theatre-
critic of the *Vossische Zeitung* had visited the London theatres, wrote of the
meticulous accuracy which was the dominant principle behind Kean's productions,

suggesting in a mildly ironic fashion that accuracy in such matters is often less relevant than visual effect. At the *Burgtheater* Laube had been regarded as something of a Spartan in such matters; his views on Hebbel make it clear that he did value the visual side of theatrical production, and he is said to have paid a great deal of attention to such things as the visual effect of groups of actors (he favoured the semicircular grouping of less important figures around the central character in a given scene, and made frequent use of steps or raised platforms); nevertheless Laube had always stopped short of elaborate decorations, feeling that they could distract the audience from the words of the dramatist. In 1876 the *Burgtheater* was taken over by Franz von Dingelstedt, who, as director of the *Hoftheater*, had been closely associated with the *Münchener Dichterschule*. With his arrival the decorative style took over in Vienna. In acting, as in production, the emphasis seems to have been on externals; Fontane wrote that Klara Ziegler 'acted Kaulbach'; and the theatre-historian, Max Martersteig, has described the Viennese actress, Charlotte Wolter, in similar terms: 'sie bot ein Wiederaufleben des klassischen Ideals der Bildnerei—aber nun in Makarts Kolorit getaucht; die schöne Pose war ihr sieghaftestes Mittel'.[12]

Once again it is a gross oversimplification to pretend that the young Naturalists responded to this trend with outright rejection. On the one hand there is the critic, Karl Bleibtreu, who attacks in the most outspoken manner the historical school: 'Unsre gesund realistische Zeit verlangt vom historischen Roman Richtigkeit à outrance. Die Folge davon ist . . ., daß ein Pseudodichter durch Kultivierung des Kostüms uns über die Mängel seiner Afterpoesie wegzutäuschen versucht' ('Our healthy realistic age demands rigorous accuracy from the historical novel. The result of this is . . . that pseudo-poets try to exploit costume in order to cover up the deficiencies of their sham-poetry');[13] on the other hand there is the dramatist, Karl Bleibtreu, who cultivates the genre, historical drama, with undiminished enthusiasm in such plays as *Harold der Sachse*, *Ein Faust der Tat*, *Das Halsband der Königin*, and *Schicksal*. Among the Berliners Otto Brahm and Arno Holz were declared admirers of Heyse and Geibel respectively; whilst Gerhart Hauptmann was strongly influenced by Felix Dahn and Wilhelm Jordan, and his early drama, *Germanen und Römer*, was very much in their style. In *Vor Sonnenaufgang*, it will be recalled, Dahn's *Kampf um Rom* is recommended by Loth to Helene as more worthy of her attention than the work of Zola and Ibsen. There is good reason to believe that this had been Hauptmann's own view in the 1880s.[14] The subject matter of the historical drama of the early Naturalist period does, however, reflect a change of outlook. A renewed political interest, which was centred on class conflicts, makes the French Revolution (Bleibtreu's *Weltgericht*; Franz Held's *Ein Fest auf der Bastille*) and the Peasants' War

(Conrad Alberti's *Brot*; Julius Brand's *Thomas Münzer*; and, later, Hauptmann's *Florian Geyer*) the most favoured topics. But the motive forces operating in these dramas still tend to be the individual passions. In Alberti's play (as in Conrad Ferdinand Meyer's story, *Der Heilige*) the historical conflict is subordinate to the romantic theme, the love of Thomas Münzer and Gerlind.

It is hardly necessary to emphasize that German unification and national pride at the outcome of the Franco-Prussian war tended to foster the creation of a national tradition, and so the cult of the historical drama. As I have already suggested, certain of the young Naturalists were not unaffected by such pride, among them Heinrich and Julius Hart (Heinrich Hart did, in fact, write a drama entitled *Sedan*). Their early agitations, which herald the beginnings of the German Naturalist movement, are an open statement of their disappointment that the national revival seemed to lack a spiritual dimension; in their more pedestrian way they, like Nietzsche, lament 'die Niederlage, ja Exstirpation des deutschen Geistes zugunsten des "deutschen Reiches" '. It is a strange accident of literary history that the Harts, and a number of German writers like them, should have come to be associated with a movement so international in character as Naturalism, for their nationalism is more than skin-deep, more than just a stick with which to beat Paul Lindau and the epigones of the French salon-dramatists. The open letter which appeared, addressed to Bismarck, in the *Kritische Waffengänge* of 1882 declares: 'wie jedes andere Gebiet, so muß auch die Literatur auf dem nationalen Staat basiren und aus seiner Kraft die ihre saugen'. Nationalist criteria are an important factor in their literary judgement, responsible for their praise of the work of Graf Schack, and the dramas of Ernst von Wildenbruch—which many detached observers might regard as another symptom of that spiritual decline of which Nietzsche complains. Nationalism is equally in evidence among the Munich writers, Bleibtreu, Conradi, and Conrad, who frequently criticized the internationalism of the *Freie Bühne*. Through one of its regular contributors, the anti-semitic Fritz Lienhardt, the periodical, *Die Gesellschaft*, is linked with the development of *Heimatkunst*; and Conrad, it appears, was one of the first to raise the subsequently notorious cry for a literature based on 'Blut und Boden'.[15] Conrad Alberti, a prominent member of this circle, and himself a Jew, argues in the pages of *Die Gesellschaft* for the complete assimilation of the Jews into the German nation—'rückhaltlos aufgehen im Deutschtum'—and conducts his argument in a particularly virulent anti-semitic tone.[16] We need not here concern ourselves further with this particular tendency, except to remark that the movement we know as German Naturalism contains elements which we do not normally associate with European Naturalism, and that in this respect German Naturalism is decidedly untrue to the spirit of one of its masters, Émile Zola.

Among the theatres which cultivated the historical-decorative style a very special place is occupied by the *Herzoglich-Meiningensches Hoftheater* (the Meiningen Court Theatre); indeed, this theatre occupies a very special place in the development of the modern European theatre, and deserves considerable attention in its own right.[17] In 1866 Herzog Georg II von Sachsen-Meiningen came to power. The Duke was a devotee of the *Museumskultur* of his age, but he was also a man of considerable natural artistic talent, and was passionately interested in the theatre, which he himself proceeded to run, with the assistance of his wife (a former actress), and the director, Ludwig Chronegk. In the first instance the contribution of the Duke himself won the company its reputation; it became renowned for the splendour and authenticity of its costume and décor; in Moscow Chronegk was heard to complain: 'I brought them Shakespeare, Schiller and Molière, and they are interested in the furniture.'[18] But the company's real importance lay in its use of all the fashionable paraphernalia to implement a radical reform in theatrical production. The Court Theatre of a small state could scarcely afford the services of the best-known star actors of the day, but this deficiency was turned to good account, for Chronegk was forced to look elsewhere than to individual talents for his successes. He was able to assume the function of the modern director, assert his authority over his actors, and approach the drama as an organic whole, rather than as a vehicle for a star performer. In particular he concentrated his attention on ensemble-playing and crowd-scenes, where he used professional actors and not, as was customary, off-duty soldiers or other makeshift personnel. This is not to say that the company never employed first-rate actors—when on tour they would engage well-known performers like Ludwig Barnay or Friedrich Mitterwurzer, and for a time the young Josef Kainz was a member of the company (although this was before he became famous)—but in general their successes seem to have been greater in those plays or scenes where stage-direction could conceal or compensate for the performers' inadequacies. Stanislavsky wrote of their Moscow performance of *Die Jungfrau von Orleans*: 'The stage-director thickened the atmosphere of the defeated court so that the spectator waits impatiently for the coming of the Maid, and he is so glad when she does come that he does not notice the cheap acting of the woman who uses the worst stage methods . . ., rolling her eyes and giving vent to vocal fireworks'.[19]

The repertoire of the company bears out this impression. Among their most popular productions were *Julius Caesar* and *A Winter's Tale*; Schiller's plays, especially *Wallenstein* and *Wilhelm Tell*, figure prominently; and the company did a great deal to popularize the work of Kleist, with their productions of *Die Hermannsschlacht*, *Das Käthchen von Heilbronn*, and *Prinz Friedrich von Homburg*.

As this cursory glance at their repertoire indicates, the Meiningen Court Theatre was a company whose importance lies in the field of theatre history. They introduced very few new works to the public (though among those they did introduce were Ibsen's *The Pretenders* and *Ghosts*), but concentrated on the serious, classical drama, at a time when the public theatre was given over to rather more frivolous fare. The manner of their presentation, and the scope of their influence are more important than the plays they produced.

This influence was very largely won by the *Gastspielreisen* which the company undertook between 1874 and 1890, which took them as far afield as London, Moscow, New York, Prague, and Copenhagen, as well as to many German and Austrian cities. In the 1880s their style was recognized to be having considerable influence on the theatres of Berlin, especially L'Arronge's new *Deutsches Theater*.[20] In Vienna, where Dingelstedt had introduced the more superficial and spectacular elements of the style, the company had less impact, and this may be one reason why Naturalism was slow to overcome the resistance of the Austrian capital; the ground had been less well prepared. Of much greater moment was the long-term influence of the Meiningen theatre on Stanislavsky and, in the German theatre, Otto Brahm. These two men, the great Naturalist directors, are the direct heirs of the authoritarian Chronegk, but they were committed to a *literary* tendency in a way he was not. As Naturalists they carried to its logical conclusion a process of which their predecessor—if his repertoire is anything to go by—had only a dim awareness. They applied his style to new subject matter in such a way as to show that the day of the great star-performer, the great individual, was past; in the Naturalist drama the hero is no longer an eloquent, articulate figure, capable of comprehending his own destiny, but is subordinate to external forces beyond his control; he is subordinate to the milieu represented in the stage-set. The Naturalists went further than the Meiningen company in establishing real relationships between setting and action, in accordance with contemporary theories of determinism, over and above the purely atmospheric or symbolic reflection of the action in a visually appropriate set.

The belief in determinism is widely and, I believe, correctly regarded as one of the key features of Naturalist theory; it is a conviction which grew very rapidly in the latter part of the nineteenth century. One field in which this growth can readily be traced is the field of historiography. Hegel can be seen as standing at the turning-point between an Idealist view of history which saw an *Idee* behind historical phenomena and actions, and a Materialist view, which tended to explain historical change by external reasons, *Ideen* by *Sein*. I have already spoken briefly of the development of cultural history in the post-1848 period, by such writers as Freytag and Riehl. The methods of such historians could readily be carried into other territories; and though, with few exceptions, literature held out for a while, there arose rapidly a school of historians who began to concentrate on the investigation of material causation. Marx's influence made economics a particularly important field of study, and in the 1870s Roscher, Schmoller, and Inama-Sternegg wrote and lectured on the economic history of Germany. In a wider European context the ideas of Taine, Comte, and Buckle are of similar importance.

The advance of cultural history did not proceed without any resistance; there was, for instance, the Gothein-Schäfer controversy of 1888–91; and Karl Lamprecht's *Deutsche Geschichte* (1891) met with some severe criticism.[21] On the whole, though, the study of history seems to have passed more smoothly through this period; the historians seem to have been more progressive and tolerant of new ideas than many of the literary historians and critics.

The treatment of the revolt of the Silesian weavers in 1844 provides an interesting parallel case. Hauptmann's *Die Weber*, completed in 1892, split the literary world into two camps, progressives and reactionaries; the play was not released for unhindered public performance until after the turn of the century. Yet this same weavers' revolt had for some time been a respectable subject of historical investigation. In 1873 Gustav Schmoller had written a study of the weaving industry which covered it; and in 1885 a pupil of Schmoller, Alfred Zimmermann, published his study, *Blüthe und Verfall des Leinengewerbes in Schlesien*, from which Hauptmann drew extensively in writing his play. Both historians are somewhat less equivocal than Hauptmann about the apportionment of blame: Schmoller expresses the view

> that the crisis was much more serious and severe than it need have been, that it was not brought about solely by irresistible forces, and that, if there can be any question of guilt, this does not reside with the individual weaver, but is to be sought in those higher circles where there were people better placed than the weavers to see the true situation;

and Zimmermann quite explicitly attributes the revolt to conditions rather than people:

> The unreasonableness of the manufacturers, together with the rapidly rising cost of food, had caused a great deal of bad feeling in the Reichenbach area. . . . Industrial progress . . . had brought along with it the evils of mass-industry, particularly since there was no factory act to impose restraint on the capitalists.[22]

Both these accounts and Hauptmann's play make an interesting contrast with the reports which had appeared in the *Vossische Zeitung* of 1844. Here the weavers' revolt is attributed to such things as hatred, the desire for vengeance, the effects of alcohol, the stubborn insolence of the Langenbielau workers, and discontent caused by agitators; the report dated June 10 asserts: 'As far as anyone can see, there is no deeper basis for these disturbances.'

The comparison between a professional social historian of 1885 and a conservative journalist of 1844 exaggerates the change of outlook which took place in the intervening years, but change there undoubtedly was. Where the two sides are not simply indulging in empty abuse, these changes are what the controversy surrounding the emergence of Naturalism is about. The younger generation of writers begins to display a scepticism about the accuracy of the picture of reality presented by its elders in their literary work. The older, idealist generation continues, for its part, to reject the principles of the new positivist thought, protesting that it takes insufficient account of the freedom of the will, and treats Man as if he were on the same level as animals. The older generation demands that such a pessimistic view of life should be excluded from the field of art; Johannes Volkelt, a generally tolerant academic critic (and a student of Schopenhauer), insists that the primary purpose of art is the manifold and exhaustive representation of that which is of human significance, 'das Menschlich-Bedeutungsvolle', and he goes on to specify that it should not therefore merely demonstrate material causation, 'naturgesetzliche Verknüpfungen'.[23] The younger generation protests that this kind of selectivity excludes whole areas of life where such causation is believed to be of major importance; and not surprisingly these, the areas which contain the great social problems of the day, are the areas which most interest the Naturalist writers. Bleibtreu voices the typical protest: 'Es ist, als wären die furchtbaren sozialen Fragen für die deutschen Dichter gar nicht vorhanden.'[24]

One of the first tasks of the Naturalist theorists, then, was to overcome prejudices against certain types of material. The aesthetic and moral objections raised by the various critics of Naturalism are countered, time and again, with an appeal to 'Truth'; sometimes with an appeal to Goethe's statement that no material is intrinsically unpoetic: 'Was der Dichter darstellt ist ganz gleichgültig . . . die Tatsache, daß kein Stoff, auch der unsittliche und gemeine nicht, an und für sich undichterisch ist, bleibt . . . zu Recht bestehen'; and occasionally a writer will go further than this, and defend an author's right to be gratuitously provocative:

Beleidigt Zola in seinen Romanen unser angeborenes Anstandsgefühl, auch dort, wo es die Dichtung nicht verlangt, aus bloßem Mutwillen, so kann ich ihn für einen ungehobelten, ungebildeten Menschen halten und für was sonst noch,

If, in his novels, Zola offends our innate sense of decency, even when it is not artistically necessary, out of sheer wantonness, then I can consider him a coarse and uncultured man, and much else besides—but it does not lessen his

—aber seine dichterische Bedeutung schmälert das in keiner Weise, der dichterische Wert des Romans wird dadurch in nichts gedrückt.[25]

aesthetic importance by one jot, the aesthetic merit of the novel is in no way reduced.

This pronounced emphasis on the subject-matter of the work of art is typical of early Naturalist theory—just as a certain sensationalism in the choice of material is typical of the practice—but it is not really typical of the Harts, who were in no sense and at no time radical representatives of the newer literary trends. They still consciously preserve a residue of the idealist tradition, and will not see it replaced by scientific rationalism:

Wir müssen wieder anknüpfen an den jungen Goethe, den Schöpfer des *Werther* und *Faust*, denn da ist nicht nur Wahrheit wie bei Zola, da ist poesiegetränkte Wahrheit. Nur dann wird unsere Poesie die rechte Mitte finden zwischen erdfrischem Realismus und hoher Idealität, zwischen kosmopolitischer Humanität und selbstbewußtem Nationalismus . . . nur dann wird sie das Höchste erreichen, nämlich aus dem vollen Born der Gegenwart schöpfend ursprüngliche, individuell gefärbte Natur zum Ideal verklären.[26]

We must look back again to the young Goethe, the creator of *Werther* and *Faust*, for there one finds not only truth, as in Zola, but truth imbued with poetry. Only then will our literature find the middle way between fresh, earthbound realism and high idealism, between cosmopolitan humanity and self-assured nationalism . . . only then will it reach the summit of artistic achievement and, drawing from the source of the present, transfigure original, individual nature to an ideal.

In the later years of Naturalism Heinrich and Julius Hart still remain true to their *Idealrealismus*, dissociating themselves from what they regarded as the extreme theories of Arno Holz, and the rigid policy of Otto Brahm at the *Deutsches Theater*; and in the 1890s they eagerly embraced the new 'subjectivism' or 'impressionism' practised by such writers as Dehmel, Bierbaum, Liliencron, Arne Garborg, and Przybyszewski:

In diesem Kreise regten sich zuerst oder doch wenigstens am stärksten und nachhaltigsten jene Stimmungen, welche über die Epoche des Naturalismus, Pessimismus und Sozialismus hinausstrebten. Man hatte sie satt, übersatt, die graue Nüchternheit der Elendsliteratur, die engbrüstige Moral der Massenprediger, den herrschenden Rationalismus und die herrschende Politisiererei.[27]

It was in this circle that there were the first, or at least the most powerful and enduring stirrings of the desire to overcome the epoch of naturalism, pessimism, and socialism. They had had enough, more than enough, of the drab solemnity of the literature of misery, the narrow moralizing of the mass-preachers, the dominance of rationalism and the dominance of politics.

The cautious and basically conservative attitude of the *Kritische Waffengänge* is widely shared in the early 1880s. In 1882 Brahm expresses much the same reservations about the interrelationship of science and literature and, far from proclaiming a rigid, doctrinaire Naturalism, he rather timidly advances Gottfried Keller as a model for the writers of the future:

Die Vereinigung dieser beiden Elemente, des Realistischen und des Phantastischen, macht den hervorstechenden Zug in Kellers Wesen aus. Hier liegt der Weg, welchen die Dichtung der Zukunft wird beschreiten müssen, wenn sie sich nicht einseitig bescheiden will, entweder auf das spezifisch 'Poetische' zu verzichten, oder auf die Gestaltung des spezifisch 'Modernen'.[28]

The combination of these two elements, the realistic and the fantastic, constitutes Keller's most prominent characteristic. This is the way that the literature of the future will have to go if it is not to make a one-sided renunciation of the specifically 'poetic' or of the specifically 'modern'.

The common concern among the more thoughtful representatives of the pro- and anti-Naturalist camps (among whom I would include Brahm, Volkelt, and Heinrich Hart) is the problem of art in an increasingly scientific climate, and the question of whether it can be preserved both as art and as a vehicle of truth. As confidence in biological, psychological, and sociological diagnoses increases, as the scientist becomes surer of his ability to discover the laws of the universe, the artist feels called upon to justify his *imaginative* creation, to ask himself the sort of questions Schiller (for instance) was asking himself a century earlier, and in a similar climate of scientific and philosophical discovery: 'Was kann die Dichtung für die moderne Welt noch bedeuten?'[29] The answer which is widely regarded as the Naturalist answer is that, to be meaningful, art must assimilate the techniques of the sciences. Such a view is incorporated in many of the programmatic writings of this period; in his introduction to *Die naturwissenschaftlichen Grundlagen der Poesie* (1887) Wilhelm Bölsche asserts: 'was ich von dem aufwachsenden Dichtergeschlecht fordere und hoffe, ist eine geschickte Betätigung besseren Wissens auf psychologischem Gebiete, besserer Beobachtung, gesunderen Empfindens, und die Grundlage dazu ist Fühlung mit den Naturwissenschaften'. Nevertheless the discussion which surrounds this issue deserves a closer scrutiny, for it tells us a good deal about the uncertainties of the German Naturalists, and the conflict between their theoretical confidence in science and their more traditional beliefs.

The basis to the discussion about the relationship of literature and science, as indeed the Naturalist answer to the problem, is provided by Zola, in *Le roman expérimental*. Now the simplified view that German resistance to Zola came only from the older generation is a mistaken one, for many of the younger writers had immense difficulty in coming to terms with his works and theories. In the essay 'Für und gegen Zola' Heinrich Hart explains the scientific emphasis in Zola's theory as a reaction against the excesses of French Romanticism; this analysis is quite erroneous, for while Zola did reject Romanticism, he also praised the movement for its contribution to artistic freedom, and so for its contribution to the development of Naturalism ('le drame romantique est un premier pas vers le drame naturaliste auquel nous marchons');[30] Heinrich Hart goes on to argue that the German literary tradition (and presumably German Romanticism) would not have called forth in Zola so violent a reaction, that it is likely to exclude the spiritual dimension from literature altogether:

Geschichtlich ist die Entstehung des französischen Naturalismus leicht erfaßlich, er ist aus dem bewußten Widerstreben gegen die Romantik, gegen die Unwahrheit und den Schwulst der Viktor Hugo, Dumas, Sue, hervorgegangen, aber die Reaktion ist so stark, daß die Literatur in Gefahr steht, unmittelbar in das entgegengesetzte System geworfen zu werden und auf diese Weise wiederum neue Lügen und statt des Schwulstes Flachheit zu gebären.	Historically the development of French Naturalism is easy to understand. It arose from the conscious reaction against Romanticism, against the lies and the bombast of Victor Hugo, Dumas, Sue; but the reaction has been so violent that literature is in danger of falling directly into the opposite extreme of telling new lies and, in place of bombast, producing dullness.

Heinrich Hart attacks Zola's theory of the experimental novel—which is at best a metaphor, at worst a polemic over-statement—with a curious literal-mindedness. Not without a certain *Schadenfreude*, he invokes the authority of Claude Bernard (whose *Introduction a l'étude de la médecine expérimentale* had prompted *Le roman expérimental*) to support his view that an experimental novel is an impossibility: 'Pour les arts et les lettres la personnalité domine tout. Il s'agit là d'une création spontanée de l'esprit, et cela n'a rien de commun avec la constatation des phénomènes naturels, dans lesquels notre esprit ne doit rien créer' ('In art and literature personality is dominant. A work of art is a spontaneous spiritual creation and that has nothing to do with the verification of natural phenomena, in which we can have no creative role'). He argues *both* that the novel can never be an experiment in the scientific sense, *and* that such novels are, in any case undesirable: 'Die Wissenschaft sucht das Allgemeine aus dem Individuellen heraus zu extrahieren und in Begriffe aufzulösen; der Roman und nicht minder die Poesie überhaupt sucht im Individuellen das Allgemeine darzustellen und in Formen zu verkörpern' ('Science seeks to abstract the general from the particular and express it in concepts; the novel, and, no less, literature on the whole, attempts to represent the general in the particular, and to incorporate it in forms').[31]

In all this Heinrich Hart does not differ radically from the more traditional critic, Karl Hillebrand (the father of the Naturalist writer, Julius Brand). Writing on the subject of the new, scientific novel in the *Deutsche Rundschau* (1884) Hillebrand declares that whereas science seeks causal relationships, ignores individuality in order to discover the operation of general laws, art tries to reproduce life in its individuality, eliminates the abstract generality in order to understand better the particular, and eliminates chance in order to grasp the essential.[32]

Heinrich Hart's own appreciation of the traditions of French and German literature may appear limited, but he is right to insist that the theoretical views of any writer should be seen against the background of his tradition. The similarity between the views of Heinrich Hart and Hillebrand is not accidental, but it is the product of a literary tradition which, a generation earlier, had borne fruit in Otto Ludwig's theory of 'Poetic Realism', a form of art midway between Naturalism and Idealism, which was to re-create the world by purging it of irrelevance and making its essential unity more visible than in the real world; a kind of art which is not yet fantastic, but which owes *more* to the creative imagination than to 'mere reason'.[33] Like Ludwig—and of course Schiller—Heinrich Hart and Hillebrand share the prejudice that Naturalism (and perhaps even Nature itself) is essentially base, and needs desperately to be refined by the artistic imagination.

Both these critics assert that there is a discrepancy between Zola's theory and practice, that there must *a priori* be this discrepancy; nevertheless they do criticize parts of Zola's work as if there were no discrepancy, and it really were scientific. Where they do speak of a discrepancy, they do not illuminate this with any appreciation of Zola's creative personality. Among Zola's more receptive German critics there is, however, an increasing tendency to recognize in him a strong imaginative personality, and to admire him for this (though without always clearly saying so).[34] That is to say Zola's German followers come to adopt a view—'une œuvre d'art est une personnalité, une individualité'—that is as much a part of Zola's personal conviction as his more famous Naturalist doctrine, but which, in a flush of enthusiasm for science, he rather played down in his reflections on the experimental novel.[35] One of the reasons for this inconsistency in Zola's theory lies in his very personality, his enormous reserves of creative energy, which consistently well up in descriptive spectacle throughout his novels, unchecked by the inhibitions of a critical intellect. Some of Zola's qualities are shared by the man who worked most energetically as his German proselytizer,

Michael Georg Conrad. In his newly-founded *Die Gesellschaft*, Conrad defends Zola's theory of the experimental novel, but the tone in which he writes of Zola effectively converts the theoretical ideal of scientific objectivity into the moral quality of fearless personal integrity:

> Zola ist die personifizierte Aufrichtigkeit, der Freimut à outrance. Nicht zufrieden mit den tausend Schwierigkeiten der delikatesten sachlichen Probleme, tritt sein ungestümer Reformdrang auch an die empfindlichsten Personalfragen heran. Er kennt nur ein Heiliges und Unverletzliches: die Wahrheit.[36]

> Zola is integrity personified, he represents the extreme of outspokenness. Not content with the thousand difficulties of the most delicate technical problems, his violent desire for reform also leads him to tackle the most sensitive personal problems. He recognizes only one thing as sacred and inviolable: the truth.

In 1886 Georg Brandes, the Danish critic (and a figure who exerted an immense influence on the development of German literature at the end of the nineteenth century), published in the *Deutsche Rundschau* an important essay in which he intelligently clarified the position of those who admired the personal rather than the scientific elements in Zola's works. Unlike Heinrich Hart, Brandes did not claim to perceive a discrepancy between theory and practice, but seized on the word 'temperament' in Zola's famous definition of the work of art as 'un coin de la nature vu a travers un tempérament', and made this, the personal contribution of the individual creative artist, the focus of critical attention. His analysis of Zola's writings leads to a diagnosis of Zola's 'romantic' temperament; Brandes draws attention to the French novelist's love of the epic, the grandiose, the monumental, his simplification of characters to make them representatives of various social groups, his use of symbols, his taste for personification. The idea of Zola, the Naturalist, as an impersonal, scientific, objective observer and recorder of external reality, hindered in his aims only by a minimal 'temperament', is seriously undermined:

> Die Frage ist . . . ob nicht das, was jetzt Temperament genannt wird, ganz wie das, was vorher der Geschmack, später die Phantasie genannt wurde, läutert und beschnidet, vergrößert und verschönert? . . . Die Antwort muß lauten: daß auch nicht der Naturalismus jener Umbildung der Wirklichkeit entgehen kann, die sich aus dem Wesen der Kunst ergibt.[37]

> The question is . . . whether that which is now called temperament, just like what was once called taste, later imagination, does not refine and condense, magnify and beautify? . . . The answer must be that Naturalism too cannot avoid that re-shaping of reality which is an essential feature of art.

The consequence of this change of emphasis was to hasten the transformation of what had been generally (and sometimes distrustfully) regarded as a stringently realist credo into a sanction for the completely subjective interpretation of nature. A subsequent chapter will show how this transformation is mirrored in the theoretical writings of Arno Holz, which date from the time when German Naturalism was beginning to stress observation less, and individual imagination very much more. While this transformation was not of course confined to the German literary scene—in France it was to lead to views like Proust's 'Le monde . . . n'a pas été créé une fois, mais aussi souvent qu'un artiste original est survenu'[38]—it was particularly welcome in Germany as a continuation of the literary tradition of which I have spoken; and whereas in other European countries this new emphasis on the imagination was a post-Naturalist trend, in Germany, it is especially important to note, the Naturalist movement did not really get under way as a creative literary movement, did not begin to produce works of literature that are in the slightest degree memorable, until after the theoretical insistence on the observed realities of the social world had been somewhat diluted. In Germany even Naturalism, far from being stricter than elsewhere, as has often been asserted, displays that tendency to dissociation from the social world which has been shown to be a recurrent characteristic in the literature of that country.[39]

To reach a full understanding of German Naturalism it is essential to realize that the ambiguities and contradictions of the movement cannot conveniently be reduced to the inevitable discrepancy between impossibly rigorous theoretical demands and the limitations of any artistic medium, between 'Nature' and 'Art', but that the ambiguities represent a genuine reluctance to embrace fully certain new views which are found intellectually attractive. One of the characteristics of the German Naturalist movement which is least widely appreciated is that this dilemma is resolved in the way which might be felt to be less likely: it is resolved in favour of the artist rather than the scientist. Even Bölsche's *Die naturwissenschaftlichen Grundlagen der Poesie*, which is presented as an apology for the scientific approach in art, leaves an opening for an artistic resolution. In a way which distantly recalls Nietzsche's admiration of the strong and healthy, his replacement of a transcendental deity with the concept of the Superman, Bölsche proclaims a new object for essentially imaginative idealization (which was soon to find a champion in Hauptmann's character Alfred Loth):

Wir haben gebrochen mit der Metaphysik . . . das Ideal geben wir doch nicht auf. Wenn es nicht mehr der Abglanz des Göttlichen sein darf, so ist ihm darum nicht benommen, die Blüte des Irdischen zu sein, die tiefste, reinste Summe, die der Mensch ziehen kann

We have broken with metaphysics . . . but we are not renouncing ideals. If our ideal may no longer be the reflection of the divine, then there is no reason why it should not be the fullness of the earthly, the purest and profoundest sum of all that man can see. . . . When he casts

aus allem, was er sieht. . . . Wenn er den Blick schweifen läßt über diese ganze Erde, über sein ganzes Geisterreich, so sieht er im Grunde all' dieser wechselnden Formen ein einziges großes Prinzip, nach dem alles strebt, alles ringt: das gesicherte Gleichmaß, die fest in beiden Schaalen schwebende Wage, den Zustand des Normalen, die Gesundheit.

his eyes over this whole earth, over his entire spiritual realm, he sees at the root of all these changing forms one single great principle, which all is striving to secure: equilibrium, the exactly balanced scales, the state of normality, health.

While this new 'realist ideal' may not be created by the imagination of the artist, he has nevertheless the special function of bringing it into the open: 'es muß heißen, den idealen Faden, den fortwirkenden Hang zum Glücke und zur Gesundheit, der an allem Vorhandenen haftet, durch eine gewisse Behandlung deutlicher herausleuchten zu lassen'.[40] Wolfgang Kirchbach's reflections on this theme lead to a similar conclusion, in which a religious or metaphysical *need* is more clearly accepted; the purpose of literature is to endow an apparently mechanical and senseless world with value and beauty, and so counteract the contemporary tendency to cynicism and nihilism.

We shall encounter this same attitude in Gerhart Hauptmann's *Das Friedensfest*, in which an old-fashioned idealist (and an artist), Wilhelm Scholz, is favourably contrasted with a cynical, modern intellectual, his brother, Robert; and in the drama, *Marianne*, by Carl Hauptmann (a pupil and friend of the biologist, Ernst Haeckel, and a writer deeply involved in the scientific and religious discussions of the day). In this play of 1894 the romanticism, which was only implicit in the theoretical works to which I have referred, becomes explicit; *Marianne* dwells very much on the distinction between the artist, with his sense of wonder ('wir denken an das Wunder—um uns—und in uns!') and the philistine, and on the duty of the gifted individual to cultivate his own imaginative potentiality regardless of others; such special-pleading is a common feature of the literature of this period.

Up to about 1887, and notwithstanding the reservations I have already made, Zola undoubtedly exerted the most powerful influence on the German Naturalist writers. Among the most obvious consequences of this was a concentration on the novel rather than the drama; this trend was also helped by the tolerance of publishers like W. Friedrich of Leipzig (the theatre-directors offered much greater resistance). These years were therefore one of the few periods in German literature when the urban novel was among the most favoured genres—although the specifically Naturalist examples are rather undistinguished: Conrad's cycle, *Was die Isar rauscht*, Max Kretzer's *Die Betrogenen* and *Die Verkommenen*, Alberti's *Riesen und Zwerge*, Bleibtreu's *Größenwahn*. But in Berlin things had been happening which were soon to change all this. A power-base was gradually being established, and in Ibsen a champion had been found who was to lead Naturalism into the theatre.

Notes to Chapter I

[1] Jost Hermand, 'Zur Literatur der Gründerzeit', *Deutsche Vierteljahrsschrift für Literaturwissenschaft und Geistesgeschichte*, XLI (1967), p. 204. See also Richard Hammann und Jost Hermand, *Gründerzeit. Deutsche Kunst und Kultur von der Gründerzeit bis zum Expressionismus*, Bd 1, Berlin, 1965.

[2] Hermand, op. cit., p. 213.

[3] 'Literarische Erinnerungen. 1880–1905', *Gesammelte Werke*, Berlin, 1907, III, 27 ff.

[4] 'Das zweite Vierteljahrhundert', *Die großen Beichten*, Frankfurt a.M., 1966, p. 645.

[5] *Dramaturgische Blätter*, Stuttgart-Leipzig, 1874, I, 209.

[6] *Freie Bühne für modernes Leben*, IV (1893), p. 593.

[7] *Dramaturgische Blätter*, I, 226–33.

[8] Lindau, *Nur Erinnerungen*, Stuttgart-Berlin, 1919, II, 317; Spielhagen, *Westermanns Monatshefte*, XLIX (1881), p. 665.

[9] Quoted from Fritz Martini, *Deutsche Literatur im bürgerlichen Realismus*, Stuttgart, 1962, p. 450.

[10] Cf. Hermand, 'Zur Literatur der Gründerzeit', p. 219: 'Nicht die Geschichte will man, sondern die erhabenen Momente. So nennt Meyer seinen "Heiligen" "ein Stück Mittelalter", in "ganz klarer Form und ohne alle überflüssige Lokalfarbe"'. Martini (op. cit., p. 222) writes similarly about Heyse: 'Durchweg geht es in Heyses Dramen . . . um den gleichen Konflikt zwischen der Innerlichkeit des edlen, freien Charakters und der ihm widerstrebenden Umwelt. Dieser Moralismus begrenzte sich auf persönliche Ereignisse und Schicksale; die Geschichte wird nur als Rahmen benötigt. Der zum Typischen formalisierte Fall bedurfte keiner Atmosphäre von historischem Raum und historischer Zeit'.

[11] Heinrich Bulthaupt, *Dramaturgie des Schauspiels*, IV, Oldenburg-Leipzig, 1901, p. 211.

[12] Fontane, 'Causerien über das Theater', *Gesammelte Werke*, Berlin, 1904–10, Ser. 2, VIII, 345; Martersteig, *Das deutsche Theater im 19ten Jahrhundert*, Leipzig, 1924², p. 512.

[13] *Revolution der Literatur*, Leipzig, 1886, p. 22.

[14] See F. W. J. Heuser, 'Frühe Einflüsse auf Gerhart Hauptmann', *Gerhart Hauptmann*, Tübingen, 1961, p. 16.

[15] See Hans Schwerte, 'Deutsche Literatur im wilhelminischen Zeitalter', *Wirkendes Wort*, XIV (1964), pp. 265 f.

[16] 'Judentum und Anti-Semitismus', *Die Gesellschaft*, V (1889), p. 1719.

[17] It also deserves a more up-to-date history than Max Grube's dutiful *Geschichte der Meininger*, Stuttgart, 1926.

[18] Constantin Stanislavsky, *My Life in Art*, London, 1962, p. 195.

[19] Ibid., p. 197.

[20] Otto Brahm, *Kritische Schriften*, Berlin, 1913–15, I, 40.

[21] See G. P. Gooch, *History and Historians in the 19th Century*, London, 1920, pp. 586–93.

[22] Schmoller, 'Die Entwicklung und die Krisis der deutschen Weberei im 19ten Jahrhundert', *Deutsche Zeit- und Streitfragen*, II, Berlin, 1873, p. 32. Zimmermann, *Blüthe und Verfall des Leinengewerbes in Schlesien*, Breslau, 1885, p. 350.

[23] *Ästhetische Zeitfragen*, München, 1895, pp. 15 f.

[24] *Revolution der Literatur*, p. 12.

[25] 'Für und gegen Zola', *Kritische Waffengänge*, 2 (1882), p. 47, p. 35.

[26] Ibid., pp. 54 f.

[27] 'Literarische Erinnerungen', *Ges. Werke*, III, 92.

[28] 'Gottfried Keller', *Kritische Schriften*, II, 140.

[29] The title of an article by Wolfgang Kirchbach, *Litterarische Volkshefte*, 6 (1888).

[30] 'Le naturalisme au théâtre', *Les œuvres complètes*, Paris, 1927–9, p. 15.

[31] *Kritische Waffengänge*, 2, pp. 51–3.

[32] 'Vom alten und vom neuen Roman', *Deutsche Rundschau*, XXXVIII (1884), p. 425.

[33] 'Poetischer Realismus', *Gesammelte Werke*, Leipzig, 1891, V, 458. It is interesting to note that Otto Brahm claimed to recognize in Ludwig a German forerunner of Zola; see Sigfrid Hoefert, 'Émile Zola dans la critique d'Otto Brahm', *Les cahiers naturalistes*, no 30 (1965), p. 150.

[34] See Winthrop H. Root, *German criticism of Zola*, New York, 1931.

[35] See F. Doucet, *L'esthétique de Zola et son application à la critique*, Paris, 1930, p. 91.

[36] 'Zola und Daudet', *Die Gesellschaft*, I (1885), pp. 747 f.

[37] 'Emil Zola', *Deutsche Rundschau*, LIV (1888), p. 30.

[38] *À la recherche du temps perdu*, IV, *Le Côté de Guermantes*, ii, Paris, 1920, p. 20. Cf. René König, *Die naturalistische Ästhetik in Frankreich und ihre Auflösung*, Borna-Leipzig, 1931, pp. 189 f.

[39] See J. P. Stern, *Re-interpretations*, London, 1964.

[40] *Die naturwissenschaftlichen Grundlagen der Poesie*, Leipzig, 1887, p. 69, p. 73.

II

Naturalism and the theatre:
from Heinrich Hart to Otto Brahm

The early period of German Naturalism was not rich in positive suggestions as to how the literature of the day should be revolutionized. There is a widespread awareness that an older reality has been called in question, and that old forms are therefore no longer viable; but there is very little agreement about how the new reality is to be handled. The emphasis placed on the contribution of the creative artist, for instance, is constantly being revised. From the theoretical writings of the time it is quite impossible to abstract a picture of the Naturalist drama about which there is any degree of conformity. Two important principles do meet with much approval: an anti-Aristotelean elevation of character over action, and a breaking-down of the distinctions between the genres, epic and dramatic; but they do not pass entirely without contradiction. It is typical of this period of transition, and of its opposition to aesthetic rules, that two attempts to formulate a literary credo, Eugen Wolff's 'Zehn Thesen' and Conrad Alberti's 'Die zwölf Artikel des Realismus', failed to attract a single endorsement other than that of their respective authors.[1]

Programmatic tracts of such a general nature are not among the most important or the most influential of the Naturalists' theoretical writings. By the time these two manifestoes had appeared the works of Ibsen were being performed in the theatres of Berlin, and the example of a successful practising dramatist was far more influential in determining the pattern to be followed by the new drama. The most important items in the mass of critical and theoretical works produced by the German Naturalists are those which are most directly concerned with specific topical issues, such as Otto Brahm's Ibsen-essay of 1886, which did so much to determine the Naturalists' view of Ibsen, and Heinrich Hart's essay of 1882, 'Das deutsche Theater des Herrn L'Arronge', which outlines for the theatre of the age a policy which actually was put into practice, and whose fulfilment is one of the great achievements of the Naturalist movement in Germany.

On the strength of this essay and the Zola-essay to which I have referred in the previous chapter, Heinrich Hart must be considered among the more important theorists of the German Naturalist movement. Like the Zola-essay, this particular work shares the moderately conservative attitude of the rest of the *Kritische Waffengänge*. There are no demands for literary revolution, but for

Idealrealismus. The drama is singled out as the noblest literary form in words which could almost have been written by Schiller in his most anti-realist mood: 'Die Schaubühne eröffnet uns . . . die reine Welt der Ideen, frei von allen Zufälligkeiten und frei vom Endlichen; sie zeigt uns den Menschen in seiner Wesenheit, in der ganzen Reihe seiner Taten und Handlungen' ('The theatre gives us access . . . to the pure world of ideas, free of trivialities and restrictions; it shows us Man in his essence, in the full range of his deeds and actions').[2] Here the drama is valued for what has widely been regarded as the quality which distinguishes it from the literary genres epic and lyric: its suitability for the creation of a complete, enclosed world, in which the part represents the whole by standing symbolically for it. This is an example of that same idealist tendency which lies behind the coolness of the Hart brothers towards the more radical scientific Naturalism proclaimed by many of their contemporaries. It also explains why they virtually disowned the later achievements of Otto Brahm who, to the detached observer, appears to have fulfilled so much of the programme outlined by Heinrich Hart in 1882. Heinrich Hart did, in fact, oppose the appointment of Brahm as the first director of the *Freie Bühne* in 1889, on the grounds that he was not enough of an idealist: 'Ich kannte ihn gut genug, um zu wissen, daß im Sinne einer feineren Idealität, einer großen Geistes und Ideenkunst nichts von ihm zu hoffen war'.[3]

In the first place, however, Brahm, the Harts, and the bulk of their contemporaries were agreed that the literature and, more especially, the theatre of the day were inadequate and trivial. They were agreed that the function of the theatre should be serious, even, in the broadest sense, didactic; it should be used to cultivate the spiritual qualities and the taste of the nation, and so to contribute to a revival of national greatness 'denn ohne die innere Größe bleiben wir immer die Sklaven fremder Nationen oder abgeschmackte Chauvinisten, nur mit ihr werden wir ein freies, großes und fruchtbares Volk'.[4] The theatre should not be simply a place of entertainment, a mere *Vergnügungsanstalt*, nor should it be a *Moralanstalt* (once again Heinrich Hart makes clear his reservations about the *pièce à thèse*; although his distinction between a work with a moral purpose, which he condemns, and a work with a moral effect, which he does not, is not a very helpful one). Broadly speaking, Heinrich Hart subscribes to that view of the work of art which we began to explore in the previous chapter: he regards it as the product of a higher perception and spiritual application, because of which the artist has the privilege of observing and lending expression to the whole of life, free from moral or aesthetic limitations; but at the same time the artist has a duty to extend the consciousness of his fellow men: 'Der Dichter ist der Spiegel der Menschheit, und bringt ihr, was sie fühlt und treibt, zum Bewußtsein'.[5]

Consequently the most important factor in judging the work of a theatre is, in Heinrich Hart's view, its repertoire. While accepting the need for a strong classic and foreign element—he mentions Shakespeare, Calderon, Lessing, Schiller, Goethe, and the newly popular Kleist—his interest is clearly in the development of the contemporary German drama. He is not enthusiastic about the historical drama, and insists that the past can only have a role in as far as it is still meaningful to the present—an insistence reflected in the theory of Bleibtreu,[6] and in plays such as Hauptmann's *Florian Geyer*. The theatre must treat specifically modern problems and ideas if it is to become a national institution, a *Volksbühne*, which stands in a living relationship to the entire nation and which unites all sections of the community; it should be democratic in character; it should not cultivate an exclusive intellectual literature, nor should it, by relying too heavily on the French salon-drama, appeal to just one section of the community, even though that section, the bourgeoisie, may well be capable of providing full houses. The ideal repertoire should engage the interest of the whole people and should show, writes Heinrich Hart, anticipating the themes subsequently to be treated by the Naturalist dramatists, serious intellectual struggles, social conflicts, and the lighter and darker scenes of family-life.[7] The democratic impulse, reflected rather nicely in the recommendation that the price of an ordinary seat should be kept low, is very precariously balanced with a certain intellectual arrogance, which is recognizably a symptom of resentment against the contemporary theatrical set-up. The theatre, Heinrich Hart argues, cannot begin to have its proper effect and influence in the community until it has won back the 'geistige Aristokratie'—a phrase which is to occur increasingly in the writings of the Naturalists. The conclusion of the essay, that the impulse for a real National Theatre must arise from the initiative of enthusiastic writers, is an important idea, and might be considered the first tentative call for the *Freie Bühne*; it also suggests who, in Heinrich Hart's opinion, constitute the 'Aristocracy of the Spirit'.

The policy outlined in 'Das deutsche Theater des Herrn L'Arronge' is, in all respects, a strong plea for the rights of the creative artist; it is a plea for drama rather than theatre; it is a criticism of the rights assumed by director, star-performer, and box-office. The desire of the Naturalists gradually 'to get rid of "theatre" from the theatre'[8] represents the wish of the writer and his ally, the serious literary critic, to break into the theatre and have some influence on re-hearsal and production. Heinrich Hart complains that actors tended to regard the dramatist as an intruder in their kingdom.[9] Eventually Gerhart Hauptmann did come to have this influence; he worked very closely with Brahm, and later with Max Reinhardt, and his contributions to the productions of various plays have been highly praised.[10] Brahm and his friend Paul Schlenther made the same sort of breakthrough; after starting their careers as literary critics they became, in the 1890s, the directors of the two most important German-speaking theatres, the *Deutsches Theater* in Berlin and the *Burgtheater* in Vienna.

Heinrich Hart holds the view that the text, the literary artist's creation, is what really matters: 'Bei der schauspielerischen Darstellung tritt der Character des Helden nicht klarer hervor, als wie ihn ein einigermaßen phantasie- und geistbegabter Mensch nach der Lektüre auffaßt.'[11] It is important that the text should come across clearly, and so Heinrich Hart demands, and Brahm subsequently makes increased use of, the *Leseprobe*. All the elements of the production should be co-ordinated in the interest of artistic unity—the lesson of the Meiningers; decorations should not contradict the knowledge of the more cultured members of the audience, but should not attract attention for themselves; above all, the individual actor should learn to restrain the declamatory style, and seek only 'Natürlichkeit in Sprache und Bewegung', 'geistige Erfassung des Characters'.[12] An urgent need is felt for an actors' school, to function in close association with the National Theatre; such a school was subsequently to be founded by Emanuel Reicher, an actor intimately associated with Brahm, and directly involved in the successes of Hauptmann and Ibsen.

Heinrich Hart had no illusions that he was proposing a popular policy. On the contrary, he took an idealistic relish in the aesthetic leadership he associated with a model theatre: 'Habe L'Arronge die moralische Kraft, eine bessere Einsicht dem Publikum auch mit Gewalt aufzudringen'.[13] L'Arronge did not, and it was only in its early years that his theatre provided the Naturalists with any sort of satisfaction. The *Deutsches Theater* did not become the centre of the modern movement until 1894, when Otto Brahm took over as director.

Otto Brahm was born in Hamburg in 1856, the son of a Jewish merchant. From an early age he had an interest in the theatre, and journalistic ambitions. On the strength of an essay on Paul Lindau, Julius Rodenberg, the editor of the *Deutsche Rundschau*, encouraged him to study, and he went to the University of Berlin in 1876. A year later he moved for a short while to Heidelberg, where he met his lifelong friend, Paul Schlenther. The style of Professor Kuno Fischer did not appeal to Brahm, who already had a pronounced dislike of rhetoric, and the two young men soon returned to Berlin, where Brahm became a protégé of the literary historian, Wilhelm Scherer. Scherer subsequently recommended Brahm to Erich Schmidt, with whom he began work on his doctoral dissertation, *Das deutsche Ritterdrama*, which was presented in Jena, in 1879. In 1881 Brahm joined the *Vossische Zeitung* as junior theatre-critic—Theodor Fontane was his senior colleague—but he was dismissed in 1885 because of a dispute over his criticisms of the *Wallnertheater*. He then worked as theatre-critic for the weekly *Die Nation* until the foundation of the *Freie Bühne*.

Brahm shared Heinrich Hart's expressed admiration for the sober, restrained, realistic style of theatre, which had been associated with the city of his birth since the time of Lessing, and which was practised in the 1880s by Adolf Ernst's company at the *Thalia Theater*. His whole disposition, his distaste for external pomp and declamatory pathos, his truth to his ideals, and his reluctance to compromise, made him just the man to force through the kind of policy which Heinrich Hart had envisaged, and which Brahm had approved in a piece he wrote welcoming L'Arronge's new theatre.[14] Brahm himself had over a decade to wait before he became director of this same theatre, and by this time the enthusiasms and tastes of his former allies were being re-directed, but his own dedication was undiminished; in the meantime he clearly established himself as the leading critic of his generation.

As a critic, Brahm is distinguished from his fellow-agitators by an ability to do more than just polemicize. While the *Kritische Waffengänge* contain masterpieces in the art of demolition, the Harts have little to put in place of Heinrich Kruse and Paul Lindau. In 1882 Heinrich Hart declares that the promising dramatists of the day are Wilbrandt, Anzengruber, Fitger, and Wildenbruch. From about 1884 Brahm begins to devote himself increasingly—and effectively —to Ibsen, Anzengruber, and Hauptmann; he discovered *Vor Sonnenaufgang* (at about the same time as Fontane) after Bleibtreu had rejected Hauptmann's play when it had been submitted for publication in *Die Gesellschaft*.[15]

Brahm's first significant contribution to the development of Naturalism in Germany was the part he played in the campaign on behalf of Ibsen, which led to the Norwegian dramatist replacing Zola as the writer most admired by the younger generation. I believe that the breakthrough of Ibsen represents an important turning-point in German Naturalism and, before going on to consider Brahm's other achievements, I wish to establish the date of this as precisely as possible. As I have already mentioned, *Pillars of Society* and *A Doll's House* reached the German theatre at a fairly early date—in fact one year after they had each been completed. Yet this early success of Ibsen's social dramas was something of a false start. In 1881 Karl Frenzel, the influential theatre-critic of the *Nationalzeitung*, was already writing of it as a thing of the past: 'Vor einiger Zeit war [Ibsens] Schauspiel *Stützen der Gesellschaft* ein Repertoirestück auf vielen deutschen Bühnen.'[16] Until 1887 there seem to have been no further public performances of any of Ibsen's social dramas.

Brahm and Schlenther together saw *Pillars of Society* when it was performed in Berlin in 1878, but their accounts of how they responded to the play are rather different. Looking back in 1904, Brahm declared that he was immediately won over by Ibsen: 'Von Stund an gehörten wir dieser neuen Wirklichkeitskunst, und unser ästhetisches Leben hatte seinen Inhalt empfangen.'[17] Schlenther recalls, however, that Brahm was rather cool about this play, and decidedly critical of *A Doll's House*, when it appeared two years later.[18] We can, I believe, confidently accept Schlenther's assertion that it was only in 1884, when he came across *Ghosts*, that Brahm began the long and loyal campaign on behalf of Ibsen, which lasted right up to the end of his career, as director of the *Lessingtheater*, for Brahm's work during the period before 1884 shows no marked interest in the Naturalist social drama with which he was to become so closely associated. Apart from his dissertation on *Das deutsche Ritterdrama* and his well-known study of Kleist, which appeared in 1884, his longer works include an article for the *Deutsches Montagsblatt* (1880), entitled 'Goethe und Berlin', in which he puts forward moderate views similar to those of the Hart brothers; here he urges his contemporaries to hold fast to the idealizing tradition in German literature, 'die das Poetische nicht in der platten Wiedergabe der allgemeinen Alltäglichkeit findet, sondern die in klassisch-durchgebildeter Form das erhöhte Abbild der edlen Wirklichkeit festzuhalten trachtet'.[19] There is a similar anti-naturalist bias behind Brahm's admiration of Paul Heyse, about whom he wrote an essay for *Westermanns Monatshefte*; and behind his early, unfavourable, criticisms of the work of Zola.[20] But in the present context the most interesting piece of criticism Brahm wrote in these years is an essay on Keller, which appeared in the *Deutsche Rundschau* of 1882. This essay concludes with a direct comparison between *Das Sinngedicht* and *A Doll's House*, which surely confirms Schlenther's statement that Brahm was, at this time, unenthusiastic about the work of Ibsen. Here again Brahm's views resemble those expressed in the *Kritische Waffengänge* for his criticism reflects the same reaction against the tendentious social drama of his own day:

Wieviel bitterer und heftiger ist die Satire des Norwegers als die des Schweizers, wieviel ernster ist er in seinem letzten Akt der Gefahr verfallen, an Stelle der Dichtung die pure unpoetische Tendenz vorzutragen . . . für uns handelt es sich nicht um das soziale Problem als solches, sondern um seine poetische Realisierung; und im Bereiche der Kunst ist es zweifellos Gottfried Keller gewesen, der die vollendetere Schöpfung gegeben hat.[21]	How much more bitter and violent is the satire of the Norwegian than that of the Swiss, and in his last act how much more seriously has he fallen into the danger of replacing poetry with pure, unpoetic tendentiousness . . . for us it is not a question of the social problem as such, but its poetic realization; and on an artistic level it is undoubtedly Gottfried Keller who has produced the greater work.

In discussing the reception of Zola by the early German Naturalists I drew attention to one issue over which the younger writers were unanimous: the question of *bienséance*. Even among those writers who have reservations about Zola's scientific approach there is an insistence on his right to complete freedom in the choice of subject matter. In the early years of German Naturalism there is a strong desire to get literature out of the 'salon'. Many writers turned to the seamier side of city life for their new material; the novelists whom I have mentioned in the preceding chapter, and a number of lyric poets, including Arno Holz. The effect of this was to give the Naturalist movement its slightly unsavoury reputation: 'Man denkt in erster Linie gewöhnlich an den Stoff, wenn man von Naturalismus oder Verismus spricht; und meist nur an eine bestimmte Art, die niedrigste Gattung von Stoff, an das stofflichste am Stoff.'[22]

Brahm was another for whom progress in art meant the extension of its boundaries: literary history, he claimed, shows 'wie die Kunst sich die Kunst aneignet, immer mehr Natur in sich aufzunehmen'.[23] Boldness in introducing new material was one of the features of Kleist's work which he singled out for praise: 'Die Grenzen des Darstellbaren sucht er zu erweitern, und das nie vor ihm dem Bereich der Dichtkunst Zugehörige für die Dichtkunst zu erobern, wie Faust sein Neuland'; and he praises the same tendency in the work of Anzengruber.[24] In his first season as director of the *Freie Bühne* Brahm presented, out of a total of ten plays, three (*Ghosts, Das vierte Gebot*, and Arthur Fitger's *Von Gottes Gnaden*) which had previously had censorship problems; the remaining seven included *Vor Sonnenaufgang, Die Familie Selicke*, and Tolstoy's *The Powers of Darkness*, which all contained the sort of material regarded as highly offensive by the audiences of 1889–90.

To a generation of writers with the sort of attitudes I have been outlining Zola clearly had more to offer than Ibsen; and I believe that this explains why his success in the early 1880s was more spectacular. Perceiving just how little Ibsen had to offer, one recent critic reflects:

> There were . . . some things which the German Naturalists, no matter how hard they tried to fit Ibsen into the framework of their own literary philosophies or prejudices, were unable to find in his work. Most conspicuously absent were any traces of 'Großstadtpoesie', and 'Armeleutepoesie' or other strongly proletarian sympathy, any real approach to 'konsequenter Naturalismus' in the dialogue. Indeed Ibsen's world was in its class framework so predominantly bourgeois, in its intellectual pretensions so persistently aristocratic, and in its speech habits so deficient in raw dialect, that one even wonders how he escaped their censure.[25]

The explanation is, I believe, the relatively simple one, that the philosophies and prejudices of the German Naturalists were not fixed and unchanging; that Ibsen's dramas did not appeal at once, largely because of the attitudes to which I have been drawing attention; but that round about 1887 a change was taking place in German Naturalism which was to make the movement very much more sympathetic to Ibsen (and, incidentally, to the work of the Goncourts) and rather less enthusiastic about Zola.[26] One of the results of this is that the German Naturalist drama comes to rely less on shocks and sensations; another is that, dialogue apart, the dramas of the 1890s are enacted in a world very similar to Ibsen's world, as McFarlane describes it. Among few exceptions *Die Weber* is the most notable; *Einsame Menschen* is more typical of the work being done at this time.

One possible objection to this hypothesis might be that Brahm's interest in Ibsen is unquestionably established with his review of *Ghosts* in 1884, and that quite a substantial campaign preceded the first performance of this play. But then *Ghosts* quite clearly *is* the sort of play which would have appealed to those among the Naturalists who were calling for new and challenging material; it is scarcely surprising that their enthusiasm should have been kindled by, and for a time have been concentrated upon, this particular play.

The search for new material is most probably what attracted Brahm to Ibsen and to Naturalism in the first place, but he soon became reconciled to the other main impulse behind this literary trend: the social-critical impulse, 'der Drang, die Wunden der leidenden Gesellschaft bloßzulegen und zu heilen'.[27] His earlier dislike of tendentious literature soon waned and he came to be an advocate of the social drama. This development is already in evidence in his Ibsen-essay of 1886, where he is disposed to interpret Ibsen predominantly as a social-realist; indeed, this essay was one of the most influential works to propagate this view of the Norwegian dramatist.[28]

Brahm sees the basis of Ibsen's social-criticism in his individualism. In his work he finds a consistent emphasis on independence and strength of character:

[Ibsen] glaubt leidenschaftlich an das Recht der starken Persönlichkeit, des Einzelnen gegenüber der Gemeinschaft . . . er hat ein tiefes Mißtrauen gegen das Recht jener Ansprüche, welche der Staat an die Bürger, die Gesellschaft an ihre Mitglieder stellt, auf Kosten der stolzen und freien Entwicklung der Persönlichkeit. Er glaubt an sein Talent, ein Mensch zu sein; und er zweifelt an seinem Talent, ein tätiger Staatsbürger und eine Stütze der Gesellschaft zu sein. Er blickt in eine ferne Zukunft, welche	Ibsen believes passionately in the right of the strong personality, in the right of the individual as opposed to society . . . he has a profound mistrust of the right of those demands which the state makes of its citizens, society of its members, at the expense of the free and proud development of the personality. He believes in his talent to be an individual; and he is rather dubious about his talent to be a solid citizen and a pillar of society. His eyes are fixed on a distant future which will shake up the world, destroy states,

den Bestand der Welt erschüttern, Staaten zerbrechen und vielleicht gar die Idee des Staates selbst antasten wird; aber vor der gegenwärtigen politischen Bewegung in seiner Heimat zieht er sich mit vornehmer Scheu zurück.[29]

and perhaps call in question the very idea of the state; but he turns away with aristocratic reserve from the present political activity in his own country.

This emphasis on a non-political individualism is an important foretaste of the development of German Naturalism in the 1890s; so also is Brahm's discussion of *An Enemy of the People*, for here he begins to convert an individualist ethic into a piece of special-pleading for the 'outstanding' individual, for 'das Recht der vornehmen Individualitäten, der einsamen Freien, die für die jungen keimenden Wahrheiten auf Vorposten stehen'.[30] Here we already have the essence of such plays as *Einsame Menschen*, Dehmel's *Der Mitmensch*, Carl Hauptmann's *Marianne*, and Flaischlen's *Martin Lehnhardt*. In the history of German Naturalism this individualist slant to the interpretation of Ibsen is more significant than the tendency to regard him as a social dramatist in a more general sense. When this ideal of the free development of the individual personality is extended, as it is by Halbe in 1889, to the sphere of artistic creation:

Wer Ibsen wirklich erfaßt hat, [sollte] vor dem Recht der Individualität, vor dem freien, schrankenlosen Sichausleben der Persönlichkeit . . . als dem obersten Gebot im sozialen und Gesellschaftsleben ebensowohl wie in Literatur und Kunst in Demut sein Haupt beugen,

Whoever has fully understood Ibsen, ought to bow his head humbly before the right of individuality, before the free, unrestrained assertion of the personality . . . as the highest law, not only in social life, but also in literature and art,

then a synthesis has been achieved between the German interpretations of Ibsen and Zola, between aesthetic and ethical individualism; for the unrestricted development of the personality here means the free activity of the artistic imagination. Where such an attitude is combined with a denunciation of the scientific attitude, the signs are that a Naturalism based on the principle of exact observation is not destined for a long reign.[31]

Otto Brahm's agitation on behalf of Ibsen, which culminated in the essay of 1886, had its reward in a single performance (the police would permit no more) of *Ghosts* at the *Residenztheater* in Berlin on January 9, 1887. The previous year had seen two private performances of this play, one at the Meiningen Court Theatre on December 22, and one in Augsburg on April 14, and both these performances no doubt had some influence in securing the Berlin production. The performance at the *Stadttheater* in Augsburg was arranged by a number of young writers from Munich, including Ludwig Fulda, Max Bernstein, and Felix Philippi, and was described as a *Generalprobe unter Ausschluß der Öffentlichkeit für geladene Gäste*, because of the problem of censorship. It was an example of the initiative demanded by Heinrich Hart, and, as such, an anticipation of the *Freie Bühne* idea. The subsequent performance of *Ghosts* in the capital was all that was needed to encourage this sort of initiative, to unite the young writers in a common purpose. In the words of Otto Brahm: 'Der Weg war gewiesen, und das Ziel war gesteckt; nun galt es, auszuschreiten und, was uns hemmen wollte, niederzurennen.'[32] From now on the novel began to give way to the drama as the most favoured literary genre; 'Die Vorstellung von *Gespenster* im Residenztheater zeigte mir das wiedererstandene Theater', wrote Gerhart Hauptmann.[33] Munich came rapidly to be supplanted by the theatre-capital, Berlin, as the centre of literary activity. Here an *Ibsengemeinde* was formed, and made its presence felt as a *claque* at the first performances of his plays.[34] These now followed in swift succession: *An Enemy of the People* and *Rosmersholm* in 1887; *The Wild Duck*, *Lady Inger*, and a revival of *A Doll's House* in 1888; *The Lady from the Sea* and a revival of *Pillars of Society*, as well as a further single performance of *Ghosts* in 1889. March 5, 6 and 7 of 1889 saw the performance in Berlin of three different plays by Ibsen.

The confidence generated among the Naturalists by the feeling that they were really on the point of breaking through led them to take matters more firmly into their own hands. By 1889 their circle of influence was large enough to support a regular programme of private performances and, modelling themselves on Antoine's Parisian *Théâtre Libre*, they formed the *Freie Bühne*. The original proposal came from Theodor Wolff and Maxmilian Harden, and the founder-members included the Hart brothers, Schlenther, and the publisher, Samuel Fischer, but the most important individual was Brahm, who was elected leader, and given almost dictatorial powers. His exercise of these powers soon led to a great deal of friction among the active members of the society, but Brahm was a difficult man to dislodge; his achievement is his justification.

The society was designed to be an exclusive organization, run by the *avant-garde* for that section of the public with a serious interest in literature. Even where the project did not gain sympathy, it did succeed in gaining support, and by the end of the first season the *Freie Bühne* had a membership of over 1,000, which included theatre-directors (Blumenthal, Lautenburg, L'Arronge) and critics (Landau, Frenzel, Lindau) who might have been expected to regard such a society with suspicion, if not downright hostility.[35] Because he did have a firm base, Brahm was able to put into practice the anti-popular policy which he and the Harts had advocated, and so to revolutionize the theatre from above. He

was also more than a little fortunate in the nature of the literary style he supported, for where enthusiasm might not quite have filled his theatre, sensation and
controversy helped out. The first play he presented was *Ghosts*, still banned from
public performance; but his real *succès de scandale*, and at the same time his
theatre's major contribution to the development of the German drama, came
with the notorious première of *Vor Sonnenaufgang* in the *Lessingtheater* on
October 28, 1889.

The Naturalist theatre in Germany was built on the twin pillars of Ibsen and
Hauptmann (Brahm was strangely unsympathetic to Strindberg and Wedekind).
By 1889 the success of the former had been secured; the purpose of the *Freie
Bühne* was to smooth the passage of just such a native dramatist as Hauptmann.
When *Einsame Menschen* was taken into the repertory of the public theatre, and
Hauptmann's next available play, *Kollege Crampton*, was given its première at
the *Deutsches Theater*, the *Freie Bühne* had served its purpose.[36] After 1891 it
was resurrected only in special circumstances, to present *Miss Julie* in 1892 (one
of Brahm's rare Strindberg productions), or in 1893, to present two plays which
had censorship problems, *Die Weber*, and Ernst Rosmer's *Dämmerung*. Subsequently it became an experimental annexe to the *Deutsches Theater*, where Brahm
could try out plays by little-known authors, occasionally transferring them from
there to the repertory of his own theatre.

One effect of the success of this particular private venture was imitation. The
Volksbühnen, which I shall discuss at some length in a later chapter, were the
most important and most enduring extension of the *Freie Bühne* idea, though
their purpose was rather different, and their audiences came from a different
section of the community. The *Verein Deutsche Bühne* was founded in direct
rivalry to the *Freie Bühne*, and with a great deal of personal animosity towards
Brahm, by Alberti and Bleibtreu. It gained the support of the Hart brothers, but
its policy of concentrating on German authors met with no success. Halbe's
Intimes Theater and the various literary societies, the most notable of which was
Walter Harlan's *Litterarische Gesellschaft* in Leipzig, were intended, without
rivalry, to achieve the same purpose as the original *Freie Bühne*, that is to provide
a modern repertoire for a select audience of enthusiasts, free from commercial
pressures, and to give to the serious young writer the encouragement of seeing
his work performed, even if only in an amateur production.

The success of the *Freie Bühne* was such that Brahm was able to do much more
than had originally been planned. In 1894 he began the first of two five-year
leases of the *Deutsches Theater* from L'Arronge, who had decided that the time
had come for him to step down. Still relying principally on Hauptmann and
Ibsen, Brahm rapidly established himself as the undisputed leader in the theatre

of the German-speaking world, until the emergence of his pupil, Max Reinhardt. That he was able to do so without abandoning his ascetic, anti-popular, and anti-theatrical style, is a clear enough indication of his personal greatness as a director, for the Naturalist impulse alone would never have sustained Brahm's theatres, the *Freie Bühne*, the *Deutsches Theater*, and finally the *Lessingtheater*, for over two decades. As we have seen, this impulse was already flagging when Brahm took over at the *Deutsches Theater*. The flexibility of the policy which Brahm, as editor, outlined in the introduction to the first number of the periodical, *Freie Bühne für modernes Leben*, showed a keen awareness of the way the wind was blowing:

> Dem Naturalismus Freund, wollen wir eine gute Strecke Weges mit ihm schreiten, allein es soll uns nicht erstaunen, wenn im Verlauf der Wanderschaft, an einem Punkt, den wir heute noch nicht überschauen, die Straße plötzlich sich biegt und überraschende Blicke in Kunst und Leben sich auftun.

> As a friend of the Naturalist movement we will go along with it a good way, but we must not be surprised if, in the course of the journey, at a point which is not yet in sight, the route takes a sudden turning, and astounding views into art and life are opened up.

But Brahm was less ready than many of his contemporaries to explore the first turning. In 1891 he was still speaking out for a Naturalism of social observation and criticism; his production of *Die Weber*, in 1893, was designed to bring out just that element of social criticism which Julius Hart sought, in his review, to play down, by subordinating it to what he called pure art and pure humanity, 'reinste künstlerische Bildung und über dem nackten Interesse schwebende Menschlichkeit'.[37] He was not very receptive to the 'impressionism' developed in the 1890s by writers such as Hermann Bahr, whose work he described as 'parfümiertes Ekel'.[38]

As editor of the periodical, *Freie Bühne*, Brahm had rather less success than as theatrical director of the organization. Already on the defensive when the periodical was founded, Brahm did not here acquire the dictatorial powers he was granted in the theatre. Discontent with his policies led to a revolt in the first year of the periodical's life, and Bahr, Bierbaum, Paul Ernst, Holz, Liliencron, and Schlaf publicly dissociated themselves from Brahm. More important, Samuel Fischer, the publisher, had rather different ambitions for his periodical than Brahm, and so Brahm also had to go, to be followed in rapid succession by Bölsche, Julius Hart, and Bierbaum, until Fischer found in Oskar Bie a rather more pliant editor. The *Neue deutsche Rundschau*, as the periodical became known in 1894 (in 1904 *Die neue Rundschau*), very soon left its programmatic origins behind to become Germany's leading literary periodical. This is a rare example of such a transformation, and the credit is Fischer's.[39] But this is pre-eminently a publisher's achievement, and as such has little to do with the literary movement, Naturalism.

In the theatre Brahm did have sufficient power, independence, and obstinacy to hold out much longer. In his ten seasons at the *Deutsches Theater* he never performed works by Strindberg, Wedekind, or the increasingly fashionable Oscar Wilde; he did not perform anything by Maeterlinck until his ninth season. Heinrich Hart, who had declared in 1890 that the time was ripe for a retreat from Naturalism and a return to the verse-drama, compares Brahm's activity in the theatre unfavourably with the development of Fischer's periodical: 'Je reicher die Zeitschrift sich entfaltete, desto ärmer schleppte die [Freie] Bühne ihr Dasein hin'.[40] In fairness it should be pointed out that Brahm did introduce Schnitzler and, rather less typically perhaps, Hofmannsthal to the German theatre; but in an atmosphere of increasing criticism he continued to build his repertoire around Ibsen and Hauptmann, performing all of the latter's plays as they became available. His last great productions were the cycle of Ibsen's dramas from *The League of Youth* to *When we dead awaken* given at the *Lessing-theater*.

The achievement of Otto Brahm in the German theatre of the 1890s resembles very closely the achievement of the late George Devine in the English theatre of the 1950s; he gave a completely new impetus to the German theatre by renewing its contact with the literature of the day; he gave to a new generation of writers encouragement and confidence; he gave to the Naturalist movement its theatres, its successes, its public controversies, he gave it a new school of actors, Else Lehmann, Rosa Bertens, Rittner, Sauer, Bassermann, and above all he gave his own services as a director. It was perhaps inevitable that this impetus should eventually lead to a point beyond which Brahm could not, or would not, himself go; it was, perhaps, inevitable that the 'Theatre' should reassert itself, and that the restraint of Brahm should give way to the rather more ambiguous splendour of Reinhardt, for Brahm's success was, in a sense, a *tour de force*. Hauptmann was a dramatist to whose work the *Brahmstil* was eminently suited, and it is arguable that his unofficial position as Brahm's resident dramatist is one of the reasons for the discipline of his best plays, and for the relatively long duration of his Naturalism; but from *Hanneles Himmelfahrt* to *Die Ratten* even Hauptmann was straining at the leash, alternately accepting and ignoring the implications of Brahm's methods. The demise of Hauptmann the dramatist after 1912 is probably not unconnected with the death of Otto Brahm.

Notes to Chapter II

[1] Wolff, *Deutsche Universitätszeitung*, I (1888), p. 1; Alberti, *Die Gesellschaft*, V (1889), pp. 2–9.

[2] *Kritische Waffengänge*, 4 (1882), p. 20.

[3] 'Literarische Erinnerungen', *Ges. Werke*, III, 71.

[4] *Kritische Waffengänge*, 4, p. 6.

[5] Ibid., p. 14. (A quotation from Schopenhauer, *Die Welt als Wille und Vorstellung*.)

[6] *Revolution der Literatur*, p. 22.

[7] *Kritische Waffengänge*, 4, pp. 24 f. This preoccupation with the family is a very important feature in the Naturalist drama of the 1890s; it was also important to Lindau, cf. above, p. 5.

[8] Arno Holz, 'Die Evolution des Dramas', *Das Werk*, ed. H. W. Fischer, Berlin, 1924–5, X, 214.

[9] *Kritische Waffengänge*, 4, pp. 41 f.

[10] See Julius Bab, 'Gerhart Hauptmann als Regisseur', *Gerhart Hauptmann-Jahrbuch*, Neue Folge, I (1948), pp. 148–53.

[11] *Kritische Waffengänge*, 4, p. 17.

[12] Ibid., p. 48, p. 51.

[13] Ibid., p. 35.

[14] *Kritische Schriften*, I, 30–36.

[15] Cf. M. G. Conrad, *Von Emil Zola bis Gerhart Hauptmann*, Leipzig, 1902, p. 80.

[16] *Deutsche Rundschau*, XXVI (1881), p. 308.

[17] *Kritische Schriften*, I, 447.

[18] 'Otto Brahm', *Das deutsche Theater im XIX Jahrhundert*, Berlin, 1930, p. 78.

[19] Quoted from Schlenther, 'Otto Brahm', p. 67.

[20] Cf. S. Hoefert, 'Emile Zola dans la critique d'Otto Brahm'.

[21] *Kritische Schriften*, II, 192.

[22] Leo Berg, *Der Naturalismus*, München, 1892, p. 23.

[23] 'Der Naturalismus und das Theater' (1891), Otto Brahm, *Theater-Dramatiker-Schauspieler*, ed. Hugo Fetting, Berlin, 1961, p. 404.

[24] See *Heinrich von Kleist*, Berlin, 1884, p. 206; and 'Der Naturalismus und das Theater', p. 404.

[25] J. W. McFarlane, 'Hauptmann, Ibsen and the concept of Naturalism', p. 50.

[26] Cf. Kurt Wais, 'Zur Auswirkung des französischen naturalistischen Romans in Deutschland', *An den Grenzen der Nationalliteraturen*, Berlin, 1958, pp. 215–33. Wais draws attention to three characteristics in the work of the Goncourts which distinguish it from Zola's, and to which the Germans became increasingly sympathetic: the Goncourts drew their material from the world of the bourgeoisie, not the proletariat; their achievement lay less in the field of concrete, visual description than in psychological perception; they adopted a consciously refined literary style; in all this they resemble Ibsen more closely than Zola.

[27] 'Der Naturalismus und das Theater', p. 403.

[28] D. E. R. George, *Henrik Ibsen in Deutschland. Rezeption und Revision*, Göttingen, 1968, pp. 34 f.

[29] 'Henrik Ibsen', *Deutsche Rundschau*, XLIX (1886), p. 193.

[30] Ibid., p. 216.

[31] Max Halbe, 'Berliner Brief', *Die Gesellschaft*, V (1889), p. 1183.

[32] *Kritische Schriften*, I, 465.

[33] Diary entry for 18. xii. 1897, Gerhart Hauptmann, *Die Kunst des Dramas*, zusammengestellt von Martin Machatzke, Frankfurt a.M-Berlin, 1963, p. 196.

[34] Cf. Halbe, 'Berliner Brief', p. 1183.

[35] Cf. Gernot Schley, *Die Freie Bühne in Berlin*, Berlin, 1967, p. 15.

[36] *Einsame Menschen* opened at the *Deutsches Theater* on March 21, 1891. It was not, as is sometimes stated, the first play by Hauptmann to be performed in the commercial theatre, though it was the first to be accepted before its private performance. *Vor Sonnenaufgang* had run—without incident—for two weeks shortly after its noisy première; see Alberti, 'Die Freie Bühne', *Die Gesellschaft*, VI (1890), p. 1112.

[37] Quoted from Gerhart Hauptmann, *Die Weber, Dichtung und Wirklichkeit*, ed. H. Schwab-Felisch, Frankfurt a.M.-Berlin, 1963, p. 195. For detailed comments on Brahm's production of *Die Weber*, see H. Henze, *Otto Brahm und das deutsche Theater*, Berlin, 1930, p. 22.

[38] Cf. W. Grothe, 'Die Neue Rundschau', *Börsenblatt für den deutschen Buchhandel*, XVII (1962), p. 2186.

[39] See Grothe, op. cit., p. 2176.

[40] 'Literarische Erinnerungen', *Ges. Werke*, III, 73.

III

Consequential Naturalism: Arno Holz

In the foregoing account of the rise of Naturalism in Germany I have placed a great deal of emphasis on the success of Ibsen after 1887 and Gerhart Hauptmann after 1889. There is no doubt that these are the most important events of the period under discussion. So far I have virtually overlooked the role of Arno Holz who, as a theorist and practising dramatist, is most closely associated with the style known in literary history as 'consequential Naturalism'. Hauptmann dedicated *Vor Sonnenaufgang*, in its first edition, to 'Bjarne P. Holmsen [the pseudonym used by Holz and Schlaf], dem konsequentesten Realisten, Verfasser von *Papa Hamlet*', and stated that the work of Holz and Schlaf had exercised a decisive influence on him. Subsequently, though, he became distinctly hostile towards Holz (he re-dedicated *Vor Sonnenaufgang*, in its second edition, to Brahm and Schlenther) and denied that his influence had ever been decisive. This later view is probably a more accurate one. Even before the publication of *Papa Hamlet*, in January 1889, Hauptmann was himself already attempting to reproduce accurately everyday speech in his works; *Fasching* (*Siegfried*, 1887) and *Bahnwärter Thiel* (*Die Gesellschaft*, 1888) had already been published, and *Vor Sonnenaufgang* had been completed. *Papa Hamlet* marks a step forward in terms of realization; it represents a difference in degree, not in kind.

An examination of the work of Holz is not thereby rendered nugatory. His aesthetic writings and, even more so, the works written in collaboration with Johannes Schlaf, occupy a central position as representative works of this period. An unprejudiced examination of them can tell us a great deal about the real quality of German Naturalism. I say *unprejudiced* because I do not share the widely held view that the importance of these works resides in their rigid adherence to extreme principles of verism. The picture of Holz as a single-minded defender and exponent of an extreme doctrine is not a convincing one. The length, the detail, and the triviality of his arguments with his critics are symptoms of anything but supreme self-confidence. Behind the apparent certainty, even arrogance, of his statements there lurk all the uncertainties and contradictions of an age in ferment. His theoretical writings occupy over 700 pages of his collected works, and they form a vast and confusing edifice. I propose to consider them, and his creative writings, only briefly, and only in so far as they are relevant to the work of the Naturalist period.

Arno Holz, like many of his contemporaries, began his literary career as an admirer and imitator of one of those established figures who soon became anathema to his generation. His early poems *Klinginsherz* (1883) and *Deutsche Weisen* (1884) owe a lot to the lyric of Emanuel Geibel, in whose honour Holz wrote a *Gedenkbuch* (1884). In 1885 he first became associated with the Naturalist movement through his contributions to the lyric anthology, *Moderne Dichtercharaktere*, and in the following year he was widely acclaimed as the leading Naturalist poet for his *Buch der Zeit. Lieder eines Modernen*. In these early works he displays a greater facility than most of his contemporaries, but, except in the 'Phantasus' poems of the *Buch der Zeit*, there is little attempt at formal innovation. As I have suggested in the previous chapter, the literary revolution for the Holz of these years amounts to finding new material for his poetry:

> Ich lache, wollt' ihr blöden Blicks
> verjährten Tand modern staffieren
> und himmelbläulich phantasieren
> vom Waldgnom und vom Wassernix.[1]

Like other young writers Holz found his new material in the city and in the struggle of the oppressed proletariat; he also came to share the general feeling of solidarity with the banned Social Democrat Party. In poems such as 'An die "obern Zehntausend" ' and 'Ecce Homo' he gave direct enough expression to the aspirations of the working-classes to win for the *Buch der Zeit* the lasting admiration of the Marxist critic, Franz Mehring. (This, is by the way, some indication of the inadequacy of Mehring's application of his critical criteria to contemporary literature.)

In 1885 Holz made a clean break with socialism—he was the first of the Naturalists to do so—and henceforward he began to indulge in aesthetic speculation and formal experiment of a kind which inevitably lost him the sympathy of his former admirers. Among the Naturalists Holz was the writer who always possessed the greatest formal awareness, and he soon came to hold the view that the revolution of the early 1880s would remain insubstantial unless it became a stylistic revolution: 'die Entwicklung jeder Kunst [beruht] in erster Linie auf der Entwicklung ihres Mittels'.[2] Heinrich Hart was also beginning to think along these same lines at about this time:

Nicht das Was bedeutet in der Literatur das Meiste, sondern das *Wie*. Die stoffliche Modernität, die Darstellung gegenwärtiger Parteikämpfe, die Verwertung 'brennender' Zeitfragen ist sehr	What counts most in literature is not the *matter*, but the *manner*. The choice of modern subjects, the depiction of contemporary political conflicts, the exploitation of the 'burning' issues of the day,

geeignet, durch sich selbst die Teilnahme weiter Kreise des Publikums zu gewinnen, aber dieser Erfolg ist ein Erfolg *für den Tag*, wenn der Dichter nur das Stoffliche bietet.[3]

can by themselves arouse the interest of large sections of the public, but this success will be a success *for today only*, if all the writer can offer is new material.

Springing, as it does, from his consciousness of form, Holz's Naturalism is much more literary than that of his contemporaries. Like a younger and, let it be said, much greater poet, who at an early stage in his career attained a remarkable facility in the lyric genre, Holz soon found himself in the predicament of the epigone, and unable to write poetry. In their dissatisfaction with a language seemingly deprived of meaning and force by the weight of traditional usage, Holz and Hofmannsthal have much in common; and they both write about their problems in an attempt to overcome them; Holz theorizes, he says, to improve his practice.[4] His aesthetic writings, therefore, are free of the nationalism of the Harts, and the moralism of the socially-committed Naturalists.

As his point of departure Holz takes the theory of Zola, concentrating in particular upon his famous definition of the work of art as 'un coin de la nature vu à travers un tempérament'. In a previous chapter we noted that by 1888 there was a tendency among German critics of Zola to admire him for his creative personality rather than for the scientific accuracy of his work or his originality as a theoretician. Holz was familiar with Brandes' important Zola-essay, and shared this particular tendency:

nicht die Funkelnagelneuheit seiner 'Ideen' war es, nicht die mehr als zweifelhafte Tiefe seiner 'Wahrheiten', die Zola auch als Theoretiker so hoch über den trivialen Haufen emporragen ließ, sondern die wunderbare Wärme seiner überzeugung, das Pathetische seiner Perioden, das ganze Machtvolle seiner Persönlichkeit, das, wie seinen übrigen Werken, so auch seinen kritischen Schriften zur Folie dient.[5]

What made Zola, as a theorist, stand out so far above the common herd was not the originality of his 'ideas', nor the more than dubious profundity of his 'truths', but the wonderful warmth of his conviction, the pathos of his sentences, the whole power of his personality, which acts as a foil to his critical writings as it does to his other works.

Holz does not feel it necessary to point out any discrepancy between Zola's theory and his practice but, like Brandes, he accepts that the concept 'temperament' can adequately—was actually intended to—embrace such things as 'Geschmack' and 'Phantasie';[6] he therefore describes Zola's definition as a trivial commonplace. Although Zola's theories are not free of ambiguity, the concept 'temperament' almost certainly did not, so far as he was concerned, include these things, and for him his definition of a work of art is part of a meaningful realist credo. While Zola was always a respecter of the strong artistic personality—'Il y a une vérité éternelle qui me soutient en critique, c'est que les tempéraments seuls vivent et dominent les âges'—he was never prepared to see it entirely free of restraint.[7] It is certainly arguable that in the case of Zola (as, I believe, in the case of Hauptmann) the discipline of Naturalism had a beneficial effect on an over-exuberant imagination; that the quality of his works derives from a certain balance that is achieved between two conflicting aspects of his character.[8] The tradition in which Zola wrote—the tradition of Balzac, Stendhal, and the French Realists—accepts that there is a substantial external reality, as distinct from our subjective image of it, and Zola's theory demands that the artist should not lose touch with this reality: 'Un jour vient où la force manque pour jouer . . . au créateur. Puis lorsque les œuvres sont trop personnelles, elles se reproduisent fatalement. La réalité au contraire est une bonne mère qui nourrit ses enfants d'aliments toujours nouveaux.' ('There comes a day when one no longer has the strength to play the role of creator. Then, when works are too personal, one goes on inevitably repeating oneself. Reality, on the other hand, is a good mother, who continues to nourish her children with fresh food.')[9]

The impression given by Holz's theory is that he is less confident about the existence of such a reality; and this is equally characteristic of the German tradition in which he stands. As his theory develops Holz displays an increasingly monistic tendency to identify nature with its reflection in the mind of the individual, or with the sensation it arouses in him; thus he can ask: 'Ist . . . die Empfindung, die ein Sonnenuntergang in mir wachruft, kein Naturvorgang?', and go on to argue that even music re-creates nature by recreating such sensations.[10] Views like this make it very difficult to define exactly what Holz means by 'Natur' in his oft-quoted statement: 'Die Kunst hat die Tendenz, wieder die Natur zu sein. Sie wird sie nach Maßgabe ihrer jeweiligen Reproduktionsbedingungen und deren Handhabung.' ('Art has the tendency to become Nature again. It becomes Nature in so far as this is permitted by the prevalent conditions of imitation and their exploitation.') One could say, as Emrich does, that by nature Holz means the whole of the spiritual, social, and physical world, including the world of imagination and dreams, in so far as it is ever experienced by any single individual or artist.[11] This would certainly mean that Holz was right when, in 1898, he reassured his critics that he had never advocated a restrictive, mimetic realism, and had never sought to inhibit the artistic individuality in the slightest degree;[12] but it also deprives Holz's 'Kunstgesetz' of any programmatic meaning; and so, once again, an apparent demand for realistic literature becomes a sanction for complete subjectivity.

In this rather cursory comparison of the theories of Holz and Zola I have sought to bring out the most consistent line in Holz's argument, the monistic line, according to which the 'temperament' is already regarded as a part of nature. I must, however, concede that Holz's theory is not remarkable for its consistency; and the inconsistency derives from a lack of clarity on the part of Holz about what he is trying to achieve. On the one hand, Holz's theory *does* amount to a programmatic demand for Naturalism, which is what his contemporaries took it for; on the other hand, it aspires to be a scientific aesthetic, and purports to reveal a law applicable to all art, whatever its particular style. The balance shifts from the prescriptive to the descriptive as German Naturalism stresses observation less and imagination more. One is therefore tempted to conclude that Holz set out to introduce into his country a modern, realist style of literature, only to find that, by the time he had evolved his theories, no one wanted to be a realist any more. He, and certain of his contemporaries, therefore spent the 1890s unsaying (or denying that they had ever said) much of what is implicit in their theoretical writings of the previous decade. This judgement is a little unjust, for the process is not that conscious a process, and the earlier writings are open to development in a number of possible directions, It is certainly not true, as Rasch and others have asserted, that the essay of 1891 quite unambiguously defines artistic activity as the exact reproduction of a physically perceivable object; nor do I accept that Holz's work can be conveniently divided into three periods, each characterized by a different view of nature; or that the later theoretical writings can be dismissed as an obstinate hanging-on to the 'Kunstgesetz' once it had been formulated.[13] When Holz claimed that he had never demanded that a work of art should be an exact imitation of nature, then, strictly speaking, his claim was just. Nevertheless he *had* dismissed as an unsound dogma the view, attributed to Taine, that the essence of art *does not* consist in the exact imitation of nature;[14] intentional or not, the implication behind these words is reasonably clear: art *does* consist in the exact imitation of nature.

The same contradiction is often present when Holz speaks of his theory as a law. In his *Die Kunst. Ihr Wesen und ihte Gesetze* (1891) he supports the deterministic view that all phenomena are subject to certain immutable laws and he sees his task as an aesthetician not in the laying down, but in the discovery of the laws of art; as he puts it in a letter of 1892: 'Wir sind keine Gesetzgeber, sondern —finder.'[15] He therefore claims that his aesthetic law, like the law of gravity, necessarily governs anything which comes within its sphere of influence: 'ein altes japanisches Götzenbild nicht minder, als eine moderne französische Porträtstatue, einen Böcklin nicht minder, als einen Menzel'.[16] Nevertheless Holz does adopt the role of proselyte in stylistic matters; in the same essay, *Die Kunst. Ihr*

Wesen und ihre Gesetze, he claims that his basic law of art can provide the artist with a method of attaining the truth; and elsewhere he speaks of his duty to teach others to apply this law.[17]

I have suggested that the contradictions in Holz's theories arise because of the developments taking place in German Naturalism at the time these theories were being worked out. As a result of these developments style is re-established as a means of expression rather than a means of precise and accurate reportage. But, curiously, the very search for accuracy and objectivity has a great deal to do with this change. I have already indicated that Holz's theory develops in an unexpected direction, and I believe that this is much more evidently true of the literary style, the *Sekundenstil*, which he and Schlaf employed.

Heinrich Hart gives an impression of what was most probably Holz's original intention in developing this style:

Er entwickelte seine Ansicht am Beispiel eines vom Baume fallenden Blattes. Die alte Kunst hat von dem fallenden Blatt weiter nichts zu melden gewußt, als daß es im Wirbel sich drehend zu Boden sinkt. Die neue Kunst schildert diesen Vorgang von Sekunde zu Sekunde; sie schildert, wie das Blatt, jetzt auf dieser Seite vom Licht beglänzt, rötlich aufleuchtet, auf der andern schattengrau erscheint, in der nächsten Sekunde ist die Sache umgekehrt, sie schildert, wie das Blatt erst senkrecht fällt, dann zur Seite getrieben wird, dann wieder lotrecht sinkt, sie schildert—ja, der Himmel weiß, was sie sonst noch zu berichten hat.[18]

He used the example of a leaf falling from a tree to explain his ideas. The old kind of art could only say of the falling leaf that it sinks to the ground in a spiralling motion. The new art describes this process second by second; it describes how the leaf, illuminated on one side, appears red, on the other a shadowy grey, and how, a second later, this is reversed; it describes how the leaf first falls vertically, then is blown to one side, then falls vertically again, it describes— heaven knows what else it has to report.

Lamprecht, writing more sympathetically of Naturalist poetry, describes its distinctive qualities as intensity and precision: 'Beobachtung von diesem Eingehen auf die Intimitäten der Erscheinungswelt ist etwas schlechthin Neues.'[19] Holz himself, when speaking of the potentiality of the new style emphasizes similar characteristics:

Was die alte Kunst mit ihren primitiveren Mitteln, an die wir nicht mehr glauben, die uns keine Illusion mehr geben, schon einmal getan, diese neue Kunst mit ihren komplizierteren Mitteln, hinter denen wir mal wieder bis auf

What the old kind of art once did, with its more primitive means, in which we no longer have any faith, and which no longer provide any illusion, this new art, with its more complex means, through which we cannot yet see, will achieve

weiteres noch nicht so die Fäden sehen, wird es noch einmal leisten: den ganzen Menschen von neuem geben![20]

once again: it will reveal the whole man anew!

In view of the scientific background to Naturalism this emphasis on accuracy, precision, and complexity is not surprising; it did not, however, feature quite so exclusively in the theory of Zola, who chose also to emphasize the opposite virtues of simplicity and amplitude, vigour and even crudity;[21] and, of course, these virtues are fully reflected in the novels of Zola, as those German critics who praised his epic breadth and grandeur were well aware.

Furthermore it is not self-evident that the precision advocated by Holz is at all likely to lead to works of art that are, in any sense, more 'objective' than the work of Zola. I should like to illustrate this by comparing a short passage from Holz's and Schlaf's *Ein Tod*, with a piece of English prose, written with a degree of precision at least equal to that of Holz and Schlaf.

Der erste Sonnenstrahl blitzte jetzt goldig über die Dächer weg in das Zimmer. Er legte einen hellen Schein auf die dunkelblaue Tapete über dem Bett und zeichnete die Fensterkreuze schief gegen die Wand. Die Bücherrücken auf dem Regal funkelten, die Gläser und Flaschen auf dem Tisch fingen an zu flinkern. Die Arabesken des blanken Bronzerahmens um die kleine Photographie auf dem Tisch mitten zwischen dem weißen, auseinandergezerrten Verbandzeug und dem Geschirre glitzerten. Auf den Dächern draußen lärmten wie toll die Spatzen. Unten auf dem Hofe unterhielten sich ganz laut ein paar Frauen.

'Donnerwetter! Ist das eine wüste Wirtschaft hier!'

Jens, der zum Sofa ging, war über ein Paar Stiefel gestolpert, die mitten im Zimmer auf dem verschobenen, staubigen Teppich lagen.

'Mir ist ganz öd im Schädel!'

Schwer hatte er sich wieder auf das knackende Sofa sinken lassen.

Olaf hatte nicht geantwortet.

Jens reckte sich.

'Übrigens . . . Es war eine schneidige

The first ray of golden sunlight shone over the rooftops into the room. It cast a bright gleam on the dark blue wallpaper and inscribed the slanting shadow of the window frame on the opposite wall. The backs of the books on the shelves glistened, the glasses and bottles on the table began to sparkle. The arabesques of the shiny bronze frame around the small photograph on the table, between the unwrapped white bandages and the dishes, glittered. On the roofs outside the sparrows were chirping madly. Down below in the yard a few women were chatting loudly.

'Good Lord! What a mess!' Jens, who was going to the sofa, had stumbled over a pair of boots which were lying in the middle of the room on the crooked, dusty carpet.

'I feel all washed up!'

He had sunk back heavily on the creaking sofa.

Olaf had not replied.

Jens stretched himself.

'By the way . . . It was a first-rate duel!'

'Yes! Very correct!'

'Yes! Very honourable!—For both!'

Mensur!'
'Ja! Sehr korrekt!'
'Ja! Sehr ehrenhaft!—Für beide!'
'Eversen ist ins Ausland, nicht wahr?'
'Wahrscheinlich!'
Jens betrachtete nachdenklich die beiden
blitzenden Pistolenläufe über dem Sofa.
'Wenn sie nun kommen?'
'Hm.'
'Ae!'
Jens gähnte nervös.
'Wo bleibt denn dieser alte—Ohr-
wurm?!'
'Wann können sie denn hier sein?'
Olaf hatte sich vom Bett in die Höhe
gerichtet.
'Ich denke, nach sechs?'
'Hm!'

'Eversen has gone abroad, hasn't he?'
'Probably!'
Jens looked thoughtfully at the two
gleaming pistol barrels above the sofa.—
'What do we do when they come?'
'Hm.'
'Ae!'
Jens yawned nervously.
'Whatever's keeping that—old woman?!'
'When can they get here by?'
Olaf had got up from the bed.
'I should say after six?'
'Hm!'

I shut the closet door and went out of the bedroom, holding my handkerchief ready
for more doorknobs.

The door next the linen closet, the locked door, had to be the bathroom. I shook
it but it went on being locked. The key for this ought to be kept on the top shelf of
the linen closet but it wasn't. I tried my knife blade, but that was too thin. I went back
to the bedroom and got a flat nail file off the dresser. That worked. I opened the
bathroom door.

A man's sand-coloured pyjamas were tossed over a painted hamper. A pair of
heelless green slippers lay on the floor. There was a safety razor on the edge of the
washbowl and a tube of cream with the cap off. The bathroom window was shut, and
there was a pungent smell in the air that was not quite like any other smell.

Three empty shells lay bright and coppery on the nile green tiles of the bathroom
floor, and there was a nice clean hole in the frosted pane of the window. To the left
and a little above the window were two scarred places in the plaster where the white
showed behind the paint and where something, such as a bullet, had gone in.

The shower curtain was green and white oiled silk and it hung on shiny chromium
rings and it was drawn across the shower opening. I slid it aside, the rings making a
thin scraping noise, which for some reason sounded indecently loud.

I felt my neck creak a little as I bent down. He was there all right—there wasn't
anywhere else for him to be. He was huddled in the corner under the two shining
faucets, and water dripped slowly on his chest from the chromium showerhead.*

The most obvious difference between the extracts is that Chandler's is clearly
structured to make a *pointe*. It is also a first-person narrative, and we see in both
structure and style a reflection of the narrator's character. The precision is the
precision of a trained observer, the detective, coolly, and detachedly taking in

* From *The Lady in the Lake*, copyright © 1944 by Raymond Chandler (Hamish
Hamilton, London).

all the details, because any one of them—at the time of the investigation he does not know which—may later prove to be a vital clue. But the time of the narration is *not* the time of the investigation; so the *narrator* does know what eventually turned out to be significant and what did not, but it is not in his interest as a story-teller to reveal this. He can best create suspense by giving the details without relating them to a whole; this is the same kind of suspense as the cinema creates by showing a scene in a series of close-ups, and keeping the audience waiting, not knowing what the next frame might bring (but suspecting that sooner or later it will be something nasty). The suspense arises largely from the audience's tendency to draw inferences from what it is shown, and, what is part of the same thing, a desire to fit all the pieces together, and so get some kind of grasp over the whole.

It is not entirely frivolous to compare the style of Holz and Schlaf with that of Chandler (many would argue that Chandler is a good enough writer for it not to be frivolous at all) for their descriptions have much in common with his, and can, I would suggest, create a similar kind of suspense. Holz and Schlaf do not tell us what any chance observer would see, but they describe with a more than ordinary precision; by bringing us so close to objects they deprive us of reassuring familiarity. The objects in this room are seen only in their immediate context— the books on the shelf, the glasses, the bottles, and the photograph on the table, the boots on the carpet—and we need to read very attentively, or to keep looking back in the text, if we are to understand the disposition of objects about the room as a whole. The dialogue of the latter half of the passage is similarly fragmented. The narrator does not distil it into a completely meaningful conversation; he does not discriminate between the incidental noises, and the articulated thoughts, but reports everything as it comes. In ordinary conversation the listener does discriminate, and eliminates the noises, unless they really are very obtrusive. By putting them down on paper, where we are not accustomed to seeing them recorded, Holz and Schlaf draw a disproportionate amount of attention to them, making conversation seem difficult, the familiar seem strange. The price of over-close scrutiny is a frightening loss of grasp. Hofmannsthal makes a similar point with a nice analogy:

Mein Geist zwang mich, alle Dinge . . . in einer unheimlichen Nähe zu sehen: so wie ich einmal in einem Vergrößerungsglas ein Stück von der Haut meines kleinen Fingers gesehen hatte, das einem Blachfeld mit Furchen und Höhlen glich, so ging es mir nun mit den Menschen und ihren Handlungen.[22]

My mind forced me to see everything in mysterious close-up; just as when I had once observed a section of the skin of my little finger through a magnifying-glass, which looked like a ploughed field with furrows and hollows, so it was now with people and their actions.

In the passage by Chandler the narrator is carefully and consciously building up excitement; he is *unwilling* to order his material in such a way that the reader can survey it in a relaxed manner; Holz and Schlaf present their story through the eyes of a narrator who is, it seems, *unable* to put things in their place, or to differentiate between the significant and the insignificant. All he can do is register everything he sees, and in so doing register his own incomprehension, as Hofmannsthal does in the first few strophes of the 'Ballade des äußeren Lebens':

Und Kinder wachsen auf mit tiefen Augen,
Die von nichts wissen, wachsen auf und sterben,
Und alle Menschen gehen ihre Wege.

Und süße Früchte werden aus den herben
Und fallen nachts wie tote Vögel nieder
Und liegen wenig Tage und verderben.

The hostility which was evident in Heinrich Hart's account of this style, which I have quoted above, is not just a personal matter; it is the hostility of the Idealist who likes to see a pattern in things or, if none is apparent, likes to see a spiritual effort made to impose one.[23] The *Sekundenstil* deprives us of the possibility of a panoramic view; it expresses, though it does not state explicitly, a sense of loss and anxiety in a fragmented world. The development in the visual arts from the impressionism of Monet to Van Gogh represents a similar development from a veristic to a clearly Expressionist style.

In developing the precise style of 'consequential naturalism' in literature Holz was probably motivated by the veristic intention common to many of his contemporaries, but this intention is irrelevant, for the quality of this style makes it more appropriate to a decidedly subjective kind of work, or one that is realistic only in the sense that it shows how certain people experience reality. In the context of German literature, with its distaste for actualities, and for the presentation of the external social world, it would indeed have been remarkable if the *Sekundenstil* had been employed principally as a means of registering visible realities, rather than the response of individuals to them. Despite their claim to have created in *Papa Hamlet* a work of complete originality, Holz and Schlaf are most definitely still within an established tradition. This emerges very clearly in the early part of Holz's essay, *Die Kunst. Ihr Wesen und ihre Gesetze*, where Holz includes a short extract from an autobiographical novel, *Goldene Zeiten*, on which he had been working. He draws attention to one sentence which gave him particular satisfaction, because it seemed to exclude the momentary temperament of himself, the writer: 'In Holland mußten die Paradiesvögel entschieden schöner pfeifen und die Johannisbrotbäume noch viel, viel wilder wachsen.'[24]

This descriptive reference to Holland, with birds of paradise and carob trees (it may owe its exotic flavour to the influence of Nerval), is manifestly not a piece of objective description; and Holz's pleasure must have derived from his rendering of the mood of boyish enthusiasm and naivety, that is to say his elimination of direct author-intervention by the use of the *style indirect libre*. The novel, then, if it had been completed, could have taken its place among those nineteenth-century German works by writers from Grillparzer to Keyserling which, according to Richard Brinkmann, tend increasingly to present a subjective view in a basically objective manner.[25] Holz rarely discussed such technicalities as the *style indirect libre* in his theory, but a comment by Schlaf shows that he did, for a time, turn his mind to its possibilities:

Holz war damals dahin gekommen, dem Zolaschen Satze 'Un chef d'oeuvre est un coin de la Nature vu à travers un tempérament' den anderen gegenüberzustellen: Ein Kunstwerk ist ein Stück Leben, angesehen nicht durch das Temperament des Künstlers, sondern aller der Personen, die er geben will.[26]

Holz had reached the point of comparing Zola's sentence 'A work of art is a corner of nature seen through a temperament', with the sentence: A work of art is a piece of life seen not through the temperament of the artist, but of all the people he wishes to present.

This brings us to the principal contribution which Holz makes in the collaboration with Schlaf. The latter's sketch, *Ein Dachstubenidyll*, which provided the basis for *Papa Hamlet*, is a completely unremarkable little story which covers the short and miserable life of the child of an unemployed actor and his wife. Holz seized on the fact that one of the main characters in the story was an actor, interwove into the narrative quotations from a role with which the actor, Thienwiebel, might have identified himself, and so produced a story with considerable satirical bite, centred on the illusory relationship of Thienwiebel to the world around him. The interruption of Thienwiebel's bombastic monologues with brief, restrained descriptive passages cuts the protagonist down to size, by enabling the reader to judge that his view of things is hopelessly incongruous:

'Armes kleines Menschenkind! Welch böser Stern verdammte dich in dieses Elend!'

Das arme kleine Menschenkind zappelte ihn an und lachte.

'Aber still! Still! Ich will alles einsetzen! . . . Ich werde dem Schicksal die Stirn bieten; ich werde ihm abtrotzen, daß du in dieser Welt dereinst jene

'Poor little mortal! What evil star condemned you to this misery!'

The poor little mortal kicked at him and laughed.

'But stay! Stay! I will venture all! . . . I will defy destiny; I will wrest from it the acknowledgement that some day you may take up a place in the world meet for someone of your talents . . .

Stellung einnimmst, die deinen Talenten gebührt . . . Ja! So macht Gewissen Feige aus uns allen . . .'

Seine Stimme bebte, seine Schlaf-rocktroddeln hinter ihm, die er sich zuzubinden vergessen hatte, zitterten.[27]

Yes! Thus conscience does make cow-ards of us all . . .'

His voice trembled, behind him his dressing-gown tassles, which he had forgotten to tie up, were shaking.

The distance between narrator and character gives the sketch a satirical dimen-sion. An illusory view of the world is ironically rejected. A critical realism in-forms the work, giving it a satisfying hardness, rare in a literary movement which is, on the whole, over-indulgent to the whims and irresponsibilities of the artist. Thienwiebel's escapism is, nonetheless, made understandable. It is only by adopting a role that he is able to attain any sort of mastery, and this an illusory one, over the world in which he lives. In the extract from *Ein Tod* which I discussed above the only flash of actual conversation is where the two characters speak of the duel, for the duel is a convention in which they each have roles they understand; the rest of the time they spend talking past each other in a painfully embarrassed way. Among Hauptmann's characters, Robert Scholz needs to adopt the role of a hard-bitten cynic, and Johannes Vockerat that of a moral pioneer, in order to find the strength to survive. The sense of exposure and isolation in an incomprehensible and therefore hostile world is responsible for these various forms of escapism. This is the only kind of resistance offered by the weak character; without his role Thienwiebel can only wander around aimlessly while the world seems to disintegrate about him. It is at this point that the satirical perspective of the story becomes blurred, and the narrator, rather clumsily, in-vites us to identify with the main character: 'Der große Thienwiebel hatte nicht so ganz unrecht: Die ganze Wirtschaft bei ihm zu Hause war der Spiegel und abgekürzte Chronik des Zeitalters' ('The great Thienwiebel was not so wrong: his whole household was the abstract and brief chronicle of the times').[28]

In the second story of the *Papa Hamlet* collection the satirical element is less important and the narrative perspective is more consistent. Here the *erlebte Rede* is allowed a greater dominance. Everything is told from the point of view of young Jonathan, a boy experiencing a very full and very frightening first day at school. His experience includes a violent assault on one of his fellow-pupils by the sadistic *Rektor*, severe intimidation at the hands of the school bully, and the terrifying discovery when he flees to an aged friend that the latter is sitting dead in his chair. More evidently and more sensationally than in *Papa Hamlet* Holz (who claimed sole authorship of this story) is concerned to create an impression of terror and to encourage the reader to share it by objectivizing it; but he still preserves some of the irony of *Papa Hamlet* by adopting the viewpoint of so obviously limited a character (although a touch of sentimentality rather softens this irony). *Ein Tod*, which is probably the best of these three sketches (although not for this reason), is free of any trace of critical irony. Here the writer, and this time it was almost certainly Schlaf alone, concentrates, as I have already begun to demonstrate, on re-creating an attitude of mind, a sense of being hopelessly trapped. For all its precision the information conveyed by the narrator's words actually amounts to very little; these words combine with silences and pauses, descriptive passages alternate with fragments of dialogue, to give expression to the predicament of characters waiting (the characteristic symbol of dependence in German Naturalist literature), watching over their dying companion, seemingly imprisoned in a dark, cheerless and silent room, cut off from the outside world, whose light and noise only penetrate as a series of fragmentary impressions of the inaccessible:

Draußen krähte wieder der Hahn. Ein leiser Windstoß strich am Fenster vorbei. In der Nachbarschaft kräuselte sich aus einem Schornstein ein feiner, weißer Rauch in das mattblaue, eckige Stück Himmel über den Hinterhäusern.[29]	Outside the cock crew again. A gentle puff of wind passed the window. Near by a thin column of white smoke wound out of a chimney into the dull blue corner of sky above the backs of the houses.

This discussion of the prose sketches of Holz and Schlaf is a convenient point at which to make a brief mention of Hauptmann's *Bahnwärter Thiel*, for it too is a work in which the point-of-view technique is used to considerable effect. As in *Papa Hamlet* and *Der erste Schultag* the point of view adopted is the obviously relative one of a limited character, whose own delusions contribute to his personal tragedy. The story is one which Hauptmann takes up again in his drama, *Fuhrmann Henschel*, that of a man unable to reconcile the spiritual and the sensual aspects of his personality, represented by his first and second wives, and failing in his attempt to order his life in such a way that they are kept strictly apart. He devotes the hours he has to spend in the lonely silence of the countryside to the memory of his dead wife, Minna, and tries to contain the more physical Lene in the home environment. But just as the train disturbs the peace of the countryside, breaking into his dreams of Minna, and demanding his attention as crossing-keeper, so Lene insists on coming out to his workplace, and defiling ground which Thiel regards as sacred:

Es war ihm plötzlich eingefallen, daß ja nun Lene des öfteren herauskommen würde, um den Acker zu bestellen, wodurch dann die hergebrachte Le-	It had suddenly occurred to him that Lene would frequently be coming out to see to the land, which was bound to disturb his customary way of life consider-

bensweise in bedenkliche Schwankungen geraten mußte. Und jäh verwandelte sich seine Freude über den Besitz des Ackers in Widerwillen. . . . Er wußte kaum warum, aber die Aussicht, Lene ganze Tage lang bei sich im Dienst zu haben, wurde ihm, so sehr er auch versuchte, sich damit zu versöhnen, immer unerträglicher. Es kam ihm vor, als habe er etwas ihm Wertes zu verteidigen, als versuchte jemand sein Heiligstes anzutasten (VI, 50f).

ably. And at once his joy in the possession of this land turned into revulsion. . . . He scarcely knew why, but the prospect of having Lene with him at work for whole days became more and more unbearable, however much he tried to reconcile himself to it. It was as if he had something valuable to defend, as if someone were trying to encroach on that which was most sacred to him.

A vague parallel is thus established in the mind of Thiel—and in the structure of the story—between Lene and the train, which becomes most evident in the description of Lene at work: 'Nachdem die Frau hastig eine dicke Brotkante verzehrt hatte, warf sie Tuch und Jacke fort und begann zu graben mit der Geschwindigkeit und Ausdauer einer Maschine' ('After the woman had hastily devoured a thick crust of bread, she threw her jacket and scarf away and began to dig with the speed and stamina of a machine') (VI, 56). While on a rational level Lene is guilty only of negligence in allowing young Tobias to play on the railway-line, in Thiel's mind she is part of those forces which are hostile to his first wife, Minna, and her child, and is therefore directly responsible for Tobias' death. In this way the symbolic meaning of the story is skilfully integrated in the psychological motivation of the central character, but to integrate it in the psychology of *this* character is to render it suspect; yet there is no explicit statement of suspicion and no irony in the actual narrative; the story-teller identifies himself completely with the symbolism.

The tendency away from critical realism which is evident here, and which we noted in Holz's and Schlaf's sketches, is taken a stage further in their drama, *Die Familie Selicke* (1890). Here again it was Schlaf who provided the material for the work, from another prose sketch of his, *Mainacht*, but in the present context Holz's contribution is more significant than would appear from Schlaf's subsequent claim that it consisted of no more than his share in a few lines on the first seven pages of Act I and the last three pages of Act III. It was on the suggestion of Holz that Schlaf altered the play by bringing in the character 'der olle Kopelke', who had already appeared in the sketch *Die papierne Passion* (1887–8; published 1892); and it is on the pages which Schlaf mentions that Kopelke appears. He is a character who is open to the same hostile treatment as Thienwiebel received in *Papa Hamlet*. By profession a cobbler, Kopelke is also an old quack who offers advice and assistance to the family of the dying child, Linchen

Selicke. He is evidently not motivated by anything but the impulse of a good-natured old man to help this wretched family, but he cannot help basking in the illusion of status that his role gives him, as the following passage rather subtly suggests:

FRAU SELICKE. . . . Und . . . na ja, wenn wir Sie nicht noch hätten . . .
KOPELKE. *leichthin.* Jo! . . . na! . . . Wissen Se: det kommt jo bei mir nich so druf an! . . . Ick . . . nu ja! Se wissen ja! Ick bin man sozusagen 'n janz eenfacher Mann . . . Abber det kann'k Ihn' versichern: jeholfen hab 'k schon manchen! . . . Jott! Ick kennt jo wat bei verdienen! Wat meen'n Se woll! Abber sehn Se . . . will 'k denn? Ick . . . nu ja! Ick bin nu mal so! *Eifrig.* Wissen Se? de Hauptsach' is jetz': man immer scheen warm halten! det Ibrije, verstehn Se, det Ibrije jibt sick denn janz von alleene! . . . man bloß nich immer so ville mang der Natur fuschen, sag ick! . . . [30]

FRAU SELICKE. . . . And . . . well, if we hadn't still got you. . . .
KOPELKE. *casually.* Yes! . . . well! . . . You know! I'm just an ordinary sort of man . . . But I can tell you, I've helped lots of people in my time! . . . Heavens! I could earn a lot like that! Don't you reckon? But you see . . . do I want to? Me . . . ah well! That's what I'm like! *Eagerly.* You know what? The main thing now is just keep her nice and warm! You see the rest will take care of itself! . . . what I say is, you don't want to keep mucking about with nature! . . .

Kopelke resembles Thienwiebel in that he too is in an illusory relationship with reality, but *his* illusions are not criticized from a rational standpoint, and are not shown as socially harmful; they are smiled on tolerantly and indulgently. In this respect *Die Familie Selicke* anticipates Hauptmann's comedy, *Kollege Crampton*.

In its basic situation *Die Familie Selicke* closely resembles the *Papa Hamlet* sketches; once again the authors choose a subject which expresses the complete helplessness of the individual in the face of his environment. The play was criticized by Carl Spitteler (one of its more sympathetic critics) for the monotony engendered by the lack of progress between the first and second acts, both of which open with the family waiting despairingly for the homecoming of Selicke.[31] The situation throughout most of the first act of *Das Friedensfest* is exactly the same; but Hauptmann's play is superior in its execution, its atmosphere is tenser. There is nothing wrong with the conception of *Die Familie Selicke* at this point. This state of nervous and anxious waiting need not be a dull and monotonous experience for reader or audience, for it is an artistically adequate expression of the predicament of the characters involved; and the message of the play is that the predicament of a family sitting at home, waiting, impotent, dependent, and imprisoned, can be a predicament of wide representative significance and interest.

If the play is looked at in this way the fate of Toni Selicke becomes more poignant, and its social implications more evident. She is the only character who is offered any chance of escape, the possibility of marriage to the *Kandidat*, Wendt, and retreat from the loathsome city (this particular nuance is recognizably a contribution of Schlaf)[32] to a comfortable country parsonage. Indirectly, but no less effectively for that, critical light is cast on the institution of marriage in a society where woman is tied to the family, and where it is thus debased to a means of escape. The situation does not, however, permit Toni to make a free choice; with the death of her younger sister, Linchen, she feels an obligation to stay with her parents, and keep the home together. The objection that this is an unlikely decision in the circumstances misses the point; it is a very likely decision, because it is shown to be hardly a conscious decision at all; it is one of those deeds 'performed without thought, without choice, perhaps even without love', an example of what Lionel Trilling has described as the 'morality of inertia'.[33] Toni is so much a prisoner of circumstance that it is simply inconceivable to her that she should now leave her parents; she does not therefore think about her position, and does not announce a decision, but simply reverts to the polite form as she speaks to Wendt: 'Sie müssen ja um elf—fort'.[34] She cannot really explain her change of mind, but can only appeal for Wendt's understanding, and strengthen herself with the brave rationalization that they would not have been happy anyway.

Holz and Schlaf are capable of revealing complex psychological motivation through very ordinary sounding language; and with this same language they are able to involve us uncomfortably in a most oppressive predicament. Within its limited range their writing can reach a high level. In *Die Familie Selicke*, and much to the detriment of this play, they do not restrict themselves in this way. Their play lacks this sort of consistency, without being an obviously inconsistent play, for it has another, lesser, sort of consistency—a sentimental appeal—running right through it. The play, if we consider its impact as a whole, does not so much ask us to share an experience of isolation, as to spare some sympathy for a family cut off by poverty from the happiness (and especially the Christmas festivities) of the world outside. In the final scene Wendt emerges as a *raisonneur* to voice this sentimental appeal in the most obvious and banal way, by drawing attention to the sacrifice made by Toni, and declaring that this has renewed his belief that life is, despite all its misery, worth while: 'Das Leben ist ernst! Bitter ernst! . . . Aber jetzt seh ich, es ist doch schön! Und weißt Du auch warum, meine liebe Toni? Weil solche Menschen wie Du möglich sind!' ('Life is serious! Deadly serious! . . . But now I see that it is also beautiful! And do you know why, my dear Toni? Because there are people like you!').[35]

By being reduced to objects of sentimental sympathy the characters are made remote, their predicament less disturbing; and this distance is increased by the conventional nature of certain aspects of the play. Among the characters the two sons, Walter and Albert, are quite finely drawn and differentiated, but the nagging mother, the drunken father, and the sceptical young *Kandidat* are from stock. The action moves very slowly, but is structured in an unoriginal way; the acts all have a strong theatrical ending, and in the last act an artificial tension is created by the announcement that Wendt's train is due to leave in two hours, and therefore Toni must hurry and decide whether she is to marry him or not; and to conclude, all the characters assemble for the *Tableau-Schluß* of a comedy (Kopelke having conveniently returned), and they hear Wendt make the comforting announcement that he will return.[36]

It cannot be stated too strongly that the major failings of *Die Familie Selicke* are not failings of the *Sekundenstil*. *Ein Tod* shows that Holz and Schlaf could use this style in a more consistent way, without any directly sentimental appeal and without such manifest concessions to traditional literary forms. As it is, these weaknesses are a reminder that, even in what are regarded as their most extreme moments, the German Naturalists can be very uncertain and timid.

Notes to Chapter III

[1] Arno Holz, *Das Werk*, Berlin, 1924-5, X, 13. Subsequent references are to this edition, unless otherwise indicated.

[2] Holz, X, 190.

[3] 'Die realistische Bewegung', *Kritisches Jahrbuch*, I (1889), p. 51.

[4] Holz, X, 105.

[5] Holz, X, 59.

[6] Cf. above, p. 18.

[7] 'Mes Haines', *Les œuvres complètes*, Paris, 1927-9, p. 241.

[8] Cf. J. H. Matthews, *Les deux Zola; science et personnalité dans l'expression*, Paris, 1957, pp. 91-93.

[9] 'Mes Haines', p. 86.

[10] Holz, X, 139.

[11] 'Arno Holz und die moderne Kunst', *Protest und Verheißung*, Frankfurt a.M., 1960, p. 165.

[12] Holz, X, 522.

[13] Cf. W. Rasch, 'Zur dramatischen Dichtung des jungen Gerhart Hauptmann', *Festschrift für F. R. Schröder*, Heidelberg, 1959, p. 245; L. Demler, *Arno Holz. Kunst und Natur*, Wien, 1938; H. Praschek, *Das Verhältnis von Kunsttheorie und Kunstschaffen im Bereich der deutschen naturalistischen Dramatik*, Phil. Diss., Greifswald, 1957, p. 17.

[14] Holz, X, 53; see also p. 364.

[15] Quoted from Dieter Schickling, *Interpretationen und Studien zur Entwicklung und geistesgeschichtlichen Stellung des Werkes von Arno Holz*, Phil. Diss., Tübingen, 1965, p. 72.

[16] Holz, X, 159.

¹⁷ Holz, X, 96; cf. Schickling, op. cit., p. 67; and Holz, *Briefe*, ed. Anita Holz und Max Wagner, München, 1949, p. 266.

¹⁸ 'Literarische Erinnerungen', *Ges. Werke*, III, 69.

¹⁹ *Deutsche Geschichte*, 1er Ergänzungsband, Berlin, 1902, p. 212.

²⁰ Holz, X, 215.

²¹ See 'Le naturalisme au théâtre', *Les œuvres complètes*, passim.

²² 'Ein Brief', *Gesammelte Werke*, Prosa II, Frankfurt a.m.-Berlin, 1951, p. 14.

²³ Hofmannsthal explains this kind of hostility in his essay 'Der Dichter und diese Zeit' (Prosa II, 287): 'Die Dichter, hören Sie mich versichern, führen alle Dinge zusammen, sie reinigen die dumpfen Schmerzen der Zeit, unter ihnen wird alles zum Klang und alle Klänge verbinden sich: und doch—Sie haben allzuviele dieser Bücher gelesen, es waren dichterische Bücher, es war die Materie des Dichters in ihnen, aber nichts von dieser höchsten Magie. Den zersplitterten Zustand dieser Welt wollten Sie fliehen und fanden wieder Zersplittertes. Sie fanden alle Elemente des Daseins bloßgelegt: den Mechanismus des Geistes, körperliche Zustände, die zweideutigen Verhältnisse der Existenz, alles wüst daliegend wie den Materialhaufen zu einem Hausbau. Sie fanden in diesen Büchern die gleiche Atomisierung, Zersetzung des Menschlichen in seine Elemente, Desintegration dessen, was zusammen den hohen Menschen bildet, und Sie wollten doch in den Zauberspiegel sehen, aus dem Ihnen das Wüste als ein Gebautes, das Tote als ein Lebendiges, das Zerfallene als ein Ewigblühendes entgegenblicken sollte.'

²⁴ Holz, X, 45.

²⁵ *Wirklichkeit und Illusion*, Tübingen, 1957, pp. 321 ff. In its own way Brinkmann's book might be said to continue the process I have been discussing here and in the previous chapter, for he, too, redefines 'realism' in such a way as to make it an essentially subjective style.

²⁶ Quoted from Holz, X, 336.

²⁷ Bjarne P. Holmsen, *Papa Hamlet*, Leipzig, 1889, pp. 34 f.

²⁸ *Papa Hamlet*, p. 72.

²⁹ *Papa Hamlet*, p. 170.

³⁰ *Die Familie Selicke*, Berlin, 1890², p. 14.

³¹ Carl Spitteler, 'Die Familie Selicke' (1890), *Ges. Werke*, Zürich, 1950, IX, 338.

³² Cf. the first act of Schlaf's play *Meister Oelze* (1894); see also below, p. 69.

³³ Cf. Lionel Trilling, 'The morality of inertia', *A Gathering of Fugitives*, London, 1957, pp. 31–40.

³⁴ *Die Familie Selicke*, p. 80.

³⁵ *Die Familie Selicke*, p. 89.

³⁶ *Die Familie Selicke*, p. 94. Cf. Wolfgang Kayser, 'Zur Dramaturgie des naturalistischen Schauspiels', *Die Vortragsreise*, Bern, 1958, pp. 220 ff.

IV

Naturalism and Socialism

In my examination of the early prose writings of Holz and Schlaf I suggested that the achievement of the style which the two writers employed was to give direct expression to the anxiety experienced in the face of a world which can be *understood* in precise, scientific detail, but whose overall purpose or shape cannot be *comprehended*. This style involved the accurate reproduction of everyday speech, and the precise inventory of physical detail; in his early theory Holz rationalized this into the doctrine of mimetic naturalism. But as Holz turned his attention to the more evidently personal genre, the lyric, it became increasingly apparent that he felt the need of this newly-won precision to express his own individual and unique sensations; he began to make the same demands on language as were made by Rilke in *Das Stundenbuch*:

Ich glaube an alles noch nie Gesagte.
Ich will meine frömmsten Gefühle befrein.

Holz's success in doing this is rather less evident than Rilke's, but however foolish his claims to have restored the 'natural value' of words, however eccentric his theories of rhythm and diction, however grotesque his *Mittelachsenverse*, there is about all these experiments a tenacious consistency of purpose: they are all part of a protest against the crushing weight of tradition, against what Holz describes as the 'tyranny' of Goethe and Heine over subsequent lyric poetry. As such, I believe they have a parallel in the various protests of Ibsen and his young German followers against the 'tyranny' of the past in the ethical sphere. The preoccupation of German Naturalist theorists with the precision of language is not just an indication of their concern over the distortion of nature by art, but it is part and parcel of an Individualism which influences their outlook over the widest area. The early Naturalist manifestoes abound with statements like the following one from Hermann Conradi's introduction to the anthology, *Moderne Dichtercharaktere*: 'schrankenlose, unbedingte Ausbildung ihrer künstlerischen Individualität ist . . . die Lebensparole dieser Rebellen und Neuerer' ('unrestrained, unconditional cultivation of their artistic individuality is the watchword of these rebels and innovators'), or Bleibtreu's 'In allererster Linie muß die Subjektivität entfesselt werden, um die Erstarrung in konventioneller Schablone zu brechen' ('As an absolute priority subjectivity must be released, in order to put an end to ossifying convention').[1] I draw attention to this attitude because in this chapter I propose to examine the political history of the Naturalist movement the flirtation with, and subsequent estrangement from, socialism; and I wish to emphasize that this latter development is no more surprising than the socialism itself.

Most of the writers associated with the Naturalist movement in Germany were born around 1860. They grew up during the years of Germany's delayed industrial revolution, during that period of intense commercial activity which saw the Buddenbrooks displaced by the Hagenströms. As young men of university age they came from the provinces to the rapidly growing cities, with their drab proletarian quarters, and their grim *Mietskasernen*; to Berlin, the great literary centre, came the Hart brothers from Westphalia, Arno Holz from East Prussia, Johannes Schlaf from Halle, Max Dreyer from Pomerania, and from Silesia, by way of Zurich, the brothers Carl and Gerhart Hauptmann. Young, idealistic, and not particularly wealthy, the natural alliance for these writers was with the underprivileged, with the people who found themselves on the fringes of society (the waitress is a favourite figure in the novels of the 1880s). These newcomers soon perceived that they were in a society whose higher ranks were indifferent, if not hostile, to the less fortunate. Max Halbe writes of his early experiences of university-life in Munich: 'I saw a large number of my fellow-students behaving in a crude, even barbaric way, and at the same time cultivating an exclusiveness which shut out every vestige of harsh reality'.[2] This critical judgement by an outsider is a common experience in this period, and is reflected in the form so closely associated with the German Naturalist drama: the play opening with a tense or 'ripe' situation, which is then set in motion by a newcomer, a *Bote aus der Fremde*.

If their natural ally is the proletariat, the young writers' natural enemy is the bourgeoisie, that section of the community which read *Die Gartenlaube*, and went to plays by Lindau and Charlotte Birch-Pfeiffer, and whose taste and influence are attacked in the *Kritische Waffengänge*. This attack was taken up by many others and so, for a time at least, the Naturalists looked to the working-classes and to socialism to bring about a cultural revival—if only by destroying the bourgeoisie.[3]

One of the principal factors which directed the attention of the young Naturalist writers to the working-classes was the anti-socialist legislation, imposed by Bismarck in 1878, which singled out Social Democracy as the enemy of the established order. In the first place this encouraged the tendency to regard the proletariat as an oppressed and persecuted 'underdog', and so fostered a certain sentimental sympathy among the Naturalists; the early resistance among some of them to the ideas of Nietzsche is symptomatic of this attitude: 'Friedrich Nietzsche decisively rejects compassion, whereas Schopenhauer regards compassion as love, love as compassion. It was to be this kind of compassion which later dictated my *Weavers*,' wrote Gerhart Hauptmann in that part of his autobiography which covers these years (VII, 1079).[4] Of more direct importance was the inhibiting effect this legislation had on political activities and, after 1886, trades unions; this meant that the energies of the more articulate members of the working-classes were directed into organizations which were—or claimed to be—primarily cultural organizations: educational societies and discussion clubs. Writers such as the Hart brothers, Bölsche, and Bruno Wille thus came into contact with a kind of socialism which seemed to correspond to every middle-class intellectual's dream: 'Never have I come across a more passionate striving for knowledge, a more fervent hunger for education and culture than among those comrades who participated in the social struggles of the eighties and the nineties,' wrote Heinrich Hart.[5] In these years of close collaboration they gained, and helped to cultivate, the impression that immediate economic improvement and eventual political power were rather minor issues in comparison with the ultimate cultural purpose of socialism.

One development from the discussion clubs of the 1880s gave the Naturalists particular, and justifiable, satisfaction: the foundation of the *Volksbühnen*. The 1880s had seen a number of proposals (including one by Heinrich Hart) for the foundation of a *Volksbühne*. In certain instances this had meant the revival of traditional *Festspiele*, but this was not the aim of the members of the Berlin discussion-club, the *Alte Tante*, who approached Bruno Wille in 1890. Their interest stimulated by contact with the Naturalist writers, they proposed that the club should join the *Freie Bühne*, and send members to its performances. Instead, Wille proposed that they should form their own organization, the *Freie Volksbühne*, and an appeal for support was published in the *Berliner Volksblatt* of 23 March 1890. The political situation of the time excluded any possible argument about how the society's aims should be defined; it was to be a cultural and educational enterprise: 'Die Freie Volksbühne will . . . erziehlich auf ihr Publikum—eine gewisse Elite des Volks—und durch Vermittlung dieses Publikums auf noch weitere Kreise wirken'. Wille vigorously defended the *Freie Volksbühne* against the charge (from right-wing opponents) that it was a front-organization for essentially political activity, insisting that the enterprise would not be taken over for party-political purposes, and quoting in support the proposed repertoire which included plays by Ibsen, Hauptmann, Zola, Gogol, Tolstoy, Ludwig, and Büchner.[6] The constitution resembled that of the *Freie Bühne* in its distinction between active and passive members; élite or not, the body of the membership was to have no direct influence on repertoire or policy: 'Der Verein besteht aus einer leitenden Gruppe und aus seinen Mitgliedern. Die Leiter wählen die aufzuführenden Stücke sowie die Darsteller aus. Die Mitglieder erwerben durch einen Vierteljahrsbeitrag den entsprechenden Theaterplatz für drei Vorstellungen.'[7] The choice of works to be performed was placed in the hand of a committee consisting of a chairman, a treasurer, a secretary and six members; Bruno Wille became the first chairman, with Karl Wildberger as treasurer, and Julius Türk as secretary; the other committee-members were Kurt Baake, Otto Brahm, Wilhelm Bölsche, Julius Hart, Conrad Schmidt, and Richard Baginski. The response from the working-class public, who were effectively excluded from the commercial theatre by the high cost of tickets, was considerable, and by the end of its first year the *Freie Volksbühne* had a membership of 1,873.

All this suggests that the 1880s were a period of fruitful and harmonious collaboration between the Naturalist movement and the organized working classes, which is superficially true. But there were special reasons why collaboration was so easy, and after 1890, when the anti-socialist laws were not continued, these reasons no longer obtained. The effect of these laws within the Social Democrat Party had been to encourage centralization, to close the ranks, and discourage public controversy. Internal disputes, such as criticisms of the *Gothaer Programm* of 1875, were left in abeyance; and because of the restrictions on the Party as a whole the *Reichstagsfraktion* was able to establish itself as the official voice of the Party leadership. The Party actually came through the period with an immensely increased voting strength: 437,158 when the laws were imposed, and 1,427,298 in 1890, when Bismarck failed to have them extended further. This was an impressive achievement, and many contemporaries were duly impressed; Fontane wrote in a letter to James Morris:

Alles Interesse ruht beim vierten Stand. . . . Die neue bessere Welt fängt erst beim vierten Stand an. Man würde das sagen, auch wenn es sich bloß um Bestrebungen, um Anläufe handelte. So liegt es nicht. Das, was die Arbeiter denken, sprechen, schreiben, hat das Denken, Sprechen und Schreiben der altregierenden Klassen tatsächlich überholt. Alles ist viel echter, wahrer, lebensvoller. Sie, die Arbeiter, packen alles neu an, haben nicht bloß neue Ziele, sondern auch neue Wege.[8]

All that is interesting now resides with the working class. . . . The new, better world begins with the working class. One would say this even if it were only a question of aspirations and beginnings. But it is not so. What the workers think, say, write, has really outdated the thinking, speaking, and writing of the ruling classes. Everything is more genuine, truer, more vigorous. The working classes attack everything in a new way; not only are their ends new, but also their means.

There can, I think, be little doubt that the success of the socialist movement during these years contributed to the optimistic—often naïvely optimistic—belief of certain of the Naturalists in the benefits to be achieved by social re-organization. This found expression in the early lyric of Holz and Henckell, and in the Utopianism of many young men, including a group with whom Gerhart Hauptmann was associated, who undertook a colonial enterprise, the *Ikarierbund* (which is referred to by Loth in *Vor Sonnenaufgang*) after the model of Étienne Cabet. It was in connection with this enterprise that Hauptmann was called as a witness in the *Breslauer Hochverratsprozeß* of 1887.[9]

However naturally it arose, this alliance with socialism was a very insecure arrangement; even at the time when it was at its strongest there were clear signs that it was not destined to last, for the writers made all sorts of reservations, sometimes about socialism, sometimes about politics in general. Max Kretzer is a writer usually associated with the Naturalist movement; yet his novel *Die beiden Genossen* (1880) is a decidedly conservative work. It is, in fact, a defence of older values against the assault of organized socialism. It shows a conflict be-tween the somewhat naïve Utopianism of Schorn, and the radical communism of Raßmann (which, for good measure, is associated with such ideas as divorce and free love), and proclaims that changes in economic conditions need to be brought about peacefully and legally. Like Kretzer, few of the Naturalists really made a radical break with their origins; they tended to cling to the traditional middle-class values of the small provincial towns from which they came, where, as Schlaf declared, 'sich das alte, idealistisch-romantische Deutschland mit seinen engeren und schließlich auch altväterlich religiösen Anschauungen am längsten und . . . am wärmsten und treuesten erhalten hatte'.[10] This pro-vincialism was, of course, bound to clash with the international character of the socialist movement.

Equally at odds with socialism was the ambivalent attitude of the Naturalists towards Bismarck. Despite their criticism of his social policy, and despite their solidarity with the Social Democrats, there were still many among the Naturalists who admired the Chancellor simply as a great personality, a great individual. His supporters included Conrad, the editor of *Die Gesellschaft*, the dramatist, Max Halbe, and, from the fringe of the Naturalist movement, one of his most ardent supporters, Maximilian Harden. Such an attitude clearly went hand in hand with the attitude adopted increasingly in the latter part of the 1880s towards the work and personality of Zola and Ibsen; not surprisingly it was accompanied during these same years by a growing interest in the ideas of Nietzsche. (The reception of Nietzsche, like the German reception of Zola and Ibsen, was decisively influ-enced by George Brandes.)[11]

These few years saw some attempts to reconcile the general individualist trend with the ideas of Marx. Gerhart Hauptmann's *Vor Sonnenaufgang* perhaps owes some of its ambiguity to an attempt to do just this; Alfred Loth, a Social Democrat, who shares much of the Naturalists' philosophy, is presented as both an altruist and an egoist, and is unaware of any conflict: 'Mein Kampf ist ein Kampf um das Glück aller; sollte ich glücklich sein, so müßten es erst alle andern Menschen um mich herum sein' ('My struggle is a struggle for the happiness of the human race; if I am to be happy, then all my fellow men must be happy first') (I, 47). At the end of the play he sees his own position as unproblematical: for him his defection from Helene is consistent with *both* his struggle for the general good *and* his refusal to become a traitor to himself. Whether he intended it or not, Hauptmann's play contains an implicit criticism that Loth's theoretically consistent behaviour is not adequate in the face of real human problems, but it is worth noting that a number of critics sympathetic to Naturalism failed to see this, among them Gustav Landauer, who praised the 'healthy disinterest' of Loth's behaviour. (Brandes, by the way, condemns what he describes as Loth's shallow theories of philanthropy, and recommends the study of Nietzsche.)[12] Another attempt to reconcile socialism and individualism can be seen in Heinrich Hart's essay of 1890, 'Die Moderne':

Nur scheinbar zielt der Sozialismus auf Uniformierung, auf eine noch drückendere Einzwängung in ein Staatsganzes hin. Sein Zweck ist es, das Individuum von der Sorge um das tägliche Brod zu entlasten, ihm seinen Lebensunterhalt unbedingt zu sichern, durch eine gleichmäßige und gerechte Verteilung von Arbeit und Arbeitsertrag, die materielle Arbeit selbst aber zu erleichtern und zu vermindern. Auf diese Weise kann es erreicht werden, daß der Mensch Zeit und Kraft gewinnt, sich in höherem Maße als heute der Ausbildung alles dessen zu widmen, was ihn wahrhaft erst zum Menschen macht.[13]	Socialism only appears to aim at uniformity, at a more oppressive subordination of the individual to the state. Its purpose is to free the individual from concern for his daily bread, to guarantee his subsistence unconditionally by a just and equable division of labour and profit, and to ease the burden of physical work. In this way a man will have more time and energy to devote to the cultivation of what really makes him a man.

The theories of the young Marx on social alienation are here combined with an attitude towards the state which is reminiscent of Nietzsche: 'Es gibt keine höhere Kulturtendenz als die Vorbereitung und Erzeugung des Genius. Auch der Staat ist trotz seines barbarischen Ursprungs und seiner herrschsüchtigen Gebärden nur ein Mittel zu diesem Zweck' ('There is nothing of greater cultural importance than the preparation and generation of genius. Even the state, despite its barbaric origins and its authoritarian gestures, is only a means to this end').[14] These are not words which show Nietzsche at his most prophetic or at his most *unzeitgemäß*. Indeed they are sufficiently typical of the *Gründerzeit* to have been echoed by Paul Heyse: 'die Aufgabe des Staatsmannes muß es sein . . . den öffentlichen Rechtssinn so zu erziehen, daß möglichst viel freie Individuen sich miteinander vertragen, und Jeder auf seine Hand . . . sich mit ewigen Aufgaben beschäftigen könne' ('the aim of the statesman must be . . . to educate the public sense of justice in such a way that as many free individuals as possible can live in harmony together, and each can independently . . . devote himself to timeless tasks').[15] Heinrich Hart's individualism is essentially a continuation of Heyse's attitude, interrupted by a socialist interlude; it is not the startling new insight he himself claims.

During the 1880s such reservations were allowed to pass because, as I have suggested, the Social Democrats were in a tight corner; they had no reason to look for a quarrel with those who supported them, however ambiguous this support may have been; and even if they had wanted to quarrel, they were not favourably placed to do so, for they had very restricted means of publicity, and, as yet, no Franz Mehring, who could attack the young writers where it hurt them most, through criticism of their literary works. But by 1890 a quarrel was brewing; throughout the period of the anti-socialist legislation the *Reichstagsfraktion* had followed a policy of restraint and moderation, rejecting anarchism and violence, and carefully not provoking any further repressive measures.[16] This policy, which had been sporadically criticized by younger socialists, came under heavy fire in 1890 and 1891 from a group, known as *die Jungen*, which included Bruno Wille and Paul Ernst, and a number of intellectuals closely associated with the Naturalist writers. The aims of the rebels were confused: the most articulate were hostile to the idea of the State as such, held individualistic or anarchistic views, and were critical of the increasingly centralized organization of the Social Democrat Party. At the same time there was a great deal of resentment between the local party leaders—many of them young men who had risen very quickly in the hierarchy—and the older, more experienced, and more cautious national leaders, who wished to reassert their authority in the new situation, and who were particularly anxious that radical minority views should not be allowed to jeopardize this new situation. The whole weight of the Party leadership was thrown against the revolutionary intellectuals; August Bebel addressed meetings in their strongholds, Magdeburg, Dresden, and Berlin, and Bebel again led the attack at the Erfurt congress in November 1891, which resulted in the withdrawal of Bruno Wille and his followers from the Social Democrat Party, and the formation of the *Verein unabhängiger Sozialisten*.

Less than a year later the same quarrel was re-enacted in the context of the *Freie Volksbühne*, for it soon became evident to the orthodox Socialists that the leadership of this organization was virtually in the hands of the 'independents', who were strongly backed up by such less politically-minded intellectuals as Brahm, Bölsche, the Hart brothers, Mauthner, Halbe, and Dehmel. A dispute arose between Julius Türk and Bruno Wille over the expense involved in the use of the *Lessingtheater*, but it soon became apparent that the real issue was the more fundamental one of who should control the society and how it should be run. The explanation of a later Marxist critic is that the influence of the 'independents' continued in the *Freie Volksbühne* and prevented this organization from becoming an instrument in the struggle for the emancipation of the proletariat.[17] The effect of this influence on the repertoire was not significant—at least not significant enough to warrant a clear change in policy after the 'independents' had withdrawn—but clearly a great deal of bitterness had been generated by a rather exclusive, undemocratic attitude on the part of the writers. In a very stormy general meeting on 12 October 1892, Paul Dupont (the leader of the *Bildhauerverband*) demanded a greater number of workers on the committee, and questioned the need for any intellectuals at all. When he was elected deputy chairman, and Bruno Wille was replaced as *Vorsitzender* by the leading Social Democrat critic, Franz Mehring (who had not hitherto belonged to the society), some two or three hundred members, led by Wille and including most of the writers, walked out.

Mehring reorganized the society on more democratic lines, attacking the paternalism of his predecessors and encouraging the active participation of the rank-and-file members; his proclaimed principle was:

daß unser Verein nur dann leben kann, wenn die Mitglieder nicht die Gegenstände einer noch so wohlgemeinten Erziehungskunst sind, sondern als freie Männer und Frauen, prüfend und wählend, erobernd und erwerbend, und sei es noch manchmal tastend und irrend, sich die Geistesschätze der Weltliteratur zu eigen machen.[18]

that our society can only prosper if the members are not treated as objects of a pedagogic exercise, however well-meaning, but as independent men and women, who by examination and selection, by effort and application, and despite occasional errors and uncertainties, are getting to grips with the treasures of world literature.

Under Mehring the repertoire continued to consist of classical and contemporary plays, with social-historical content, such as *Emilia Galotti, Kabale und Liebe, Egmont*, and *Pillars of Society*; plays by Naturalist writers were not excluded, but the performance of *Dantons Tod*, planned by Wille, was cancelled thanks to Mehring's negative appraisal of Büchner's play. An arrangement with Oskar

Blumenthal, the director of the *Lessingtheater*, enabled the *Freie Volksbühne* to present a programme of popular and well-performed plays from the repertoire of the commercial theatre, and by 1895 it had a membership of 7,600, principally wage-earners. During this year the *Freie Volksbühne*, which was being increasingly harassed by the authorities, who wished to class it as a political organization, went into voluntary dissolution.

Wille and his friends reacted to the events of October 1892, by forming a rival organization, the *Neue Freie Volksbühne*, an avowedly 'non-political' organization, with an individualist emphasis, 'die an der Spitze Persönlichkeiten und nicht Vertreter dieser oder jener Mehrheit braucht'.[19] Their appeal for members, published in *Vorwärts* and *Der Sozialist*, complained that the original pedagogic and artistic aims of the *Freie Volksbühne* had become subordinated to political ends, and emphasized that the members of the *Neue Freie Volksbühne* were to be 'Zöglinge im volkspädagogischen Sinn'. Accordingly the constitution did not even grant them the right to elect the committee—the founders, who included Bölsche, Julius Hart, Hartleben, Hanstein, Wolzogen, George Ledebour and Gustav Landauer, formed a self-perpetuating oligarchy whose proposals could be rejected only by a two-thirds majority of the membership. It is hardly surprising that this new organization failed to arouse the confidence of the working class in the way the older *Freie Volksbühne* was able to do; and with a smaller membership it could not afford to present performances of a comparable standard to those at the *Lessingtheater*. *Die Weber*, which the *Neue Freie Volksbühne* was able to perform before its rival, boosted membership to about 2,000, but in 1895 it numbered scarcely 1,000.

The foundation of the *Volksbühnen*, and through them the popularization of the theatre, can reasonably be considered one of the most substantial achievements of the German Naturalist movement, but the subsequent history of these institutions, their re-amalgamation in Berlin, their extension to the provinces, in short, their emergence as an important, enduring, and occasionally influential feature on the German theatrical scene, need not concern us further in these pages. My purpose in discussing this controversy, and the struggle between *die Alten* and *die Jungen* which triggered it off, was to show how two rapid blows brought to a sudden end the Naturalists' attempts to align themselves with a political tendency for which they had some sympathy, leaving the way clear for the increasingly fashionable cult of individualism.

It is true that there was a further unsuccessful attempt by Edgar Steiger, an early historian of the Naturalist drama, and the editor of the socialist literary journal, *Die neue Welt*, to align Naturalism and socialism, but the events of 1891–2 had effectively put an end to the political aspirations of the Naturalists.

This is reflected in the introductory article to the fourth volume of the *Freie Bühne* (1893), which runs:

kraftvolle Individualitäten der Zeit, die direkt nichts mit irgendeiner politischer Partei zu tun haben, erheben ihre Stimme unnachsichtig vor den öffentlichen Schäden unserer Kultur und suchen Wege zur Besserung auch aus einer Reformierung der Geister, nicht bloß aus Besserung der Verhältnisse heraus. Solche Stimmen zu sammeln—zumal wo sich der Kritik ein positives, aufbauendes Element beimischt—erachten wir nach wie vor für unsere wesentliche Aufgabe.

energetic modern individuals, who have no connection with any political party, unsparingly denounce the manifest ills of our culture, and are seeking ways of improvement by spiritual reform, not just by the improvement of material conditions. We continue to regard it as our fundamental task to provide a forum for such voices—especially when the criticism contains a positive, constructive element.

The socialists for their part could not reconcile themselves to the pessimism of their Naturalist contemporaries, and their 'faithlessness' to the belief that improvement in social conditions can bring about a real improvement to the lot of mankind. Then, as now, pessimism and tragedy were not compatible with a Utopianist ideology; Mehring's diagnosis of the principal shortcoming of Naturalism has become very familiar from twentieth-century Marxist criticism:

Es ist ein Verdienst des heutigen Naturalismus, daß er den Mut und die Wahrheitsliebe gehabt hat, das Vergehende zu schildern, wie es ist . . . Aber die *ganze* Gesellschaft ist *nicht* verfallen, und das Schicksal des Naturalismus hängt davon ab, ob er den zweiten Teil seines Weges vollenden, ob er den höheren Mut und die höhere Wahrheitsliebe finden wird, auch das Entstehende zu schildern, wie es werden wird und täglich schon wird.[20]

It is to the credit of contemporary Naturalism that it has had the courage and the integrity to describe decaying phenomena as they are. But the *whole* of society has *not* decayed, and the fate of Naturalism depends on whether it can fulfil the second part of its task, on whether it will summon up the greater courage and the greater integrity to describe nascent phenomena as they will be, and as they are already emerging.

After the breach had taken place the tendency among the socialists was to dismiss the earlier political activity of the Naturalist writers as opportunism. Mehring, with his customary delicacy, calls them

Bourgeoisknaben, die sich . . . an die Socialdemokratische Partei heranzuwerfen versuchen, und wenn ihnen hier keine Extrawurst gebraten wird, sich durch die straffe Disziplin der Arbeiterklasse in ihrer 'genialen Individualität'

Bourgeois youths, who . . . attempted to throw themselves at the Social Democrat Party, and when they did not get special treatment here, felt that their 'brilliant individuality' was endangered by the strict discipline of the working

bedroht fühlen und sich zu 'höheren Gesichtspunkten entwickeln', das heißt . . . reumütig zu dem alten Troge der kapitalistischen Schlagworte zurück- kehren.[21]

class, and so 'developed more elevated points of view', that is to say . . . they contritely returned to feed from the trough of capitalist slogans.

Nor were such views confined to those as directly involved as Mehring. In 1896 Arno Holz, who had been one of the first of the Naturalists to turn his back on socialist ideas, and Paul Ernst, who by then had also retreated from his Marxist position, collaborated on a satirical comedy, *Sozialaristokraten*, in which Wille (Gehrke) is presented as a turncoat politician who moves from an extreme left-wing to an extreme right-wing position, merely to satisfy his desire for public recognition.

The authors of *Sozialaristokraten*, however, do rather less justice than even Mehring to a dilemma which Wille shared with many of his contemporaries. Certainly there is much that is comic in the spectacle of the clumsy Wille being outmanoeuvred by the more skilful and nimble professionals, Bebel and Mehring, and reacting with resentful denunciations of party-politics and demagogy; but Wille and his contemporaries were attempting something which they personally found very difficult. Instead of retreating from the struggles of industrial society to indulge in the private, inward speculation so valued by many German artists, they attempted to engage themselves in social and political activity; when others had settled in Worpswede they had remained in Berlin. But all the time they had remained conscious—perhaps over-conscious—of the effort involved, the risks to themselves and the integrity of their own personalities. This is evident in all their reservations about socialism, in their attempts to reconcile Marx with Nietzsche, in their admiration of Ibsen, especially his *Enemy of the People*, in their—essentially defensive—anti-democratic organization of the *Volksbühnen*, and, most catastrophically, in their incompetence at political infighting, their unresisting collapse before the first serious political attack.

In Gerhart Hauptmann's case this dilemma is reflected in that indecision which is so characteristic of many of his works, and was characteristic of many of his public actions. Two recent studies draw on his biography to explain Haupt-mann's professed inability to come down firmly on either side in social and political conflicts. Hans Mayer explains this as an imprint left by Hauptmann's early familiarity with two distinct social groups, and the conflicting loyalties which thus arose; the irreconcilables, he argues, do not derive from insoluble social conflicts, but from conflicts within the poet himself, expressed in the following comment on the dramatic genre: 'Die dramatische Kunst ist gleichsam auf einer produktiven Skepsis errichtet: sie bewegt Gestalten gegeneinander, von denen jede mit ihrer besonderen Art und Meinung voll berechtigt ist. Wo aber bleibt die gesunde rechte Art und die rechte Meinung?' ('Dramatic art is erected, so to speak, on productive scepticism; it brings into conflict characters, of whom each is fully justified in his opinions and his behaviour. But which behaviour and which opinion is correct?') (VI, 698).[22] W. G. A. Shepherd draws extensively on Hauptmann's autobiography, *Das Abenteuer meiner Jugend*, to give a fuller psychological picture of Hauptmann. He has no difficulty in tracing in Hauptmann's account of his life an insecurity which amounts to persecution mania on the one hand, and, on the other, compensatory delusions of grandeur, which are reflected in the movement and counter-movement of his works between an introspective and an expansive mood, between individualism and social-consciousness.[23] These particular studies, enlightening though they often are, have a certain limitation which will be apparent in the present context: Hauptmann's personal psychological constitution may well seem to 'explain' his dilemma, but this should not blind us to the fact that it is very much the dilemma of his generation. Franz Servaes sums it up in words which could well have come from any of a number of the Berlin Naturalists:

sich selbst zu finden, ohne in die Einsamkeit zu flüchten—sich mit anderen zu vereinigen, ohne sich selbst zu verlieren: das ist das Problem, das jeder Schaffende zunächst bei sich zu lösen hat, und das im großen Ganzen dann noch einmal gelöst werden muß— 'Genosse und Einsiedler sein', wie Bruno Wille sagt.[24]

to find oneself, without retreating into isolation—to unite with others, without losing oneself: that is the problem which every creative artist has to solve privately, and which will then have to be solved again in the community at large— 'to be a comrade and a hermit', as Bruno Wille has put it.

It is this problem, the preoccupation of the artist with his own difficulties over the question of social involvement, which provides the political dimension of many of the plays of the Naturalist period. In works like Georg Hirschfeld's *Die Mütter* and Gerhart Hauptmann's *Einsame Menschen* (which I shall discuss at length in a subsequent chapter) the hero is a tortured individual who is asked to give up his own comfort and his own security for the sake of others. But the breadth of this issue is restricted by the widespread tendency of the Naturalists to concentrate on the *Künstlerdrama*, and to make general problems, like the inhibiting effect of middle-class upbringing on progressive ideas, or the rights of the individual within a programme of socialization, into special cases in which the hero is (or is said to be) a more than ordinary man who merits extraordinary consideration. It is not difficult to find some sympathy for Mehring's tendency to dismiss the problems treated in plays like *Einsame Menschen* as the problems of a small literary coterie. At the same time one senses that special—pleading of this kind, and in this quantity, is the symptom of a bad conscience. Whether it is because socialism had indeed had some effect on them, or because they were far too conservative by nature to embrace a consequential individualism, is not clear, but in their individualist phase the German Naturalists never created ruthlessly self-assertive individuals who act with anything like the self-confidence of Wedekind's Lulu. Hartleben's Hanna Jagert, Hirschfeld's Robert Frey (*Die Mütter*), and Hauptmann's Johannes Vockerat are weighed down and inhibited by feelings of indebtedness to their benefactors. For all their increasing scorn of the masses, the Naturalists' views never harden into the exclusive aestheticism of certain of their contemporaries; where the views expressed in *Die Blätter für die Kunst* were known, they were rejected.[25]

I have suggested that political activity was something about which the Naturalist writers always had certain reservations, and that this was the case even before 1891-2. The disputes of these years were the last straw, and accelerated the withdrawal—the literal withdrawal—of even the most politically dedicated among them. In Friedrichshagen, which even today is a relatively peaceful and rural suburb of Berlin, the onetime pioneers of the Naturalist movement assembled to form a community of artists very similar in spirit to the more famous Worpswede community. For both groups of artists the sandy moors and heaths meant freedom from the increasing pressures and social demands of life in the industrial metropolis. In the 1890s Friedrichshagen, which provides the setting for Gerhart Hauptmann's *Einsame Menschen*, became a centre for the discussion of personal and ethical rather than more broadly social issues. In his autobiography Max Halbe tells us that the principal topic of conversation was the 'new morality', the relationship between the sexes, and the question of free love; numerous articles in the *Freie Bühne* confirm the growing interest in such issues.[26] The literature of the Friedrichshagen period was very much more introverted than that of the previous decade; it consisted largely of plays concerned with ethical problems and the psychological analysis of the inner life, of poems and prose-poems of a pantheistic or quasi-mystical character. Some of these works, Gerhart Hauptmann's *Die versunkene Glocke*, or his brother Carl's *Sonnenwanderer*, have very little recognizable connection with the early impulses behind the Naturalist movement. Otto Brahm, who continued to champion the realistic social drama, was criticized for the narrowness of his policy at the *Deutsches Theater*, as his former allies, led by the chameleon-like Hermann Bahr proclaimed the 'Überwindung des Naturalismus', and began to look with admiration at other foreign writers than Ibsen: Huysmans, Bourget, Remy de Gourmont, Whitman, Maeterlinck, and Strindberg. And while not all of Bahr's contemporaries were wont to move on to the latest literary mode with the same rapidity as he, the traditional valuation of the inner life, and the old suspicion of the documentation of the social world meant that there was less resistance in Germany to the new 'impressionism' or 'Neu-Idealismus' than there had been to the innovations of the previous decade.

Much of the work of these years, even where it continues to be in a Naturalist vein, is tinged with a radical cultural pessimism; it is not just critical of particular social or historical manifestations, but tends towards the criticism of civilization as such. Looking back nostalgically to Friedrichshagen and his years of companionship with Wille, Bölsche wrote:

Von dieser Rekreation aus bin ich heute nicht nur der Weltstadt entfremdet, sondern ich meine auch, daß sie ein wahrer Kraken ist, der an unserem geistigen Leben saugt. Je höher die Etagen unter den Rauchhimmel steigen, desto flächer wird die Gemütsbildung und desto mehr keucht jede Geistesäußerung vom Treppensteigen. Der Sinn geht verloren für die feinen Werte in Natur und Kunst, also gerade für das, worin die Entwicklung ansteigt.[27]

Thanks to this recreation I am now not simply alienated from the city, but I also believe that it really is a monster, which drains away our spiritual life. As the buildings rise higher into the smoke-laden sky, so our sensitivity becomes shallower, and all the stairs to be climbed leave us out of breath for spiritual utterances. We lose all sense of the finer values of nature and art, and so for the very source of progress.

Such an attitude was already implicit in Hauptmann's *Bahnwärter Thiel*, in which the train disturbs both the mystical inward life of Thiel and the peace of the countryside; but it becomes a dominant feature in the literature of the 1890s. In this respect the later works of German Naturalism diverge considerably from their European predecessors; there is nothing here to compare with Ibsen's biting condemnation of his narrow provincial homeland, nothing to compare with Zola's great urban novels and their exuberant depiction of a vast social panorama in all its concrete detail. The German Naturalists came positively to fear the city; Schlaf shares Bölsche's fear that urban growth will mean the extinction of all 'reliable values'—such as racial values—which, he says, are the product of nature and the countryside, and he criticizes those of the Naturalist writers who allowed themselves to become reconciled to the city.[28] It is not easy to know which writers he meant; certainly Gerhart Hauptmann and Max Halbe are second to none in their anti-urbanism, and in their dramas they rely increasingly on set responses to the concepts town and country. Of Hauptmann it has been said that he was never a real city-dweller, and that he was constantly in need of 'elemental contact with nature', in order to renew his spiritual powers.[29] (In one of his less successful stage-directions, at the beginning of Act II of *Vor Sonnenaufgang*, Hauptmann shows Alfred Loth, the visitor from the town, in just such 'elemental contact with nature'.)

One rather curious result of the constant recurrence of this anti-urban theme in the plays of this period was its effect on Rudolph Rittner, perhaps the greatest actor of the Naturalist school. His diaries show a sense of remorse at having left his native Silesia, and of guilt over the independence he achieved through success in society; and it is very likely that these feelings prompted his retirement in 1906, at the height of his powers. A diary entry written twelve years earlier runs:

Die Berliner Luft ist mir zu schlecht, moralisch schlecht und unrein, es liegt soviel moralischer Staub und Schmutz in der Luft, daß es mir oft den Atem verlegt, daß ich fühle, hier seelisch krank werden zu müssen. Ich möchte fort, in reinere Himmelsstriche, wo reines, edles Kunstschaffen gedeiht, dort möchte ich, losgelöst von allem Welt-und Großstadtschmutz, ganz der Kunst leben, so wie ich sie mir denke, der reinen, großen, ewigen Kunst, die ihre treuesten Jünger zu Halbgöttern adelt. Hier in der Großstadt kann ich nicht für immer leben, das fühl ich klar,—hier geh ich zu Grunde.[30]	The Berlin air is bad for me, morally bad and impure, there is so much moral filth in the atmosphere that it often takes my breath, so that I feel as if my soul must sicken. I should like to go somewhere else, under a cleaner sky, where pure and noble art can flourish; there, released from all the dirt of society and the metropolis, I should like to devote myself entirely to art, as I imagine it, pure, great, eternal art, which raises its most faithful disciples to demi-gods. I cannot always live here in the city, I feel that clearly, —here I shall be ruined.

It is very easy to see in all this nothing but the natural reaction of sensitive people to the very ugly effects of Germany's industrial revolution; but this is not all there is to be said, even on the subject of causation. The anti-urbanism of the German Naturalists is at the same time a continuation of the prejudice of a number of German writers—some of them great writers like Jean Paul, Gotthelf, and Stifter—who persistently warned against the town as a threat to the beauty of nature and the independence of man. It is, in part at least, a continuation of that tendency to idealize the peasant, which is characteristic of much nineteenth-century German literature, and which results in a view of the peasant as a timeless embodiment of Man, rather than the product of a particular social-historical situation.[31] The Naturalist writers do not, on the whole, consider town and country rationally, as two distinct modes of *social* existence, neither of which is inherently superior to the other; for them the country is not a milieu which can affect people's lives in much the same way as the town, but an absence of milieu, an unresisting natural environment, in which the real or pure character of an individual can freely unfold. Once again the attitude finds a naïve echo in the longing of Rittner, to retire to a Silesian farm where the pressures of society are not felt, 'auf einem Dorfhofe zu sitzen und den Begriff "Müssen" draußen vor der Mauer zu lassen'.[32]

This irrational response to social phenomena accords ill with a literary style which in many other respects owes much to rational social observation. To say that the sociologists provided the rational, sociological response and the poets a poetic one is to miss the point. Balzac found poetry in Paris, Dickens in London, and Döblin found it even in Berlin.

The political attitude embraced by the Naturalists in the 1890s—the advocacy of withdrawal from social involvement, the hostility to party politics, the appeal to man's spirituality for social improvement, the conservative emphasis on home and provincial roots, the slogans like 'Aristocracy of the Spirit', the cult of freedom and the open air—suggests (particularly to the mid-twentieth-century observer) an attitude at the opposite end of the political spectrum to the egalitarian socialism with which German Naturalism was associated in its infancy. I have been at pains to show that this was not a totally new attitude, and it had never been entirely rejected by many of the Naturalists, but it received a fresh impetus in 1890. A cause, or perhaps only a symptom, of this was Julius Langbehn's immensely successful book, *Rembrandt als Erzieher*.

One thing about Langbehn's book is certain: it was an appallingly bad book, and its success had nothing to do with its quality—that is unless one shares the view of Leo Berg: 'Wo ein Bierbaum und Held als Dichter wirken, da gehört auch ein Langbehn als Philosoph dazu'[33]—but it was one of those books which appeal immediately because they bring together so much of what is vaguely in the air at a particular time. In a fascinating study of Cultural Pessimism Fritz Stern describes the atmosphere in which Langbehn's book was launched as follows:

> The decade of the 1890s was one of strife and unrest, when the cultural discontent which previously had been the complaint of a few artists and intellectuals became the faddish lament of the many. The revolt against modernity, the attack on civilization gathered force, hundreds of voices inveighed against all sorts of evils and repressions, and multitudes of people everywhere were repeating these imprecations. Nietzsche, ignored during his creative period, was suddenly read and admired, Ibsen was played and praised, Nordau's *Degeneration* vehemently debated. Everywhere . . . sprang up the cry for greater freedom, for self-expression, for more experience and less theorizing, for a fuller life, for the recognition of the tortured, self-torturing individual. The intensity of this awakening in Germany can be gauged by the instantaneous success of Langbehn's book.[34]

The pages of the *Freie Bühne*, in which *Rembrandt als Erzieher* was favourably reviewed, are full of the sort of manifestations about which Stern is writing. The book could number among its admirers the influential critic, Georg Brandes; in fact Theodor Fontane, who wrote a satirical review, 'Nante Strump als Erzieher', was one of very few to withhold approval.[35] As an apostle of 'Germanic Individualism' Langbehn goes rather further than the Friedrichshagen circle in anticipating the violent irrationalism of the twentieth century, but not so far as to disguise a basic similarity in outlook and aspiration. *Einsame Menschen*, which was probably written too soon to have been directly influenced by Langbehn's book (but which is recognizably a product of the same period), draws attention by its very title to that isolation which Langbehn commends. His insistence that political and social renewal can only arise from the private exertions of a few élite pioneers who are able to retreat from society, could well have come straight from Friedrichshagen:

Der Weg von der heutigen Majoritäts-zur künftigen Minoritätsherrschaft führt, wenn er eingeschlagen werden soll, durch die Isolirung einzelner Deutscher; das heißt eine neue und feinere und wahrhaft selbständige Lebensrichtung wird sich zunächst abgesondert von und im Gegensatz zu der Masse des Volks entwickeln müssen.[36]

The way from today's majority-rule to tomorrow's minority-rule leads, if it is to be taken, through the isolation of individual Germans; that is to say, a new, more refined, and truly independent style of life has, in the first place, to be developed separately from and in opposition to the masses.

It is equally true that much of what Bruno Wille wrote in his *Philosophie der Befreiung durch das reine Mittel* would not have been out of place in Langbehn's book.[37] A coincidental confirmation of the striking similiarity between the attitudes of Wille and Langbehn comes from Fritz Stern's study of the latter. In his researches Stern came across a play to which I have referred above, *Sozialaristokraten*. He remarks: 'between the type portrayed by Holz in this play and Langbehn, whom he certainly did not have in mind, there was a strange resemblance'.[38] The main character in *Sozialaristokraten* was, as I have said, modelled very closely on Bruno Wille.

The political development of the German Naturalist writers from socialism to a supposedly non-political individualism is closely, but not obviously, related to the development of the literary movement, Naturalism, in Germany, and contributes significantly to one of the shortcomings of this movement, its lack of breadth when compared with European Naturalism. I do not wish to advance the crude view that the movement away from socialism is *per definitionem* a shortcoming, rather that in its early days Naturalism attempts to bring literature into society, the writers make contacts with politics and politicians, and in consequence a certain tension is generated; but this tension is never allowed to become a productive tension. Defeated over a specific issue, the response of the Naturalists was not to continue the fight on a political level, but to withdraw, and denounce politics from a safe distance, that is to slide back into the rather depressing old attitudes. *Die Weber* is the pinnacle of the Naturalists' achievement, and is a very fine social drama (although even in this it is something of an exception), but there is no Naturalist drama of this stature concerned with the issues of political priorities, choices, or means and ends. Gustav Landauer wrote in 1890:

> I wish our young authors would free themselves from the constraining bonds of the family; I wish they would go out into the street and among the public, so that if the power of fate is still to be effective then we will not simply be shown 'family-tragedies', but we will witness the effect of that power which, according to a famous statement, is the modern equivalent of fate: politics and society.[39]

Landauer's contemporaries, the Naturalist dramatists, did not respond; there is no Naturalist equivalent of Schiller's *Wallenstein*.

Notes to Chapter IV

[1] Conradi, 'Unser Credo', *Moderne Dichtercharaktere*, ed. Wilhelm Arent, Leipzig, 1885, p. iii; Bleibtreu, 'Andere Zeiten, andere Lieder!' *Die Gesellschaft*, I (1885), p. 892.

[2] *Scholle und Schicksal*, München, 1933, p. 280.

[3] Alberti, 'Die Bourgeoisie und die Kunst', *Die Gesellschaft*, IV (1888), p. 840.

[4] Cf. Bruno Wille, 'Erinnerungen an Gerhart Hauptmann und seine Dichtergeneration', *Mit Gerhart Hauptmann*, ed. W. Heynen, Berlin, 1922, p. 98.

[5] H. Hart, 'Literarische Erinnerungen', *Ges. Werke*, III, 78.

[6] See S. Nestriepke, *Geschichte der Volksbühne Berlins*, I, 1890–1914, Berlin, 1930, for a full history of the *Volksbühnen* during this period.

[7] Quoted from Nestriepke, op. cit., p. 11.

[8] *Ges. Werke*, Ser. 2, Briefe II, 380. Cf. Käthe Kollwitz: 'Das eigentliche Motiv. . .', warum ich . . . zur Darstellung fast nur das Arbeiterleben wählte, war, weil die aus dieser Sphäre gewählten Motive mir einfach und bedingungslos das gaben, was ich als schön empfand'; *Aus meinem Leben*, München, 1957, p. 50.

[9] See H. Lux, 'Der Breslauer Sozialistenprozeß', in *Mit Gerhart Hauptmann*, ed. Heynen, pp. 69–82; and A. Ziegelschmidt, 'Gerhart Hauptmanns Ikarier', *Germanic Review*, XIII (1938), pp. 32–39.

[10] 'Die Freie Bühne und die Entstehung des naturalistischen Dramas', *Der Greif*, I (1914), i, 404.

[11] For comments on the growth of Nietzsche's influence at this time, see M. Boulby, *Optimism and Pessimism in German Naturalist writers*, Ph.D. Diss., Leeds, 1951, pp. 534–41.

[12] Gustav Landauer. 'Gerhart Hauptmann', *Die Neue Zeit*, X (1891–2), pp. 615 f. See also F. A. Voigt, 'Die Aufnahme von "Vor Sonnenaufgang" ', *Hauptmann Studien*, Breslau, 1936, pp. 63–85.

[13] *Der Kunstwart*, IV (1890–1), p. 149. Cf. Bruno Wille, *Philosophie der Befreiung durch das reine Mittel*, Berlin, 1894, pp. 298–9.

[14] 'Nachträge aus einer erweiterten Form der Geburt der Tragödie. Vorwort an Richard Wagner', *Werke*, Stuttgart, 1921, IX, 141.

[15] Quoted from Hermand, 'Zur Literatur der Gründerzeit', p. 208.

[16] See Gerhard A. Ritter, 'Die Arbeiterbewegung im wilhelminischen Reich', *Studien zur europäischen Geschichte aus dem Friedrich-Meinecke Institut der Freien Universität Berlin*, III, Berlin, 1959.

[17] Hans Koch, in Franz Mehring, *Ges. Schriften*, Berlin, 1960–3, XII, 327.

[18] Quoted from Nestriepke, op. cit., p. 98 and p. 85.

[19] Ibid., p. 68.

[20] 'Der heutige Naturalismus' (1892), *Ges. Schriften*, XI, 133.

[21] 'Hanna Jagert' (1893), *Ges. Schriften*, XI, 372.

[22] Cf. Hans Mayer, 'Gerhart Hauptmann und die Mitte', *Von Lessing bis Thomas Mann*, Pfullingen, 1959, pp. 338–55.

[23] W. G. A. Shepherd, *Social Consciousness and Messianic Vision. A study in the problems of Gerhart Hauptmann's individualism*, Ph.D. Diss., Edinburgh, 1962.

[24] 'Nietzsche und der Sozialismus', *Freie Bühne*, III (1892), p. 205.

[25] H. E. Haß, 'Zur Kunstanschauung Gerhart Hauptmanns', *Jahrhundertfeier für Gerhart Hauptmann, 15–21 November, 1962*, Köln, 1962, pp. 29–35; see also Arno Holz's letter to Bölsche, 30. iii. 1903, *Briefe*, p. 141.

[26] *Jahrhundertwende*, Danzig, 1935, p. 39.

[27] *Hinter der Weltstadt*, Leipzig, 1901, p. viii.

[28] *Maurice Maeterlinck*, Berlin, 1906, pp. 20–22.

[29] C. F. W. Behl, *Gerhart Hauptmann. Überblick über sein Leben und Werk*, Kitzingen a.M., 1956, p. 10.

[30] Quoted from H.-A. Schultze, *Der Schauspieler Rudolph Rittner, (1869–1943), ein Wegbereiter Gerhart Hauptmanns auf dem Theater*, Phil. Diss., Berlin, 1961, p. 117. See also Rittner's drama, *Narrenglanz* (1907).

[31] See Friedrich Sengle, 'Wunschbild Land und Schreckbild Stadt', *Studium Generale*, XVI (1963), pp. 619–30.

[32] Quoted from Schultze, op. cit., p. 134.

[33] *Der Übermensch in der modernen Literatur*, Paris–Leipzig–München, p. 213.

[34] *The Politics of Cultural Despair*, Berkeley, 1961, p. 97.

[35] This appeared anonymously in the journal *Deutschland*, I (1889–90), p. 493.

[36] *Rembrandt als Erzieher*, Leipzig, 1890², p. 280.

[37] There is a particularly close resemblance between Langbehn's comments on 'Majoritätsherrschaft' and Wille's on 'Parteiherrschaft'; both writers make similar references to Ibsen's Dr Stockmann, and both give Cologne Cathedral as an example of a positive mass achievement. Wille's work is, on the whole, coloured by a more personal resentment about the way he and his supporters (e.g. Gustav Landauer) had been treated by the Social Democrats.

[38] Fritz Stern, op. cit., p. 137. In the 1890s Moeller van den Bruck, a Cultural Pessimist of Langbehn's stamp, began his career—as an admirer of Johannes Schlaf. See his article in *Die Gesellschaft*, XIII (1897), iv, 154–62. Moeller occupies a place alongside Lagarde and Langbehn in Stern's penetrating study.

[39] 'Das neue soziale Drama', *Deutschland*, I (1890), p. 478. Landauer is, of course, referring to the words attributed by Goethe to Napoleon.

PART TWO

The plays

V

Vor Sonnenaufgang

The first performance of *Vor Sonnenaufgang* on 20 October, 1889, in Berlin's *Lessingtheater* marks the real breakthrough of the German Naturalist drama. This, the second production under the auspices of the recently-formed *Freie Bühne*, was one of the noisiest and most violent premières in the history of the German theatre. Gerhart Hauptmann's play had been published in the summer of 1889 by C. F. Conrad; sides had already been taken, and this first performance thus became a veritable trial of strength between the young Naturalists and the literary establishment.

Vor Sonnenaufgang, subtitled 'soziales Drama', is set in Hauptmann's native Silesia. It opens with the arrival of Alfred Loth, a sociologist and a socialist, in the mining village of Witzdorf; he has come to investigate the conditions under which the local miners live and work. It so happens that two former friends of Loth now live in the district he is visiting. In the course of the play we learn that one of them, Hoffmann, has given up the ideals he shared with Loth in their student days, has married into a farming family recently enriched by the discovery of coal under their land (industrialization disturbing the peace of the countryside), and by a piece of sharp practice has secured a monopoly of the local retail coal trade. His views on social reform have been modified accordingly: 'Ich bin der letzte, der es an Mitleid mit dem armen Volke fehlen läßt, aber wenn etwas geschieht, dann mag es von oben herab geschehen!' ('I should be the last to be found wanting in sympathy for the poor, but if anything is to be done, then let it come from those in authority'!) (I, 20). The other friend, Dr Schimmelpfennig, has reacted in a different way. He recognizes the corruption and injustice of the society in which he lives, but dismisses the possibility of effecting any root-and-branch change; as a doctor he confines himself to alleviating the most immediate suffering and making life as bearable as possible. Loth's active socialism represents a third response, and necessarily makes him an intruder in a way his friends are not. He threatens to break the enclosing circle which for Hoffmann and the landowners has meant freedom from the pressure of discontented workers, from outside public opinion, and from the assaults of their own consciences. The true significance of Loth's arrival is made abundantly clear in the brilliant opening scene in which he calls at the Krauses' house to look up his old friend, Hoffmann, and is greeted with a torrent of abuse from his friend's mother-in-law, who takes him for a beggar.

The dramatist, then, has skilfully placed Loth in the centre of a social conflict. On the one side are the landowners and their spokesman, Hoffmann, who attempts by bribery, by appealing to past friendship, by intimidation, to secure Loth's departure; on the other side are the miners, the servants, the labourer, Beibst, to whom Loth feels a social duty. The only character to change sides is Helene Krause, Hoffmann's sister-in-law. At the outset she is in an unnatural alliance with Hoffmann and her family; but she is a comparative new-comer, since she was educated at the Herrenhut convent, and still finds her family environment abhorrent. For Helene, as for Toni Selicke, the only escape from the family is through marriage; but Hoffmann, who would like to set up a *ménage à trois* with her, has discouraged any potential suitors from the immediate neighbourhood, and in the background is her cruel and moronic cousin, Wilhelm Kahl, to whom the family have betrothed her, and who is having an adulterous affair with her stepmother. Loth therefore has little difficulty in winning her over, both for himself and for his cause; and in the structure of the play Helene thus becomes the representative, if not the spokesman, of the underprivileged classes. To the one as to the other it is Loth's duty to stay and complete his work; as the curtain falls on Act I, Helene pleads: 'Oh! nicht fort, geh nicht fort!' (I, 38).

This clear and straightforward structure is, however, complicated by the scope of Alfred Loth's optimism. Not only does he believe that man's social life can be improved by direct action, he also believes that the quality of the human race can be improved by prudent marriage.[1] Loth, who, like Hauptmann's friend Bölsche,[2] worships the immanent ideals of health, strength and normality, is not prepared to jeopardize future generations either by drinking himself, or by marrying into an unhealthy family. Alcoholism and intermarriage are said to have been significant causes in the degeneration of the families of the Witzdorf area, and the Krause family now contains two helpless dipsomaniacs, Helene's father and her sister, Marthe. Marthe's affliction has already caused the death of her first child; in the fifth act of the play her second is stillborn. In all consistency (which, in this case, has nothing to do with plausibility) Loth cannot marry Helene; he abandons her—and (to Hoffmann's great relief) his sociological investigation—and the play ends with her suicide. The 'hero' of the play therefore fails significantly in the individual tasks which face him; what are we to make of such a hero, and what are we to make of such a play? The simplest answer, that the play is a critique of the mentality of the theoretical reformer, is I believe, too simple. An analysis based on this belief—and there have been a number—is likely to suggest the Hauptmann's first play is a better play than the *Vor Sonnenaufgang* one *feels* one has read. *Vor Sonnenaufgang* is a problematical play, and it is better that the problems it poses should be recognized, for they are crucial to the understanding of the transitional nature of the German drama of this period.

Josef Chapiro reports Hauptmann as once saying: 'Das ideelle Drama, das ich schreiben möchte, wäre eines, das keine Lösung und keinen Abschluß hätte. Ich habe viele meiner Stücke nach ein oder zwei Akten abgebrochen, weil ich mich nicht entschließen konnte, ihnen eine Lösung aufzuzwingen.' ('The ideal drama that I should like to write would be one with no dénouement and no conclusion. I have left many of my plays incomplete after one or two acts, because I could not make up my mind to force a conclusion upon them.')[3] Hauptmann omits to say that on a number of occasions he did just this; his first four plays suddenly accelerate in the last act, and come to an end with more or less violent deaths. Nor is this just true of Hauptmann's work; it happens also in Schlaf's *Meister Oelze* (1892), Max Halbe's *Jugend* (1893), Max Dreyer's *Winterschlaf* (1894), and Holz's and Schlaf's short story, *Papa Hamlet* (1889). But nowhere is the ending of a play more blatantly 'aufgezwungen' than in *Vor Sonnenaufgang.*

From the outline I have given above it will be evident that *Vor Sonnenaufgang* is what R. M. Meyer called a 'drama of ripe situation', the form so often used by the German Naturalist dramatists, and derived directly from Ibsen.[4] Into the atmosphere of oppression and dormant tension suggested by such titles as *Stickluft, Winterschlaf,* and *Tote Zeit,* there comes an outsider, 'der Bote aus der Fremde', who releases the latent conflict. By analogy with Zola, Halbe described this type of drama as an 'experimental drama'; the dramatist experiments by adding a further ingredient, or a catalyst, to a given mixture.[5] In demanding that a drama should consist, from beginning to end, of exposition (VI, 1037) Hauptmann was almost certainly thinking of this kind of drama, which so frequently involves gradual revelation as the newcomer makes his discoveries. This can lead to a kind of drama in which descriptions of conditions have rather more importance, inter-personal conflicts rather less importance, than in the classical drama, and in which individual scenes are not related by a closely-knit plot, but by a common theme, as in J. M. R. Lenz's *Die Soldaten.* Thus the earlier part of *Vor Sonnenaufgang* consists of the gradual uncovering of the social conditions in Witzdorf, as Loth makes his investigations, or explains what he has seen. Tension, conflict, drama, arise from the giving and receiving of information, from the way Loth reacts to what he discovers, and from the way the various characters react to the challenge presented by the new-comer: the suspicious aggression of Frau Krause, the evasive façade of Hoffmann, Helene's desperate yearning for escape. This technique does not require that information be concealed from Loth. But in *Vor Sonnenaufgang* there is cultivated another, more superficial, and more obviously theatrical kind of tension, which arises from the artificial extension of the question: Will Loth find out about the alcoholism in the Krause family? This begins to take effect from the dinner scene of Act I, when Loth states his convictions, and when Kahl nearly gives everything away by his tactless mutter: 'Euer Aler, dar treibt's au a wing zu tull' (I, 35), which Loth does not hear; this tension is increased at the end of the act by Helene's plea that Loth should not depart, and it recurs with every successive attempt Helene makes to tell Loth about her father.

The latter part of the fourth and the whole of the fifth act differ from the rest of the play in that this second kind of suspense ceases to be an episodic feature; once obtained it is very carefully carried right through to the conclusion. Towards the end of Act IV, when the love scenes, which in many other respects are very moving, have reached the rather absurd point where Loth asks Helene whether her parents are healthy, and Helene anxiously asks: 'Aber wenn sie es nicht wären— ?' ('But what if they weren't— ?') (I, 80) their dialogue is interrupted by the screams of Frau Krause, announcing that Marthe is in labour. The act then comes to an end with Helene on her way to fetch the doctor. There now follows the first meeting between the old friends Schimmelpfennig and Loth, and so more delayed exposition, in which the doctor explains the extent of the degeneration among the local farming families. He just reaches a point which could have some bearing on the situation of Loth and Helene—and hastily leaves the room to attend to his patient. In the meanwhile the anxious Helene comes in, only to leave the room once the doctor returns. Schimmelpfennig continues his revelations a little further, and again has to leave at the crucial moment; again Helene comes in, fearful lest Loth has already gone, and he promises her that they will leave together that night. From Schimmelpfennig's third entry what dominates the play is not a conflict of ideas, since the two men share the same views, nor is there any real personal struggle for Loth. What the dramatist now relies on to hold his audience's attention is the quite trivial question of whether Marthe Hoffmann's labour will last long enough for the doctor to say what he has to say, or whether he will be called away first to deliver the baby, so giving Helene an opportunity to leave with Loth as planned, and explain her situation to him herself. At this point during the first performance of the play a member of the audience, a certain Dr Kastan, stood up and impatiently offered Schimmelpfennig a pair of forceps—which he had had the foresight to bring into the theatre with him.[6]

After Loth's departure a similar kind of suspense is again contrived. The discussion between the two friends has made it reasonably clear that Helene's situation *vis à vis* Hoffmann resembles that of Emilia Galotti *vis à vis* the Prince towards the end of Lessing's play, and so the audience has every reason to fear that she will commit suicide. Any hope that this can be avoided must rest with Schimmelpfennig, who has promised to explain Loth's decision as best he can. A letter from Loth is therefore positively dangerous, unless it is left in Schimmelpfennig's hands; but Hauptmann exploits this old device to the full. In the final scene Helene enters, looks round, and leaves in search of Loth without seeing his letter (she makes her exit by the 'Tür des Wintergartens' and must pass immediately behind the table on which the letter is lying); she returns by the same door and, when she hears her father approaching, makes to rush out again through the 'Mitteltür' (upstage, centre) from where she sees the letter on the table (downstage, left), she reads it, and takes the step we have been dreading.

The 'love-interest' in the play, the Loth-Helene aspect, provides a forward-moving plot, conceived in terms of arrival—involvement—perception—departure on the part of Loth; or, to put it differently: a man called Loth goes to a place which (more or less) resembles Sodom, and departs rather hastily, leaving his wife—or, in this case, the woman who might have been his wife—in a rather unfortunate predicament. Hauptmann thus uses the plot-structure of the 'well-made play', to round off *Vor Sonnenaufgang*, and in doing so destroys the formal unity of the work, which had hitherto relied principally on the loose, expository style of the epic theatre. The finality of Helene's death elevates an unmastered problem into an insoluble one; for its force is quite enough to nullify completely Loth's optimistic words: 'Leben! kämpfen!—Weiter, immer weiter' ('Live! Fight! Forward, ever forward') (I, 95). A more consistent drama might, a more consistently *social* drama would certainly have left this issue more open.

If in this formal respect, its reliance on a conventional plot-structure, and on skilfully contrived suspense, *Vor Sonnenaufgang* falls short of the theoretical ideals of Naturalism—though let us not forget that inconsistency of this order is a shortcoming by any standard—Hauptmann's first play is, in another respect, aggressively Naturalistic. Following the example of Ibsen's *Ghosts* and Tolstoy's *The Power of Darkness*—two plays which he knew and admired—Hauptmann joins in the attack on those who held that certain material was not suitable for the stage. And yet compared with Wedekind's *Frühlings Erwachen*—a startlingly modern play, written only one year later—the shock tactics of *Vor Sonnenaufgang* are rather dull and rather predictable. The reason is, no doubt, that Hauptmann tells us a lot, but shows us little of various forms of immorality; in a synopsis of the play it is almost as difficult to avoid the impression of parody as it is in a synopsis of one of Miss Iris Murdoch's novels, with their 'sombre, and often symbolic handling of adultery, incest, castration, sexual confusion and suicide'. In fact, Hauptmann's play raises so many issues that it is hardly possible for him to treat any single one in depth, and it is only in his next three plays that he really begins to get to grips with these issues. The question of free will and determinism looms very large in *Das Friedensfest*; the conflict of individual freedom and the traditional demands of the middle-class family is the central theme of *Einsame Menschen*, and probably the most important theme in the German Naturalist drama as a whole; whilst *Die Weber* treats the problem of the relationship between the oppressed and resentful working classes and their exploiters, the problem which the sensitive Helene experiences most poignantly:

Wie sie einen immer anglotzen, so schrecklich finster—als ob man geradezu was verbrochen hätte.— —
    Im Winter, wenn wir manchmal Schlitten gefahren sind, und sie kommen dann in der Dunkelei in großen Trupps über die Berge, im Schneegestöber, und sie sollen ausweichen, da gehen sie vor den Pferden her und weichen nicht aus. Da nehmen die Bauern manchmal den Peitschenstiel, anders kommen sie nicht durch. Ach, und dann schimpfen sie hinterher. Hu! ich habe mich manchmal so entsetzlich geängstigt (I, 27).

How they stare at you, so awful and grim—as if you'd committed some crime.— —
    In winter, when we've been on our sleighs, and they're coming in the darkness in gangs over the mountains, through the snow, and they ought to get out of the way, they walk in front of the horses and won't stand to one side. Then the farmers sometimes use the handle of their whip, otherwise they wouldn't get past. Oh, and then they swear at you. Hu! I've sometimes been so dreadfully scared.

Vor Sonnenaufgang also treats, in passing, such topical subjects as the emancipation of women, the 'marriage-lie', and the function of literature in the modern world.

In view of this thickness of texture the lack of clarity in Hauptmann's play is not very surprising. A further reason lies in the nature of the dramatist's talents; Hauptmann's characterizing impulse was such that it would almost always assert itself over his much weaker sense of a message, or his control of plot.[7] In this Hauptmann had considerable support from the dramatic theory of the Naturalist period; Arno Holz, for instance, writes: 'Nicht Handlung ist das Gesetz des Theaters, sondern Darstellung von Charakteren.'[8] It is perfectly understandable that in the course of composition the interest of a dramatist whose strength is in characterization should fall to Helene. Her fate is still in doubt, whereas the remainder of the Krause household has already sunken unknowingly and unresistingly into dissipation and animality. Hoffmann is intelligent enough to know better, but intelligence allied with weakness of character has led him to the conviction that resistance is futile. His chief concern seems to be to anaesthetize any vestiges of the capacity to feel pain; hence his increasing reliance on tobacco and alcohol, and his attempts to seduce Helene. In the interests of theatrical suspense Loth is kept in ignorance of certain facts until the end of the play, which not only makes him appear a little obtuse, it also effectively excludes him from the sort of inner conflict which Helene is capable of experiencing. Her knowledge is greater (quantitatively) than Loth's and her personality is more naïve than Hoffmann's and so she is not disposed to resignation. At the crucial moment in the play, immediately after Loth has departed, it is Helene who enters to make the announcement that Marthe's second child has been stillborn; this confirmation of Loth's fears, at *this* point in the action, and by *this* character, can hardly mean anything but that Loth's course of action is the right one. Nevertheless, so much sympathy has by this time accrued to Helene, against an overall design which would suggest that Loth is, in principle, right, that the ultimate meaning of the play is obscured.

Whilst the drawing of the wide range of characters—and special mention should be made of Hoffmann—is this play's greatest virtue, the central character, Loth, is without depth. His psychology is flat, and we are left with the feeling that his motivation is inadequately explained. It is true that Hoffmann describes him to Helene as ruthless and inhuman, but Hoffmann is an interested party on more than one count. It is also true that Loth does utter certain rather crass clichés, such as 'Nur wer mich zum Verräter meiner selbst machen wollte, über den müßte ich hinweggehen' ('I wouldn't trample on anyone, unless they wanted to make me become a traitor to myself') (I, 80); but if these words are to be seen as a sham rationalization, we need some more positive indication of the shortcoming they rationalize. Moreover, the words are spoken before there is any question of departure—they are not offered as an excuse—and they are, to some extent, taken back by Loth's subsequent words, as he begins to reflect on his attraction to Helene:

es ist mir vielleicht nicht ganz so klar bewußt geworden wie jetzt, daß ich in meinem Streben etwas entsetzlich Ödes, gleichsam Maschinenmäßiges angenommen hatte. Kein Geist, kein Temperament, kein Leben, ja wer weiß, war noch Glauben in mir? Das alles kommt seit . . . seit heute wieder in mich gezogen. So merkwürdig voll, so ursprünglich, so fröhlich! (I, 92)	it has perhaps never been so clear to me as it is now that my activities have become terribly barren, almost mechanical. I was lacking in spirit, in energy, in life, and who knew if I still believed in it all? Since . . . since today all of this has welled up in me again. It is so wonderfully rich, so fresh, so joyful!

It does not seem likely that Hauptmann could have given Loth these words at this point if it had been his conscious intention to condemn him later as a cold doctrinaire and an automaton.

A diary-entry of 1897 (VI, 1043) makes it clear that Hauptmann soon came to realize the problems attendant on treating a character such as Loth in a drama. And subsequently, in the conversations with Chapiro (p. 164), he argues that an absolutely consistent character, such as a fanatic, can have no place in a drama, because his behaviour is totally predictable:

> Personen aus einem Guß, abgerundeten Formen gleich, sind keine Gestalten für die Bühne. Fanatiker zum Beispiel, also einer, der die absolute Wahrheit zu besitzen glaubt, kann an einem Drama nur episodisch teilnehmen . . . Er nimmt dem Selbstdialog die suggestive Kraft des Unerwarteten. Für ihn ist alles schon entschieden.

The function of the 'Bote aus der Fremde', which is to produce rather than to undergo a change, tends to make him a character of this kind; and it is, indeed, a precondition of the tension which informs the last act of *Vor Sonnenaufgang* that we can rely on Loth's response. The nearest such a character can come to the centre of the action is probably in one of the classic patterns of the 'Western': in a primitive, lawless community it takes a strong and disinterested individual to impose law and order, but once this is done there is no place in that community for the man who has subdued it; hence the final sequence shows the hero riding out, alone, into the sunset. Such a role demands emotional asceticism as well as physical courage, for emotional involvement distracts from the concentration which is necessary to complete the task. There is in *Vor Sonnenaufgang* just a hint of this problem when Loth shows how unimportant the friendship of Hoffmann is to him, or when he explains to Helene that his own personal happiness is a very distant prospect: 'Ich könnte mich sozusagen nur als letzter an die Tafel setzen' (I, 47).

In *Winterschlaf*, a play strongly influenced by *Vor Sonnenaufgang*, Max Dreyer avoids the ambiguities of Hauptmann's play by treating his new-comer in the way Hauptmann was later to suggest such figures should be treated. Hans Meincke, like Loth a socialist, a sociologist, and just released from gaol, is rescued from the snow by *Förster* Ahrens, in whose isolated home he remains for three days to recover—just long enough for the *Förster's* daughter, Trude, to fall in love with him, and to acquire a longing to escape from her rather brutal fiancé and her restricted home environment to the wider outside world. Trude's evil old aunt stirs up the jealous fiancé, and provokes him into raping Trude, who gives up her plans to leave for Berlin, and commits suicide immediately after Hans' departure. There is no question of Hans' departure being seen as a defection, because, plausibly enough, he does not feel any emotional attachment to Trude; love is all on one side, and the girl has, in fact, been at pains to conceal her feelings in order to secure her father's permission to leave for Berlin. Her 'unworthiness' is a purely subjective matter; Hans never knows of the rape, or her suicide, and there is no reason to believe he would have rejected her in the way Loth rejects Helene. We can therefore concentrate with undivided attention on the single issue, the question of self-determination and self-fulfilment, for which Hans emerges as the spokesman: 'Ob Mann—ob Weib—niemand darf eine Kraft unterdrücken, die in ihm lebendig ist.'[9]

In this simplified scheme there is no opposition between social altruism and the ideal of self-realization. When Hans reproaches Trude for her passivity he is criticizing her both for failing to fulfil herself and for failing to take up the 'great social task'. Toni Selicke's dilemma is avoided, for Trude has no duty to stay with her family. Hans shows some awareness of a potential problem in his account of his period of imprisonment: for the authorities he was an agitator, and was imprisoned as such, but the workers he had come to help suspected him of being an *agent provocateur*, and therefore ostracized him; but the tensions of this situation are not examined. *Winterschlaf* is a simplified *pièce à thèse*, in which the situation is presented from one point of view; it is unquestionably a superiority of Hauptmann's play that it begins, at least implicitly, to illuminate the ambiguities of Loth's approach to social problems, and to suggest that Helene's perspective is worthy of consideration.

There is one indisputably great drama of this period which, it has often been suggested, may have influenced Hauptmann in the writing of *Vor Sonnenaufgang* —Ibsen's *The Wild Duck*. In Ibsen's play there is no doubt that Gregers Werle's intervention in the Ekdal family is misguided, and that he himself is a prig, with complex psychological problems which the dramatist, by skilful use of retrospective exposition, illuminates with immense subtlety. Hauptmann's own comments on *Vor Sonnenaufgang* would seem to confirm the view that Loth is to be seen rather differently and rather more sympathetically. Writing shortly after the first performance, Hauptmann expresses some dissatisfaction with the actor who took the role of Loth, and made him appear both naïve and pretentious, whereas he was *intended* to be an intelligent and original character:

Alfred Loth redet nirgend zum Publikum. Er redet zu Hoffmann von Dingen, wie man sie nach einer langen Trennung notwendigerweise zur Sprache bringt . . . Er redet dann mit Helenen, einem guten naiven Kinde, und gibt ihr die ihm selbst alltäglichen Gedanken in einer leicht faßlichen Form, um sie ihr nahezulegen . . .

Wie soll es anders als lächerlich wirken, wenn der Schauspieler mit

Alfred Loth never addresses the audience directly. He speaks to Hoffmann of things which will necessarily come up after a long separation . . . And then he talks to Helene, a good, simple girl, and tells her what for him are commonplace ideas, in an easily comprehensible form, in order to convince her.

How can it be anything but laughable if the actor pretentiously enunciates deliberate simplifications and throws

gewollten Simplizitäten prätentiös her-
austritt und sie wie Offenbarungen
höchster Weisheit ins Parkett hinunter-
predigt.[10]

them down into the auditorium as if
they were manifestations of the highest
wisdom.

There is, however, another point in the play where a comparison with *The Wild Duck* is more illuminating. The discussion between Schimmelpfennig and Loth links the fifth act to the first, in which Hoffmann and Loth discussed different attitudes to social reform. Hoffmann's attitude is clearly a contemptible piece of hypocrisy; and even now, his wife in labour, he shows more concern about Loth's sociological investigation than does Loth himself. But Schimmelpfennig's attitude has a certain superficial attraction, in much the same way as Dr Relling's has in *The Wild Duck*; he is a bluff and good-natured man, with no illusions, dedicated to alleviating mortal pain: 'Es ist eine ganz simple Sache: die Menschheit liegt in der Agonie, und unsereiner macht ihr mit Narkoticis die Sache so erträglich als möglich' ('It's quite simple: mankind is in agony, and it is our job to drug them, and make their condition as bearable as possible') (I, 92). One might therefore expect him to be in favour of the marriage of Loth and Helene, for this would certainly make Helene's life more bearable, but he is instrumental in preventing it, and we are led to believe that this is because of his convinced and dogmatic opposition to the institution of marriage as such. His suggestion that the companionship of Hoffmann might provide Helene with some consolation for the loss of Loth is quite consistent with his views on the function of medicine, but reveals the total inadequacy of his thinking, and his total failure to understand Helene's character. Like Relling (and like Robert Scholz in Hauptmann's next play, *Das Friedensfest*) he responds to idealism with wounding mockery: 'Daß ihr Kerls doch immer bis über die Ohren in Dinge hineingeratet, die ihr theoretisch längst verworfen habt, . . . Was ihr alles nötig habt, um flott zu bleiben, Glaube, Liebe, Hoffnung. Für mich ist das Kram' ('You fellows keep getting involved up to the neck in things which you have in theory long rejected, . . . what a lot of things you need to keep afloat, faith, hope, charity. For me that's all a load of rubbish') (I, 92); but in doing so he invites the answer of Gregers Werle: 'If *you* are right and *I* am wrong, life will no longer be worth living.'

If *Vor Sonnenaufgang* has indeed been influenced by *The Wild Duck*, then, I believe, Hauptmann's play is to be seen as an idealist's attempt to rescue something from the jaws of Ibsen's grim pessimism. During his years in Zurich in the 1880s Hauptmann and his friends had shared the attitude which lays Loth open to Schimmelpfennig's mockery: 'Das Frühlinghafte jener und besonders der Zürcher Zeit bestand in einer immanenten Gläubigkeit. Soll ich die abgegriffene

Dreizahl Glaube, Liebe, Hoffnung für sie beanspruchen? Ja! denn wir waren davon erfüllt' ('What made those days, especially the days in Zurich, so spring-like, was our immanent belief. Shall I call it the old trinity, faith, hope, and charity? Yes, for we were filled with them') (VII, 1060). And in the play it is this attitude which makes Loth an optimist, who sees in medicine—as his comments on the work of Zola and Ibsen reveal—a means of *curing* mankind. This optimism enables Loth to change the situation he finds, to detach Helene from her alliance with the party of Hoffmann, to awaken her social conscience (her defence of the dismissed maidservant), to break down the repressive defence-mechanisms she is in the process of building up (evidence of which is to be found in her description of the mine-workers), and to convert her from a limited reliance on alcohol to complete abstinence.

Loth is typical of Hauptmann's heroes in that he stands for *exposure* in both its senses: the exposure of unpalatable circumstances, and the complementary exposure of the self to suffering. Knowledge may bring suffering, but both are to be avoided only at great cost in terms of basic humanity. Hoffmann, for instance, remains human only in as much as he is still capable of suffering: 'Das ist tragisch an dem Menschen, er leidet . . ., so viel er überhaupt leiden kann' ('That is what is tragic about the man, he suffers . . ., he suffers as much as he still can') (I, 93–4). It is Loth, the idealist, and not Schimmelpfennig, the cynic, who anticip-ates that his departure may be disastrous to Helene, for she too is an idealist. As a woman she lacks the opportunity to change an evil world, and suicide is her only way of rejecting it. This suicide, unlike that of Johannes Vockerat in *Einsame Menschen*, is not simply an act of despair at being left by someone she loves, but an assertion of all that is best in her, a refusal, comparable, as I have suggested, with that of Emilia Galotti, to sink slowly into a world of unfeeling and anonym-ity.

Without being fundamentally altered the play's idealist message is, as it were, transferred from Loth to Helene. Loth's 'immanent religion' is not in the end quite religious enough to provide a convincing motive for the course of action he takes. *Vor Sonnenaufgang* shows signs of a disenchantment with scientific ration-alism, but this disenchantment is, as yet, not strong enough to have more than a negative influence, that is to say, to distract the author's interest from a character whose action is rationally thought out and to leave it, in consequence, on one who acts from an elemental impulse of horror.

Notes to Chapter V

¹ Loth was, to some extent, modelled on Hauptmann's friend, Alfred Ploetz, whose views on this subject are recorded in the article 'Alkohol und Nachkommenschaft',

Neue deutsche Rundschau, VI (1895), pp. 1108–12. Ploetz's reaction to the play was that a type such as Loth is unsympathetic, but rather rare, that the situation was presented in an unnecessarily pessimistic light, but that so long as birth-control remains undeveloped Loth's behaviour would, in principle be correct; see F. A. Voigt, 'Die Aufnahme von "Vor Sonnenaufgang" ', *Hauptmann Studien*, p. 66. Hauptmann himself denied sharing Ploetz's (erroneous) views on hereditary alcoholism (VII, 1065), but the evidence of contemporaries suggests that he did; see A. von Hanstein, *Das jüngste Deutschland*, Leipzig, 1905², p. 171, and Bruno Wille, 'Erinnerungen an Gerhart Hauptmann', *Mit Gerhart Hauptmann*, ed. Heynen, p. 106.

2 Cf. above, p. 19.

3 *Gespräche mit Gerhart Hauptmann*, Berlin, 1932, p. 166.

4 *Die deutsche Literatur des XIX Jahrhunderts*, Berlin, 1900, p. 833.

5 'Berliner Brief' *Die Gesellschaft*, V (1889), p. 1180.

6 Cf. Peter Szondi, *Theorie des modernen Drama*, Frankfurt a.M., 1959, p. 56. Dr Kastan must have read the play very diligently, for Marthe's cries of pain, required by the stage-directions (I, 86) were omitted for the first performance; see Paul Schlenther, *Wozu der Lärm? Genesis der Freien Bühne*, Berlin, 1889, pp. 28 f.

7 Cf. K. S. Guthke, *Gerhart Hauptmann. Weltbild in Werk*, Göttingen, 1961, pp. 58 f. Cf. also the letter of James to Stanislaus Joyce, quoted by K. L. Tank, *Gerhart Hauptmann in Selbstzeugnissen und Bilddokumenten*, Hamburg, 1959, p. 167.

8 Holz, X, 224; Hauptmann himself frequently expressed the view that characterization is more important than action; e.g. VI, 1043.

9 Max Dreyer, *Winterschlaf*, 1904³, p. 61.

10 *Die Kunst des Dramas*, pp. 94–95. In the first performance the actor concerned was Theodor Brandt, but the same thing seems to have happened a year later when the *Freie Volksbühne* gave a performance with a different actor in the role; the critic of the *Berliner Volksblatt* (12 November 1890) wrote: 'Herr Hagemann ist kein realistischer Schauspieler . . . Herr Hagemann verstand es ganz aus dem Rahmen des Kunstwerkes heraustretend, gleichsam agitatorisch, als stände er auf der Rednertribüne . . . zur Menge zu sprechen, und verschmähte dabei keinen noch so wohlfeilen Kniff'.

VI

Das Friedensfest

Hauptmann's second play, *Das Friedensfest*, was first performed on 1 June 1890, bringing to an end the first season of the *Freie Bühne*. There was no repetition of the scandal which had accompanied the first performance of *Vor Sonnenaufgang*, but once again the dramatist had reason to be unhappy with the performance of his leading actor, the celebrated Josef Kainz, who arrived for the performance without having memorized his part.[1] Critical response to the play ranged from lukewarm to hostile, and it is only in recent years that it has come to be regarded as a key work in Hauptmann's *œuvre*.

Das Friedensfest is a much more tautly constructed and firmly circumscribed work than its immediate predecessor. The broad social problem which lay in the background of *Vor Sonnenaufgang* is here abandoned in favour of greater concentration on the central issues of marriage and the family, and the interior struggles of the characters. Coherent argument between people of equal intelligence has a much larger role, as it does in the following play, *Einsame Menschen*; indeed, both plays illustrate the preference of the Naturalist dramatists for the middle-class, intellectual sphere, and they are, at the same time, the two of Hauptmann's plays in which the resemblance to Ibsen is most marked. *Ghosts* and *Rosmersholm* are the plays which most readily come to mind in this connection. Both had been performed in Berlin in 1887, and Hauptmann is known to have been present at the performance of *Ghosts*, at least. The superficial similarities between this latter play and *Das Friedensfest* are indeed considerable; the two plays share the same technique of analytical exposition, they reveal the tyranny of the past in hereditary disease, and they condemn the 'lie' of modern marriage. But, despite all this, they remain characteristically different, as two plays by Hauptmann and Ibsen inevitably are different. It is strange that Hauptmann should have said: 'Ibsens Stücke enthalten eine gewisse unentschiedene Moral' ('Ibsen's plays point a certain vague moral') (VI, 1043), for without ever degenerating into the flat tendentiousness of many of his German imitators, Ibsen can convey with absolute clarity the rights and duties of a character such as Mrs Alving. It is no value judgement to say that in *Das Friedensfest* Hauptmann does not, but gives a demonstration of determinism, the loss and exposure of man in the world as he understands it, the quality of his suffering, and considers the price it is necessary to pay to ensure survival.

The plot, the family-catastrophe of the sub-title, is based closely on an account of Frank Wedekind's home-life—so closely that Wedekind was deeply offended by what he considered to be a betrayal of confidence. (Wedekind's riposte was a parody of Hauptmann in his early play, *Die junge Welt* (1889). The quarrel lasted many years, and left its traces in the prologue to *Erdgeist* (1896).)[2] This plot is centred on an ill-conceived and unsuccessful attempt by Frau Buchner and her daughter, Ida, to bring about a reconciliation among the divided Scholz family. As a result, it is suggested, of an ill-advised marriage of convenience between Dr Scholz and a woman twenty-two years his junior, and very much inferior to him in intellect and experience of life, the Scholzes are a family ridden with strife and nervous disorder. As in the opening scene of *Vor Sonnenaufgang*, the atmosphere of the household in which the drama takes place is established brilliantly and quickly as Auguste (who must have seen her father waiting around outside the house) enters:

AUGUSTE, *in Hast und Bestürzung von draußen herein. Innen angelangt, schlägt sie die Glastür heftig ins Schloß und stemmt sich dagegen, wie um jemandem den Eintritt zu verwehren* (I, 106).

AUGUSTE, *enters from outside in haste and panic. Having got inside, she slams the glass door violently shut and leans against it as if to prevent someone from coming in.*

The culmination of the family quarrels was reached some six years before the play opens, when Wilhelm struck his father. The occasion of the blow was a visit which Wilhelm made to his mother, during which he introduced a musician-friend into the house, his aim being to provide 'eine Auffrischung für Mutter' (I, 133), whose musical interests were not shared by her husband. Both Wilhelm and his father left the house on the same day, and have not subsequently been back. Robert, the elder brother, has taken a job which keeps him away from home, though he has been returning every Christmas; Auguste, the unmarried daughter, has remained with her mother.

In the intervening years Wilhelm has recovered a certain amount of equanimity through friendship with Frau Buchner and Ida, whom he now intends to marry. Frau Buchner, anxious to complete the cure of her prospective son-in-law, has persuaded the reluctant Wilhelm to return home and celebrate Christmas with his mother. Quite by chance Dr Scholz, now aged and sick, has also decided to return, and so a happy coincidence sees the whole family reunited. The Buchners urge Wilhelm to take this opportunity of begging his father's forgiveness, and, in a silent scene of intense conflict, father and son are reconciled. It seems as if the Buchners have been successful beyond their original expectations when a state of harmony embraces the entire family; but they have underestimated their task; the old antagonisms destroy this superficial harmony;

Robert and Wilhelm quarrel violently, the others take sides. Dr Scholz succumbs to a stroke. Robert, embittered, resolves to leave home once and for all. Frau Buchner regrets her interference, and departs in tears. Wilhelm decides that it is his duty to give up all ideas of marriage. But at the last moment the pessimism is muted as Ida, now almost in the position of the abandoned Helene Krause, persuades Wilhelm to have confidence in the power of love, and the final curtain falls as the two walk resolutely together into Dr Scholz's death-chamber.

The subject of family-relationships and parental authority had provided the theme of a play much admired by the Naturalists, and performed four months earlier than *Das Friedensfest* by the *Freie Bühne*—Ludwig Anzengruber's *Das vierte Gebot*. Surprisingly, it is the earlier dramatist who is the more radical critic of social institutions, and the more clearly tendentious. Anzengruber argues that the fourth commandment (the fifth according to the reckoning of the reformed churches) has no absolute validity. The young pastor, Eduard Schön, follows it with confidence because his own parents have always acted with wisdom and understanding; but his advice to a young girl to marry a man of her father's choice brings disaster to herself, her parents, her child, and the man she loved. All those involved come to agree that insistence on filial duty was misplaced, and that each case must be decided on its merits; Eduard confides to his parents:

Ich hätte mich erst ganz genau mit den Verhältnissen vertraut machen sollen, und dann wäre es am Platz gewesen, ohne der Neigung irgendwie das Wort zu reden, dem Vater Hedwigs die geplante Verbindung auf das eindringlichste abzuraten . . . Ich dachte damals nur an euch und mich und ich war gewohnt, euch immer zu gehorchen.[3]	I should have enquired into all the circumstances first, and then it would have been proper, without speaking in favour of Hedwig's inclinations, to advise her father most strongly against the marriage . . . But at the time I only thought of you and me, and I was always accustomed to obey you.

The moral is reinforced in the concluding scene of the play, in which the central character of the sub-plot, Martin Schalanther, now under sentence of death, gives the modified version of the commandment for which this play became famous: 'Wenn du in der Schul den Kindern lehrst: "Ehret Vater und Mutter!" so sag's auch von der Kanzel den Eltern, daß s' darnach sein solln' ('If you teach children at school: "Honour thy father and thy mother", then you should also tell their parents from the pulpit to behave accordingly').[4]

Among other plays of the Naturalist period in which the father, the representative of the authority of the older generation, is called to account for the sufferings of the children are Ernst Rosmer (Else Bernstein)'s *Dämmerung* (1893) and Wilhelm Weigand's *Der Vater* (1894), but it is *Das Friedensfest* which takes up this theme with the greatest subtlety and the greatest force, and which, at the same time, anticipates most markedly the protests—and the *topoi*—of the Expressionist drama. Both in the 1890s and in the Expressionist period the conflict of fathers and sons is of particular importance in the field of education. Dr Scholz is described as having submitted his sons to a particularly brutal regime:

Volle zehn Stunden täglich hockten wir über Büchern . . . Wenn ich das Kerkerloch sehe, heutigen Tags noch . . . es stieß an sein Arbeitszimmer . . . Wenn wir in diesen Raum eintraten, da mochte die Sonne noch so hell zum Fenster reinscheinen, für uns war es dann Nacht (I, 131).	For ten whole hours a day we sat over books . . . When I see that prison, even today . . . it was next to his study . . . When we stepped into that room, no matter how brightly the sun was shining outside, for us it was night.

Unimaginative rationalism, the rigour of philological drill, the tyranny of systematic education ('Hier hat man mir das . . . Leben . . . systematisch verdorben', says Wilhelm [I, 126]), are also severely criticized in *Der erste Schultag* by Holz and Schlaf, in Holz's and Jerschke's *Traumulus*, in Wedekind's *Frühlings Erwachen*, and, most notably perhaps, in Heinrich Mann's novel, *Professor Unrat*.

In *Das Friedensfest*, as in *Frühlings Erwachen*, it is the mother who intercedes on behalf of the children to offer something other than discipline and systematic knowledge. Three decades later, that is after the educational system of Germany has been subject to the criticisms of Julius Langbehn, Ellen Key, the *Jugendbewegung*, and numerous others, the same motif is taken up by the Expressionist, Arnolt Bronnen, in *Vatermord*. Here the father, symbolically named Fessel, wishes to make his son become a lawyer, despite the boy's own longing for the career of a farmer, in the free, open-air atmosphere of the countryside. Education, for the father, means breaking his son's will, and imposing his own:

> Er soll nur in den Himmel wachsen!
> Ich werd ihn brechen.[5]

The effect of the father's pressure on the son is to produce in him a state bordering on insanity; and after a cruel and brutal assault, Walter eventually gives his father a single blow in self-defence. The play ends with the consummation of the sympathetic relations between mother and son in an act of incest, Walter's killing of his father, and his jubilation at his attainment of freedom.

Bronnen's crude play does not treat characterization and motivation with any degree of subtlety; one cannot expect this of an Expressionist drama;[6] but this is the field in which Hauptmann excels. *Das Friedensfest* derives its considerable merits from Hauptmann's evident understanding of the potentiality for love and feeling which, because of its range and intensity, is responsible for both the mutual antagonism and the continued family solidarity of the Scholzes. Hauptmann once wrote: 'Es gibt nichts so Grauenvolles wie die Fremdheit derer, die sich kennen' ('There is nothing so terrible as the estrangement of intimates') (VI, 1014); this is the problem he is dealing with in *Das Friedensfest*; the play which most resembles it in this is one by Eugene O'Neill, not *Mourning becomes Electra* (which Hauptmann subsequently came to know and admire) but the more personal *Long Day's Journey into Night*, in which a situation of crisis has the same effect of uniting a strife-ridden family.

There is little opportunity for weighing the conflicting arguments and judgements in *Das Friedensfest*, and so social criticism (of marriage) has only a limited role. We can readily accept that there is some justification for Robert's criticism of his parents' marriage; but as far as Wilhelm and Ida are concerned, this issue is evaded: despite the quarrel which flares up briefly in the final scene, there is no reason to assume that they are mismatched in the way Wilhelm's parents were. The conclusion of the play leaves their future in doubt, but there is some hope for Wilhelm's survival in the environment to be provided by Ida. At the same time the argument between the pessimist, Robert Scholz, and the optimist, Frau Buchner, is not conclusively resolved, despite the apparent defeat of Frau Buchner; in short, the attitude behind the play would seem to be entirely consistent with Hauptmann's words:

Optimismus an sich hat etwas Verdächtiges . . . mehr: etwas Vulgäres . . . mehr: etwas Banales . . . mehr: etwas Gemeines!—aber der Pessimismus wirkt abgegriffen und in jeder Beziehung als geforderter Gegensatz zu dem vorherigen (VI, 998).	There is about optimism something suspect . . . worse: something vulgar . . . worse: something banal . . . worse: something base!—but pessimism seems hackneyed, in all respects an opposite provoked by optimism.

The form of *Das Friedensfest* is that of the typical German Naturalist drama, with Frau Buchner and her daughter sharing the role of *Bote aus der Fremde*, though another way of looking at the play might see Dr Scholz in this role; in any event, the Buchners have very little real influence on the causal structure. What really brings the family together this Christmas Eve is the strength of those bonds which have preserved them as a family until now. There is a certain irrational quality about these bonds, but Hauptmann, treating his subject naturalistically, shows how they operate in the social sphere to produce the family unit and the tensions peculiar to it.

There are a number of signs of affection, strenuously suppressed, beneath the brittle surface of the Scholz family. Ida probes, and Wilhelm concedes that Dr

Scholz's behaviour cannot be attributed solely to the desire to dominate over his sons: 'Bis zu einem gewissen Grad mag er ja auch damals eine gute Absicht vielleicht gehabt haben' (I, 131). If this grudging admission means little, there is some evidence that the father's affection was recognized and returned: on different occasions Auguste and Robert speak up for their absent father. Most significant is Frau Scholz's spontaneous reaction when her husband unexpectedly comes through the door:

FRAU SCHOLZ, *den Doktor wie eine überirdische Erscheinung anstarrend.* Fritz!	FRAU SCHOLZ, *staring at the doctor like a supernatural apparition.* Fritz!
. . . .	. . . .
vor Staunen außer sich. Aber sag mer nur Fritz! sag mer nur . . . die Gedanken fliegen mer davon. *Ihn weinend umhalsend.* Ach Fritz! was hast du mir für Kummer gemacht in der langen Zeit! (I, 113).	*beside herself with astonishment.* But tell me Fritz! just tell me . . . I'm all confused. *Embracing him in tears.* Ah, Fritz! What a lot of worry you've caused me all this time.

The same instinctive affection characterizes Frau Scholz's relations with her children. Wilhelm left home some years ago, but in her own *kleinbürgerlich* way his mother is still concerned about his future happiness: 'Du kannst dem lieben Gott schon danken, da kannst du lange warten, bis du wieder eine wie Ida findst! . . . *Vorsichtig, vertraulich*: . . . Sag doch mal, sind die Buchners gut situiert?' ('You ought to thank God, you could wait a long time till you found another like Ida! . . . *cautiously, confidentially*: . . . but tell me, how well off are the Buchners?') (I, 153). In the past she intervened to protect them from the harshness of their father's discipline; simple person that she was, intellectual persuasion was not a course that was open to her, and so violent scenes resulted. Again it seems that this affection has been returned. Robert, outwardly, cynical and cold, has returned every Christmas during the long lonely years to visit his mother and sister; and Wilhelm's account of his feelings at the time of the quarrel suggests an almost guilty excess in his affection for his mother: 'Damals kam mir's vor, als ob er [Dr Scholz] Mutter widerrechtlich hier gefangen hielte. Ich wollte geradezu, sie sollte sich von ihm trennen' ('It seemed to me at the time as if he [Dr Scholz] was illegally holding mother prisoner here. I actually wanted her to become separated from him') (I, 132). It was in his mother's name that Wilhelm struck his father; just as it is in his father's name that Robert now hates his brother:

Seh ich ihn . . . , dann geht alle meine Überlegung zum Teufel, dann bin	If I see him . . . , I'm not rational, I become something . . . something . . .

ich etwas . . . etwas . . . na, wie soll ich sagen? dann seh ich nur den Menschen, der meinen Vater—nicht seinen, sondern meinen—Vater ins Gesicht geschlagen hat (I, 122).

well, how shall I put it? then I only see the man who struck my father—not his father but my father—in the face.

The strikingly coincidental reunion of the Scholz family is not an implausibility in the action of the play, but an indication that the Scholzes are once again ready to come together as a family, indeed, are irresistibly drawn to do so. There is only the most superficial conflict of interest between them and the Buchners. Christmas for Robert, illness for the Doctor, and the Buchners for Wilhelm, all serve as excuses or provide opportunities for the assertion of an impulse that is normally feared and therefore suppressed. Because Frau Buchner is a superficial woman she does not realize this. A similar situation occurs in a very different play, Racine's *Phèdre*. As the play opens Phèdre is already tormented and dying because of her guilty love for her stepson, Hippolyte; the false report of the death of her husband, Thésée, does not alter the morality of the situation in the least (Phèdre did not need A. W. Schlegel to point this out to her), it merely provides the queen with a reason for seeking out Hippolyte, whom she has hitherto shunned. She insists: 'Je vous viens *pour un fils* expliquer mes alarmes' (Act, III, scene v; my emphasis); but it is her terrible passion which steers the course of their interview. Without the false report, this meeting could not have taken place, but it is in only the most limited sense the cause of the tragedy.

The Buchners have little real influence in bringing the family together, and equally little on the act of reconciliation itself. The explanation of this is only to be found in the feelings of the various characters, and their continued family devotion.[7] The very fact that the family is assembled is a first step—and the first step towards a family reconciliation is the most difficult one—a tentative admission of affection and mutual dependence, an esoteric signal which can be recognized only within the family, and which itself calls forth the next step.

This second step, the confrontation of father and son, is very nearly thwarted because of Frau Buchner's interference. Wilhelm threatens to leave, suspecting that his father's presence has been engineered by her. When father and son do meet, Wilhelm's behaviour bears little resemblance to the dramatic, almost biblical instructions which Frau Buchner gave him at the end of Act I. From his words and demeanour at this point it does appear to be Wilhelm's intention to do more or less as she instructs him, that is to say to act out the role of Prodigal Son, in which he has been cast—not out of conviction, but for the sake of Ida. It is clear from his conversation with Ida at the beginning of Act II that he is still intellectually convinced of the justice of his attack on his father; he still describes it as a punishment. Yet instead of a pious, but hypocritical plea for forgiveness, we witness an instinctive awakening of sympathy, a relenting by two characters weary of maintaining a cramped and meaningless hostility; and this happens before a single word has been uttered. The relaxation spreads, to involve the whole family in a way which Frau Buchner did not anticipate, because the quality and quantity of the feeling in this particular family is something which is not within the range of her experience, lived or imagined, as she subsequently concedes:

nun habe ich so viel gesehen hier und erfahren. Da ist mir vieles von dem, was Sie [Wilhelm] mir früher gesagt haben, erst verständlich geworden. Ich verstand Sie nicht. Ich hielt Sie für einen Schwarzseher. Ich nahm vieles gar nicht einmal ernst. Mit einem festen frohen Glauben kam ich hierher. Ich schäme mich förmlich (I, 155).

I have now seen and experienced so much here. I now understand much of what you told me earlier. I didn't understand you before. I thought you were just prone to look on the gloomy side. There were many things I did not even take seriously. I came here with a firm and joyful faith. I am positively ashamed.

Robert, however, confirms that the brief interlude of peace and happiness was not entirely a surprise; that the potentiality was present before the intervention of the Buchners: 'Es ist doch jetzt in uns lebendig geworden, es war doch also in uns, warum ist es nicht schon früher hervorgebrochen? . . . Es war doch in uns!' ('Now it has come to life in us, so it was in us, why did it not break out sooner? . . . It was in us!') (I, 138).

Frau Buchner's admission of shame is an admission of excessive trust in the power of the conscious will. In *Das Friedensfest* Hauptmann is very much concerned with exposing the limitations of this force, and with revealing the unconscious motives which lie behind even the most considered words. The spoken words of the Buchners and the Scholzes—even the intelligent Robert's—are seldom effective in helping the characters understand what is driving them; they are only rarely significant for the information they convey directly. This distrust of the spoken word was already evident in *Vor Sonnenaufgang*; Hoffmann, for instance, could be seen rationalizing his designs on Helene with the help of Dr Schimmelpfennig's suggestion that she might make a suitable foster-mother for his second child. This later play probably owes more to Schopenhauer's view of the intellect as an instrument in the service of deeper impulses;[8] there are also traces of Nietzsche's suspicion of the self-gratification derived by the altruist from his task: 'Es gibt in der Tat noch immer naive Seelen, die sich nicht wohl fühlen, wenn sie nicht an ihren Mitmenschen herumbessern und herumflicken können' ('There really still are naïve souls, who are not happy unless they can meddle around trying to improve their fellow men') (I, 118), complains Robert. The point is emphasized in the argument between Auguste and Frau Buchner over the dispensation of charity by the local priest:

AUGUSTE. So viel steht fest: wenn ich arm wäre, ich hätte auf die Rede des Großmann hin . . . wahrhaftig den ganzen Bettel hätte ich ihnen vor die Füsse geschmissen.
FRAU BUCHNER. Es ist aber doch ein großer Segen für die armen Leute.[9]
(I, 108)

AUGUSTE. One thing is certain: if I were poor, when that man spoke . . . really, I should have chucked all his charity at his feet.
FRAU BUCHNER. But it is a great blessing for the poor.

Frau Buchner's affection for Wilhelm is revealed as a particularly important motive for her actions, her optimism, and her gross underestimation of the task she has taken upon herself. Her first moment of self-awareness is a disastrous blow for her:

FRAU BUCHNER, *unter Tränen*. Ich weiß nicht! Ich weiß das selbst nicht! Ich habe das Kind erzogen. Es ist mir alles in allem gewesen; an seinem Glücke zu arbeiten ist auf der Welt mein einziger Beruf gewesen. Nun kamen Sie in unser Haus. Ich gewann Sie lieb. Ich dachte auch an Ihr Glück, ich . . . Das hätte ich vielleicht nicht tun sollen . . . Ich dachte vielleicht ebensosehr an Ihr Glück—und wer weiß—am Ende—zuallermeist—an Ihr Glück. *Einen Augenblick lang starren beide einander bestürzt in die Augen.*
WILHELM. Frau Buchner!!
FRAU BUCHNER, *das Gesicht mit den Händen bedeckend wie jemand der sich schämt, weinend ab durch den Treppenausgang* (I, 156).

FRAU BUCHNER, *in tears*. I don't know! I just don't know! I brought the child up. She was everything to me; my sole earthly vocation was to work for her happiness. Then you came into our house. I became fond of you. I began to think of your happiness too, I . . . Perhaps I shouldn't have done that . . . Perhaps I thought equally of your happiness—and who knows—in the end —of your happiness—most of all. *For a moment they both look into each other's eyes in astonishment.*
WILHELM. Frau Buchner!!
FRAU BUCHNER, *covering her face with her hands like someone who is ashamed, goes off, in tears, by the staircase-exit.*

This revelation of her hitherto unconscious motives casts a radically different light on the whole of Frau Buchner's behaviour. It ironically underscores her claim: 'ich fühle mich im Dienst einer bestimmten Sache. Das feit mich' ('I feel that I am acting in a specific cause. That fortifies me') (I, 118). It strengthens the authority of Robert as a judge of character, for he has all along been reluctant to take her actions at their face value: 'Was die Buchner hier eigentlich beabsichtigt, möchte ich gern wissen' ('I should very much like to know what this Frau Buchner is really doing here') (I, 123); and it lends a greater significance to Auguste's insistence that the Scholz family is not so bad after all: 'Wir sind, wie wir sind. Andre Leute, die wer weiß wie tun, sind um nichts besser' ('We are what we are. Other people, who put on all sorts of airs, are no better than us') (I, 118). For Frau Buchner to judge and to strive to change others is presumption; her self-satisfied equanimity, based as it is on the conviction that she is engaged on an altruistic task, is a quality to which, by her own moral standards, she is not entitled.

Yet the progressive devaluation of Frau Buchner's efforts, the justification of the Scholzes' views of the Christmas festivities: 'Wenn man's recht bedenkt: eigentlich ist das doch auch nichts für Erwachsene' ('If one stops to think about it, this isn't really something for adults') (I, 109), and, at first sight, of their pessimistic despair, are not enough to support the interpretation of the play as the tragedy of Frau Buchner's kind of optimism. There is a brief scene, analogous to the one in which we are made aware of Frau Buchner's feelings for Wilhelm, in which Robert's authority is undermined. He creeps stealthily to the table of Christmas gifts and passionately imprints a kiss on the purse which Ida has placed there for Wilhelm, knowing himself to be unobserved. In this unguarded moment he reveals a more yielding side to his character, which is normally masked by his brutal cynicism; a side whose existence Frau Buchner has perceived: 'Es ist wirklich nicht Ihr wahres Gesicht, was Sie herauskehren' (I, 120). Robert's pessimism is, as Wilhelm remarks, a product of disappointment and envy; he may be right in his assessment of Wilhelm's future prospects, but it is purely coincidental if he is:

Was dich auf den rechten Gedanken gebracht hat, das sag' ich dir ins Gesicht, das ist jämmerlicher Neid . . . das ist einfach tief klägliche Mißgunst! . . . Du willst mich nicht gereinigt wissen. Warum willst du es nicht? Nun, weil . . . weil du selbst so bleiben mußt, wie du bist; weil sie mich liebt und nicht dich! (I, 163).	I tell you straight, what has put you on the right lines is pitiful jealousy . . . sheer, wretched envy! . . . You don't want to see me healed. And why not? Well, because . . . because you'll have to stay as you are; because she loves me and not you.

The pessimism of Robert Scholz and the optimism of Frau Buchner are each undermined to such an extent that there can be no talk of a clash of *Weltanschauungen* in *Das Friedensfest*. And it is precisely this lack of ideological discussion and guidance in Hauptmann's works which was to be criticized by the Expressionists; the third critic in Act I of Sorge's *Der Bettler* says:

Wir warten auf einen, der uns unser Schicksal neu deutet, den nenne ich denn Dramatiker und stark. Unser Haupt-Mann, sehen Sie, ist groß als Künstler, aber als Deuter befangen. Es ist sehr an der Zeit: einer muß einmal wieder für uns alle nachsinnen.[10]

We are waiting for someone who will interpret our destiny anew; such a man I will call a dramatist, and a powerful one. Our leading dramatist [Haupt-mann], you see, is a great artist, but a limited interpreter. It is high time: someone must come and think for us all once again.

These younger writers had an ally and an antecedent in Wedekind, for in *Schloß Wetterstein* (1910) (a counterpart to *Das Friedensfest* in that Wedekind here gives his own 'views about the inner necessities on which marriage and the family are based'),[11] he parodies the Naturalists' undermining of intellectual convictions. At the beginning of Act III, the heroine, Effie, is reduced to despair because medical diagnosis has robbed her of the self-assertive individualism to which she felt she owed her happiness:

Mein starkes
Verlangen ist die Folge, wenn ich recht
Verstanden, von Verdauungsstörungen?
. . . Und meiner Augen Schimmer,
Aus dem der Mann sich, was weiß ich
                        verspricht,
Verdank ich also einem Leberleiden?
. . .
Und daß so leicht und plötzlich mein
                        Gesicht
Die Farbe wechselt, und der matte Ton
Der Haut, das alles kommt von Gallen-
                        steinen,
Wenn nicht ein Lungenleiden gar dran
                        schuld?[12]

My strong desires are, if I have understood aright, the consequence of indigestion? . . . And the sparkle in my eyes, in which men read promises of I know not what, I owe to a liver-complaint? . . . And the way my face changes colour so easily and suddenly, and the paleness of my skin, all that is the result of gall-stones, if it isn't a disease of the lungs?

Effie pulls herself together when she is assured that, diagnosis notwithstanding, no one will notice any difference in her, and she refuses to be crushed by circumstances. In Wedekind's work it is the strength of the will over such chance circumstances which ensures human dignity; no force, not even love, should be allowed to restrict its free activity: 'In dem Augenblick, da man sich durch etwas Mächtigeres, als durch seinen freien Willen gebunden glaubt, tritt die ganze fluchwürdige Entsetzlichkeit der Ehe zutage.'[13]

This free and powerful will to self-assertion is very different from the scarcely comprehended force which determines the actions of Hauptmann's characters. As a Naturalist, Hauptmann shows this motive force operating through social phenomena;[14] although in this he does not differ radically from (say) Kleist, for in *Das Erdbeben in Chili* or *Penthesilea*, where a moment of crisis unites all in a common bond of feeling, the consequent harmony produces a complete, if temporary, reorganization of society. Given the more restricted scope of Hauptmann's play, the response of the Scholzes to Wilhelm's collapse before his father amounts to a similar reorganization.

Das Friedensfest resembles the work of Kleist in another important respect: in the limited and tentative evaluation of human conduct which (*pace* Sorge) it does contain. A heroine such as Penthesilea derives much of her beauty and value from the intensity of her feelings, from the totality of her exposure to those forces which, in others, are normally held at bay, from her very inability to restrain herself in the way Prothoe advises. Exposure and suffering *can* be avoided—by restraint or repression. And the difference between the brothers Robert and Wilhelm Scholz lies in the extent to which each is capable of defending himself from suffering. Repression of the self has played a part in the experience of Wilhelm, but it is something which he now rejects: 'Mich selbst fürcht ich. Vor sich selbst auf der Flucht sein; kannst du dir davon einen Begriff machen? Siehst du, und so fliehe ich mein Leben lang' ('I am afraid of myself. To be running away from oneself, can you imagine it? And don't you see, I've been running like this all my life') (I, 129). He longs for rest from this flight; he remains naïvely hopeful, and therefore exposed, unable to resist the promise held out by the Buchners. He is willing to risk disappointment in an attempt to change his life; with the optimism of the Expressionist generation he can assert: 'Jeder Mensch ist ein neuer Mensch' ('Every man is a new man') (I, 161). Even after his final conversation with Robert, when he has been convinced by his brother's grim arguments:

Du hast ganz recht! Ich bin ein durch und durch lasterhafter Mensch. Nichts ist mehr rein an mir. Besudelt, wie ich bin, gehöre ich nicht neben diese Unschuld, und ich bin fest entschlossen kein Verbrechen zu begehen; (I, 164)	You are quite right! I am a thoroughly depraved man. There is no longer anything clean about me. Sullied as I am, I do not belong near this innocent creature, and I am firmly resolved not to commit a crime;

he still gives in to Ida, and to her confident assertion that things will be different.

Robert, too, might well have behaved in this way in these circumstances; but with Ida so strongly committed to his brother, there is no evident escape for him. Intelligence, for a character in his situation, can soon be perverted to provide an excuse for withdrawal; the doctrine of determinism provides a ready justification for inaction. The reproach made to Gabriel Schilling, the hero of a later play by Hauptmann, could, with equal justice, have been made to Robert Scholz: 'Man kann auf das Fatum vieles abwälzen' ('One can blame a lot onto destiny') (II, 436). Experience has taught him that emotional involvement means risk. The admission of affection renders one vulnerable; and so Robert's surly behaviour on his first appearance seems to contradict the fact of his having come home to see his family at all. (His father is also reluctant to see any display of emotion when he arrives. He asks for his old manservant, Friebe, and returns to his old room upstairs.) He cynically trivializes any display of emotion; his difficult and moving apology to Wilhelm (I, 139) is followed by the wry comment: 'Akrobatenseele'. His every concession to his feelings is costly in terms of personal composure; he cannot therefore bring himself to accept a Christmas gift from Ida; when he comes in to take leave of Wilhelm for the last time, he finds himself stammering with emotion, and rapidly changes the subject:

Ich habe genug, über und über sogar! Mutter wird künftig . . . wird künftig die Weihnachtstage ohne, ohne mich auskommen müssen. *Nach dem Ofen umblickend.* Es ist kalt hier (I, 158).	I've had enough, and more than enough! Mother will in future . . . will in future have to get along at Christmas without, without me. *Looking round at the stove.* It's cold in here.

In the end Robert's fears prove to have been well-founded. Reconciliation and happiness can only be achieved briefly and with great risk; but it becomes evident that life without the attempt and the risk is a poor thing indeed. In opting for such a life, Robert makes a choice which Wilhelm regards as cowardly; he intends to repress all his feelings in work in a cold urban environment:

Ich gehe jetzt in ein kleines, geheiztes Comptoirchen, setze mich mit dem Rücken an den Ofen, kreuze die Beine unter dem Tisch, zünde mir diese selbe Pfeife hier an und schreibe, in aller Gemütsruhe hoffentlich . . . wenn ich da so sitze, siehst du . . . und die Gasflamme den ganzen Tag so über mir fauchen höre, von Zeit zu Zeit so'n Blick in den Hof—so'n Fabrikhof ist nämlich was Wunderbares! was Romantisches, sag' ich dir . . . mit einem Wort, da summt mich keine Hummel an. . . . Soll man sich immerfort aus dem Gleichgewicht bringen lassen, soll man sich denn kopfverwirrt machen lassen? Ich werde sowieso zwei bis drei Tage brauchen, um mich auf mein bißchen Lebensweisheit zu besinnen.[15] (I, 159)	I'm now going into a cosy little heated office, I shall sit with my back to the stove, cross my legs under the table, light this pipe here, and write, peacefully and quietly, I hope . . . when I sit like that, you see . . . and listen to the gaslight burning above me, and look out now and again into the yard—a factory-yard is something wonderful, something romantic, I tell you . . . to put it briefly, nothing bothers me . . . Ought one continually to let oneself be put off balance, ought one to let oneself be driven mad? As it is I shall need two or three days to collect myself again.

The idealism which Wilhelm has inherited from his father, has turned sour in Robert to produce a cynic, not unlike Büchner's Danton:

Vater und du [Wilhelm], ihr ähnelt einander zum Verwechseln. Ihr seid dieselben Idealisten. Anno 48 hat Vater auf den Barrikaden angefangen, und als einsamer Hypochonder macht er den Schluß.—Man muß sich an die Welt und an sich selbst beizeiten gewöhnen, du!— eh' man sich die Hörner abgelaufen hat (I, 159).

You [Wilhelm] and father, you are absolutely alike. You are both idealists. Father began on the barricades in '48, and he's come to the end of the road as a lonely hypochondriac—one has just got to get used to the world and to oneself, don't you see—before one has finished sowing one's wild oats.

Robert's nihilistic mockery corresponds, as a manifestation of the Naturalist period, to the dramas of Otto Erich Hartleben. If we are to believe his friend Cäsar Flaischlen, the bitterness of Hartleben's works is the bitterness of just such a disappointed idealist, and his irony is the defence of a sensitive mind: 'Je feiner und empfindsamer . . . jemand veranlagt[ist], um so leichter wird er dazukommen, sich mit Ironie zu wappnen zu suchen. . . . Anstatt sich verspotten zu lassen, spottet man lieber selbst'.[16] Hauptmann, a greater artist than Hartleben, can do justice to this attitude without adopting it.

Circumstances alone do not explain the difference between the two brothers; for certain innate differences of character explain why their circumstances are so different. Robert possesses a greater share of the discursive, analytical intelligence of his father, whilst Wilhelm has the musical interest of his mother. Robert, without an outlet for his emotions, was forced to fall back on himself when he left home, and pursue a hectic urban career, for which he had no positive inclination. The elder brother's grounds for envy of his more talented and more favoured junior are intensified by their contrasting fortunes in this period. Wilhelm's talent enabled him to approach others on an emotional level, and to gain access to the Buchner household, finding there a second mother-figure and a second home.

The initial natural parity lying deep below the differences is thus disturbed, as it is in the traditional drama of the hostile brothers. Of the works in this tradition Schiller's *Die Braut von Messina* provides the closest parallel to *Das Friedensfest*, because it shares the ambiguity of the Naturalist work.[17] The relationship between the two comparatively similar brothers, and especially the envy of the underprivileged for the privileged, provides the motive for Don Cesar's suicide; but, all the same, Schiller seems to evaluate this suicide as he would a voluntary, disinterested, and 'sublime' act. Despite the 'tout comprendre, c'est tout pardonner' which is implicit in the play's motivation, Hauptmann's *Das Friedensfest* ends with what looks very like an explicit judgement of Wilhelm's moral superiority. Ida, now independent of the manipulation of her mother, confident in the intuition that all will be well, proclaims: 'Vor dir bin ich klein, ach wie klein! wie eine kleine Motte bin ich nur. Wilhelm, ich bin nichts ohne dich! ich bin alles durch dich! Zieh deine Hand nicht von mir armseligem Geschöpfe!' ('Beside you I am small, oh how small! I am no more than a tiny moth! Without you I am nothing! Through you I am everything! Do not withdraw your hand from me in my misery!') (I, 165). But doubt must remain about this judgement; for what authority can be allowed to the views of a young girl, anxious not to be abandoned by the man she loves, given like her mother, perhaps, to dramatizing a situation, and speaking in this literary way?[18] What guarantee can there be that Wilhelm is not right to condemn her hopes as 'platte Backfischillusionen'?

It is one of the virtues of this play that Hauptmann has refrained from intruding at this point, for any authoritative statement would be inconsistent with the scepticism which is characteristic of the rest of the play. As intelligent persuasion Ida's words cannot compete with the devastating analysis of the situation just presented by Robert; but to be *dramatically* effective they do not need to compete on the same terms. It is quite plausible that they should have their effect as persuasion, *tout court*. As an expression of Ida's desire to take Wilhelm as he is, without presuming to change him, as an expression of her own anxiety, Ida's words are convincing; just as Wilhelm's response to them, his decision to give in to her, to take his chance, despite his apparent intellectual conviction that he has none, is convincing. One of the most significant advances of *Das Friedensfest* over *Vor Sonnenaufgang* is the realization that decisions are taken in this way, and not in the cold rational way Alfred Loth takes his. This realization is summed up by Hauptmann with a (not entirely appropriate) comment about Ibsen:

Ibsen gibt Gedankenwandlungen, das setzt Personen voraus, die über sich reflektieren. Das tun nur bestimmte Individualitäten. Die Gefühlswandlungen sind die tiefsten.[19]

Ibsen presents intellectual transformations; that presupposes people who think about themselves. Only certain individuals do that. Emotional transformations are deepest.

Notes to Chapter VI

[1] Gerhart Hauptmann, 'Das zweite Vierteljahrhundert', *Die großen Beichten*, Berlin, 1966, p. 659. Hauptmann's complaints about Kainz are confirmed in Maximilian Harden's review, *Die Gegenwart*, 7 October 1890.

[2] See F. W. J. Heuser, 'Gerhart Hauptmann und Frank Wedekind', *Gerhart Hauptmann*, pp. 226–46.

[3] *Sämtliche Werke*, Wien-Leipzig, 1920–28, V, 226.

[4] Ibid., p. 235.

[5] *Vatermord*, Berlin, 1925, p. 50.

6 Cf. W. H. Sokel, 'Dialogführung und Dialog im expressionistischen Drama', *Aspekte des Expressionismus*, ed. W. Paulsen, Heidelberg, 1968, pp. 59–84.

7 The family, of course, is not what it was; thus Margaret Sinden can attribute Wilhelm's 'undue self-castigation' (for having struck his father and broken up his home!) entirely to inherited nervous disorder; *Gerhart Hauptmann. The Prose Plays*, Toronto-London, 1957, p. 30.

8 See Hans M. Wolff, 'Das Friedensfest', in K. S. Guthke and Hans M. Wolff, 'Das Leid im Werke Gerhart Hauptmanns', *Univ. of California Publications in Modern Philology*, XLIX (1958), p. 55.

9 Wedekind, incidentally, makes a similar point in a short exchange between Melchior Gabor and Wendla Bergmann in *Frühlings Erwachen*; *Gesammelte Werke*, München, 1920–21, II, 114–16.

10 R. J. Sorge, *Der Bettler* (1912), Emsdetten/Westf., 1954, p. 26.

11 Wedekind, VI, 5.

12 Wedekind, VI, 59.

13 Wedekind, VI, 43.

14 Wilhelm Emrich plays down the Naturalist side of the play, to concentrate on the 'eternal power-struggle' of love and hate, guilt and reconciliation, etc., which he perceives beneath its surface; 'Der Tragödientypus Gerhart Hauptmanns', *Protest und Verheißung*, pp. 193–205. Cf. N. E. Alexander, *Studien zum Stilwandel im dramatischen Werk Gerhart Hauptmanns*, Stuttgart, 1964, p. 36.

15 In Max Halbe's *Mutter Erde* (1897), the hero, Paul Warkentin, echoes Robert Scholz's sentiments: 'Leute, die fertig sind mit sich, gehören aufs Land! Andre nicht! . . . Die andern, die brauchen Lärm, Zerstreuung, Menschen um sich herum. Man muß doch etwas haben, damit man vergessen kann. Irgend so ein Schlafpulver, womit man sich einwiegt. . . . Dazu ist die Großstadt gut. Zum Betäuben und Vergessen' (*Ges. Werke*, München, 1917–23, II, 364). In *Vor Sonnenaufgang*, it will be recalled, alcohol and tobacco provide relief from suffering by numbing the sensibilities; here Robert Scholz is a heavy smoker, and his father smokes and drinks excessively.

16 *Otto Erich Hartleben*, Berlin, 1896, p. 20.

17 The basic situation of the two plays is very similar: a mother unsuccessfully tries to use her daughter to bring about a family reconciliation. The title which Hauptmann originally planned to give this play, 'Der Friedensengel', may well derive from *Die Braut von Messina*, where Beatrice is thus described.

18 Ida's speech recalls some words spoken by Heinrich, shortly after his meeting with Mathilde in Novalis' *Heinrich von Ofterdingen*.

19 *Die Kunst des Dramas*, p. 189.

VII

Einsame Menschen

The decade of the 1890s saw the beginnings of a decisive retreat from the scientific positivism which had dominated the second half of the nineteenth century and which, in its time, had been one of the most significant factors in the emergence of European Naturalism.[1] It also saw the collapse of the provisional alliance between the German Naturalist writers and organized socialism.[2] These two developments are reflected in a number of the dramas of this period, the best of which is almost certainly Gerhart Hauptmann's third play, *Einsame Menschen*.

Einsame Menschen is a representative work in another, more superficial, but not entirely unconnected sense. Like *Das Friedensfest*, it has a factual basis; the dedication of the first edition runs: 'Ich lege dieses Drama in die Hände derjenigen, die es gelebt haben', and refers to Hauptmann's elder brother, Carl, his wife Marthe (sister to Gerhart Hauptmann's first wife, Marie Thienemann), and a young Polish student, Josepha Kodis-Krzyzanowska.[3] It also anticipates the problems which subsequently arose in Hauptmann's own marriage, and which he discusses in *Das Buch der Leidenschaft* (1929); and which, according to Max Halbe, were shared by a number of the young writers of the Naturalist generation.[4] The subject of the play, the ever-popular theme of the man between two women, may have had something to do with the play's success; at all events the première of *Einsame Menschen*, on 11 January 1891, provided Hauptmann with his first undisputed success.

The central character in *Einsame Menschen* is Johannes Vockerat, a brilliant young scholar, the son of devout middle-class parents, struggling in a transitional age to achieve intellectual freedom and moral independence. He is but one representative of a type proclaimed by the contemporary critic, Edgar Steiger, as the characteristic hero of the 'new drama': 'der moderne Übergangsmensch', or (in a moment of impatience, no doubt,) 'das Kind des Jahrtausendendes'.[5] His kindred include Ejlert Lövborg in Ibsen's *Hedda Gabler*, Glockengießer Heinrich in Hauptmann's own *Die versunkene Glocke*, and even Wilhelm Scholz in *Das Friedensfest*. The play opens shortly after the birth of a son to Johannes and his wife, Käthe. She is six years younger than her husband, and, like Frau Scholz in *Das Friedensfest*, intellectually far from being his equal—although she remains consistently the most sympathetic character in the play.

There is a suggestion in the third act that this marriage was arranged without very much reference to the young Käthe, and it soon becomes evident that it has not been a great success. It is the hope of Frau Vockerat, Johannes' mother, that the birth of the child will bring the couple closer together, and give her son some peace of mind, but Johannes' first entry suggests that it is having the opposite effect. For the sake of his parents he has made a compromise: despite his rejection of Christianity he has had the child christened, and he arrives directly from the ceremony in a state of irritability and self-pity; this is not the kind of first entry which will make an audience respond sympathetically. His friend, the sceptical Braun, is there to taunt him still further: 'Alter Hypochonder. Kohl nicht! Iß was! Die Predigt sitzt dir in den Knochen' ('You old hypochondriac. Stop that nonsense and eat something! It's the sermon that's upset you'); and Johannes' reply sums up, implicitly, the dilemma which forms the central theme of the play: 'Aufrichtig gestanden . . . du sprichst so von der Taufe. . . . Wie ich zu der Sache stehe, weißt du. Jedenfalls nicht auf dem christlichen Standpunkt. Aber's bleibt doch immer 'ne Sache, die so und so vielen heilig ist' ('Frankly speaking . . . you talk like that about baptism . . . you know my point of view, and it's not the Christian one. But it is still something which is sacred to many people') (I, 175). This dilemma between respect for traditional beliefs, consideration for the feelings of others on the one hand, and progressive thinking and truth to one's own convictions on the other, is reflected, with all the pedantry of Naturalism, in an introductory stage-direction, which prescribes photographs of Darwin and Haeckel alongside those of theologians on the wall of the room.

Once again it takes Hauptmann no more than a few pages of stage-direction and dialogue to introduce us, in masterly fashion, to a situation charged with tension. The hero, Johannes, is threatened on the one side by the orthodoxy of a conservative generation, by the tyranny of his family; but there is an equal threat from the opposite flank, from the radical socialism of the shaven-headed Braun. Into this tense situation comes the young student, Anna Mahr, an old acquaintance of Braun. She embodies a third attitude which is attractive to Johannes; she is sympathetic towards his work and shares his interests: philosophy, music, love of the open air. Anna supports Johannes in his desire to develop his individual freedom; she appears to be a natural partner for him. But Johannes is indecisive, and will not accept that he must choose between Anna and his wife. This indecision extends over four acts, until Johannes' father returns to assert his authority, and secure his son's assent to Anna's departure.[6] As he hears her train pass, Johannes is overcome with grief, and leaves the house to commit suicide. Käthe's reaction is a reproach to his parents for driving him to this extreme step: 'Mutter! Vater! Ihr habt ihm zum Äußersten getrieben. Warum habt ihr das getan . . . ?' (I, 258).

Käthe's judgement of her parents-in-law is the judgement with which the play concludes; her words come in a position of emphasis, and go unchallenged; it is self-evident that they are important words in the design of the play; and it follows that the play ends with the condemnation of the sacrifice of an individual to a rigid moral convention; Paul Schlenther, Gerhart Hauptmann's friend and first biographer, confirms that this was the author's conscious intention. But here, as in *Vor Sonnenaufgang*, Hauptmann's characterizing impulse inhibits the clear development of such a unilinear argument. If one pursues the question, 'why have you done this?', which Käthe asks of her parents, if one examines the complex motivation of all the characters in this play, one discovers, as in *Das Friedensfest*, a primitive trial of strength between characters whose means are devious, and whose ends are only very rarely clear to themselves. It is very much to the advantage of the play that this is so, for this is the ground on which Gerhart Hauptmann moves most surely.

When the play opens the relationship between Johannes and his parents is clouded. The deference which Johannes still shows—for instance by having his child christened—is not enough to pacify them, and they are constantly exerting pressure on him to give up his work. His mother blames all his discontent on his lack of religion, and his espousal of modern ideas: 'Der alte Haeckel und der tumme Darwin da: die machen dich bloß unglücklich . . . Sei ein klein bißchen fromm—Tu's deiner alten Mutter zuliebe' (I, 208). The possessive concern of a mother for her young, implicit in these words, is the most striking feature of Frau Vockerat's whole manner: her conversations with Käthe are punctuated with diminutives: 'Käthchen', 'Käthinkerle', 'liebes, gutes Kindchen'. She treats her daughter-in-law as a child, and tries to treat Johannes similarly, addressing him as 'alter Junge', thinking back longingly and proudly to the uncomplicated days when he was a brilliant young schoolboy: 'Das reine Wunderkind war er': she even tells him not to wear his best suit so much for Anna's benefit, in case he wears it out, whereupon Johannes feels the need to protest: 'Ich bin doch kein kleines Kind mehr, Mutter' ('But mother, I'm not a child any longer') (I, 208). Johannes' wife, Käthe, has never represented a threat to Frau Vockerat's possession of her son in the way the new-comer, Anna, does; Anna is not to be treated as a child, she encourages Johannes to think, to assert his independence in every respect, and so to break with the past, with tradition, and with the ties of the family. The conflict between old and new takes the form of a simple struggle for possession of Johannes, the man. For the Vockerats Christianity is a weapon in this struggle—just as in *Die Weber* it is a weapon in the hands of the property-owning classes. Occasionally Frau Vockerat will use this weapon to assert her own authority: 'Du sprichst in einem Tone mit deiner Mutter, der wider das vierte Gebot verstößt' ('You are speaking to your mother in a way which is forbidden by the fourth commandment') (I, 227); but in her moment of profoundest crisis she speaks to Anna more directly, and more honestly:

Ich will nicht richten in diesem Augenblick. Ich will zu Ihnen sprechen, eine Frau zur Frau—und als Mutter will ich zu Ihnen sprechen. *Mit tränenerstickter Stimme*: Als Mutter meines Johannes will ich zu Ihnen kommen. *Sie erfaßt Annas Hand.* Geben Sie mir meinen Johannes. Geben Sie einer gemarteten Mutter ihr Kind wieder! *Sie ist auf einen Stuhl gesunken und benetzt Annas Hand mit Tränen* (I, 243).

I don't want to pass any judgements at this moment. I want to talk to you as one woman to another—and I want to talk as a mother. *In a voice choked by tears*: I come to you as the mother of my Johannes. *She takes Anna's hand.* Give Johannes back to me. Give an unhappy mother her child back! *She has sunk down onto a chair and sheds tears over Anna's hand.*

This sincere and profound affection is so stifling because it forces Johannes off the intellectual ground on which he is reasonably sure of himself; as Anna sees immediately, she cannot defend herself for there is no *argument* against Frau Vockerat: 'Was Sie auch sagen, . . . ich kann mich nicht verteidigen gegen Sie . . .' (I, 243).

A similar family conflict provides the central theme of Georg Hirschfeld's play *Die Mütter* (first performed by the *Freie Bühne*, 12 May 1895). A young musician, Robert Frey, has been turned out of his home by his authoritarian father, and lives with a working-class girl, Marie Weil. After the death of his father, Robert's mother is anxious that her son should return home: the two women understand much more clearly than Robert what is involved; Marie abruptly rejects the suggestion that she can return with Robert and be accepted into his family; while Robert's mother states unequivocally that if he comes back, this means he has given Marie up: 'Wenn er kommt . . ., dann hat er sie aufgegeben'.[7]

In these two plays, as in *Das Friedensfest*, the mother tries to act as a buffer between a sensitive son and an authoritarian father. Frau Vockerat therefore sends for her husband only as a last resort. The interview between father and son at the beginning of Act V is only a slight variation on the earlier exchanges between mother and son in the previous part of the play. For him, too, orthodoxy is a means of maintaining his authority: when he sees Johannes he announces: 'Der Wille Gottes führt mich zu euch' ('The will of God has brought me to you'), whereupon his son very perceptively asks: 'Hat Mutter dich gerufen?' ('Did mother send for you?') (I, 248).[8] The old man reveals his stereotyped way of thinking in the clichés with which he addresses his son. There is no argument, no question of the two men reaching any understanding, for what old Vockerat requires is nothing less than total obedience: 'Es ist hier gar nicht vom Verstehen die Rede . . . Auf das Einigen kommt es nicht an. . . . Auf den Gehorsam, mein ich, kommt es an' (I, 249). He reminds Johannes of the concern his parents bestowed on him when he was young and when he was ill, and demands more than just gratitude in return. And yet there is no question of hypocrisy on the part of Vockerat, any more than there is on the part of his wife. The scene of his return at the end of Act IV, the details of which Hauptmann handles beautifully, reveal him as a thoroughly genuine old man, with a real concern for his family, but with no feeling for the complexities of his son's situation.

His final appeal to his son is a clumsy threat, which is immediately effective, but in the long run proves disastrous. He decides there is nothing left for him to do but to take his wife and go, whereupon Johannes capitulates:

JOHANNES, *nach kurzem Kampf.* Vater!! Mutter!!	JOHANNES, *after a brief struggle.* Father!! Mother!!
FRAU VOCKERAT und VOCKERAT *wenden sich. Johannes fliegt in ihre Arme.* Johannes! *Pause.*	FRAU VOCKERAT and VOCKERAT *turn round. Johannes throws himself into their arms.* Johannes! *Pause.*
JOHANNES, *mit leiser Stimme.* Nun sagt, was ich tun soll.	JOHANNES, *in a low voice.* Now tell me what to do.
VOCKERAT. Halte sie nicht. Laß sie ziehen, Hannes.	VOCKERAT. Don't keep her. Let her go, Hannes.
JOHANNES. Ich verspreche dir's. *Er ist erschöpft und muß sich auf einen Stuhl niederlassen. Frau Vockerat eilt freudig bewegt ins Schlafzimmer.*	JOHANNES. I promise. *He is exhausted and has to sit down on a chair. Frau Vockerat rushes off joyfully into the bedroom.*
VOCKERAT *streichelt den Dasitzenden, küßt ihn auf die Stirn* (I, 251).	VOCKERAT *strokes his head, kisses him on the brow.*

This sudden change of heart by Johannes is no tribute to his father's arguments; it is not the kind of response which suggests intellectual conviction. In a moment of physical weakness, which in Hauptmann's works, as in Kleist's, so often indicates a breakthrough to a deeper emotional level, Johannes gives in utterly, to become no more than a child, fearful of being abandoned by its parents.

At the opposite pole to the conservative Vockerats stands the artist, Braun. As an advocate of political commitment he is an example of a type of character who occurs rarely in the work of Hauptmann, and is never treated sympathetically. The altruistic socialism which Braun practises (or at least preaches) represents a stage which Johannes once passed, but which he now claims to have outgrown;

that is to say the friendship between the two men was once a good deal closer than it is when the play opens. Braun is most probably one of the friends to whom Käthe refers when she complains that Johannes has never really belonged to her: 'Hab' ich ihn denn überhaupt jemals besessen? Erst haben ihn die Freunde gehabt, jetzt hat ihn Anna' (I, 223). Braun dislikes the compromises Johannes makes—for instance the christening—because they indicate a weakening of his influence over his friend. He is, of course, a natural rival of Frau Vockerat, but shares her hostility to Johannes' work, because this symbolizes his independence of both of them; and he shares her hostility to Anna. Indeed Braun and Frau Vockerat recognize in Anna such a serious threat that they form a provisional alliance against her, combining, in Act IV, to persuade her to depart. Braun makes the first attempt, using the very un-radical argument that she should go for the sake of the Vockerat family; Anna deliberately and scornfully closes her ears to this appeal to her conscience, although she has, in fact, already told Johannes that they must part. Anna, it seems, can see through to Braun's real motives and is not disposed to listen to moral lectures from *him*. She can see that he is jealous of Johannes' increasing independence and resentful of the encouragement Anna has given him; in Act II she describes Braun as follows: 'Herr Braun ist ja noch so unfertig in jeder Beziehung—so . . . ich will nicht sagen, daß er Sie [Johannes] beneidet, aber es ärgert ihn . . . Ihr zähes Festhalten an Ihrer Eigenart ist ihm unbehaglich. Es mag ihn sogar ängstigen' ('Herr Braun is so immature in every respect—I won't say he envies you [Johannes], but it irritates him . . . The tenacity with which you preserve your independence disturbs him. Maybe it even frightens him') (I, 206).

It has been suggested that Anna is herself a similar character, and that she also contributes to Johannes' destruction by fighting for possession of him; that she is a tough, scheming, emancipated woman, like Laura in Strindberg's *The Father*, who deliberately and maliciously isolates Johannes until she can extract no more from him, whereupon she abandons him to despair and suicide.[9] Such a woman is to be found in the person of Hanna Elias in Hauptmann's later play, *Gabriel Schillings Flucht*, and in Hella in Max Halbe's *Mutter Erde*, who entices the young Paul Warkentin from his provincial home to the city, where he works for the emancipation movement; but Anna is surely a more sympathetic and more complex character. Her hardness, like that of Robert Scholz in *Das Friedensfest*, is a mask, a defence against suffering. She is sensitive and lonely; a homeless young girl, with a cosmopolitan background, forced to make her own way in a world which looks with suspicion on self-reliant women, and so forced to toughen herself for the sake of bare survival. Her assertions of the value of independence and the need for ruthlessness are brave rationalizations of a predicament she can do nothing to alter: 'Man muß frei sein in jeder Hinsicht. Kein Vaterland, keine Familie, keine Freunde soll man haben.' Nevertheless the loneliness of freedom and independence does clearly frighten her: 'Ich komme zu früh nach Zürich. Acht volle Tage zu früh. Wenn nur die Arbeit erst wiederanfängt' ('I'm going to be back in Zurich too soon. A whole week too soon. If only work were beginning again') (I, 220); like Robert Scholz, she needs some kind of activity to sublimate her personal anxieties. Aware that she is not wanted in the Vockerat household, she is ready to depart; proudly she resists Käthe's suggestion that she suffers—to admit to others is to admit to oneself—but she is easily persuaded to return to a house in which she has enjoyed some moments of relaxation and happiness. She has enough self-knowledge to appreciate eventually that the *ménage à trois* cannot last; she therefore decides independently that she will bring her association with Johannes to an end, and contrives to do so in a way which leaves Johannes his self-respect. By clumsily interfering after the decision has been reached, Johannes' parents deprive him of this, and to this extent they are responsible for his death. Nevertheless the play does not leave one with a feeling of undivided sympathy for Johannes, as my analysis might hitherto have suggested. The reason for this lies with Hauptmann's treatment of the two remaining characters.

Käthe Vockerat is, it should be remembered, a young wife, obsessed by feelings of inadequacy *vis à vis* her more intelligent husband, who is not only physically weak from the recent birth of her first child, but is also suffering from the depression which affects many women in her situation.[10] She is anxious, unsure of herself, unwilling to accept responsibility, almost always on the verge of tears; it is a situation in which she needs the support, the encouragement, and the interest of her husband, but none is forthcoming:

Anstatt daß du mal gut zu mir wärst, mein Zutrauen zu mir selbst——bißchen stärktest . . . Nein, da werd' ich nur immer kleingemacht—immer klein— immer geduckt werd' ich. Ich bild' mir weiß Gott nichts ein auf meinen großen Horizont. Aber ich bin eben nicht gefühllos.—Nee, wahrhaftig, ich bin kein Licht. Überhaupt: ich hab's schon lange gemerkt, daß ich ziemlich überflüssig bin (I, 211).

Instead of being nice to me, boosting my confidence a bit . . . No, I'm always being made to feel small—always small —I'm always being belittled. God knows, I don't deceive myself that my horizons are wide. But I'm not exactly without feelings.—No, really, I'm not brilliant. In fact, I've noticed it for some time, I'm more or less in the way here.

Johannes, who makes such great demands on the consideration of others, has himself very little to spare for his wife: 'wir passen wirklich nicht zusammen! . . . meine Arbeit geht vor! Sie kommt zuerst und zuzweit und zudritt, . . .

Du hast eben immer deine Familieninteressen, und ich habe allgemeine Interessen. . . . Ich bin überhaupt kein Familienvater' ('We are really not suited! . . . I'm doing my work. My work comes first, second, and third, . . . You have your family interests, and I have universal interests. . . . I am simply not a family man') (I, 209–10). The arrival of Anna at this time intensifies Käthe's need for her husband's consideration; the added responsibility of a guest in the house is itself no light matter, but Anna can offer Johannes everything that Käthe cannot. Her very presence reminds Käthe constantly of her own inadequacy, and the cruelty of Johannes' implied comparisons does not help her: 'Du solltest geradezu fieberhaft jede Gelegenheit ergreifen, geistig 'n bißchen weiterzukommen. Du solltest treiben dazu. Du solltest das Fräulein hier festhalten. Ich begreife nicht, wie man so gleichgültig sein kann' ('You ought to be eager to grasp any opportunity for intellectual improvement. You really ought to make the effort. You ought to keep the young lady here. I don't understand how anyone can be so indifferent') (I, 193).

These words reveal not only insensitivity on the part of Johannes, but also a certain lack of honesty with himself, for it is apparent to all the other characters in the play, and to even the most casual reader, that it is for himself that Johannes desires Anna to stay in the house. In *Das Friedensfest* a similar lack of self-knowledge on the part of Frau Buchner was revealed in a sudden flash; the structure of *Einsame Menschen* allows for a more gradual and more subtle illumination. Whereas *Das Friedensfest* and, to a rather lesser extent, *Vor Sonnenaufgang*, related the concluding chapter of a story which depended significantly on events which had taken place in the past, the action of *Einsame Menschen* does add up to a more or less complete story. We therefore see fully and immediately the catalytic effect of Anna's arrival on Johannes. His 'new morality', his sudden aggressive defiance of the philistines, are an *ad hoc* arrangement, adopted because they suit his present predicament. In a review of the first Frankfurt performance of the play one critic wrote disapprovingly of the behaviour of the audience, complaining that a large part of the public was amused by Johannes' assertion that his interest in Anna Mahr was purely spiritual, and attributing this to what he described as the miscasting of the more attractive actress in the role of Anna.[11] The audience was quicker to perceive Hauptmann's irony than the critic. When Johannes speaks rather foolishly and very pretentiously of his vision of a new, non-physical relationship between man and woman—'Nicht das Tierische wird dann mehr die erste Stelle einnehmen, sondern das Menschliche. Das Tier wird nicht mehr das Tier ehelichen, sondern der Mensch den Menschen. Freundschaft, das ist die Basis, auf der sich diese Liebe erheben wird' (I, 238)—he is availing himself of certain ideas associated more with the old Tolstoy than with the German Naturalist movement, in order to rationalize an emotional and sexual attraction into a spiritual friendship. He instinctively chooses the easiest line of defence, because an outspoken advocacy of free-love—which would be typical of the Friedrichshagen circle with whom Hauptmann has associated Johannes— would involve him in an immediate and head-on clash with his parents.[12] Anna is quicker to perceive the truth, and to remind Johannes that they are both prone to the same human desires as everybody else: 'In mir . . . in uns ist etwas, was den geläuterten Beziehungen, die uns dämmern, feindlich ist, auf der Dauer auch überlegen' (I, 240). Braun, too, sees more clearly, and justifiably reproaches Johannes with refusing to face up to the truth: 'Du hast den Dingen niemals gern nüchtern ins Auge gesehen. . . . Du willst Dinge vereinen, die sich eben nicht vereinen lassen' (I, 230).

Hauptmann's critique of Johannes is twofold; where it depends on the appeal of the unfortunate Käthe, the play tends to that sentimentality which is not an uncommon feature in Hauptmann's work; but where it is concerned with the deflation of a weak and self-deluding man, *Einsame Menschen* has some superb moments. In this play Hauptmann displays an intelligence and an irony which critics have often found wanting in his work; for instance: Johannes appeals for support to a new, individualist morality which he has not yet made his own, but his phraseology gives him away: 'aber *Sie sagten doch selbst* immer, man soll die Rücksicht auf andre nicht über sich herrschen lassen' ('but *you said yourself,* one should not be inhibited by consideration for others') (I, 238; my emphasis). There are moments when one thinks Hauptmann was on the way to creating a literary form of which there is no notable example in German literature, a satirical *Künstlerdrama.* It seems, however, that he did not have the nerve to carry through this project consistently; *Das Wunderkind* (the ironic title which Hauptmann originally planned to give his play) became the more pretentious (and cacophonous) *Einsame Menschen.* The play in its final form is a rather ambiguous mixture of criticism and special-pleading on behalf of the artist or outstanding individual. As such it reflects the changing political attitudes among the Naturalist writers, the retreat from social commitment to the cult of individualism, particularly in the Friedrichshagen circle.

One aspect of Johannes' character which is constantly stressed is his restlessness. On the wall of his room is a picture of Jacob struggling with the angel: 'Ich lasse dich nicht, du segnest mich denn' (I, 178). The self-torturing Johannes glorifies in his discontent, saying to his mother: 'Die zufriedenen Menschen, das sind die Drohnen im Bienenstock' (I, 182).[13] As I have suggested above, the action of the play arises out of Johannes' attempts at reorientation. He has broken with the traditional outlook represented by his parents, and has been through a period of socialism in his friendship with Braun. He has now grown beyond this, and is working his way forward to a new position of independence: 'Die ausgetretenen Wege, die sind eben nicht für jeden. Herr Johannes gehört eben auch unter diejenigen, welche neue Wege suchen' ('Familiar paths are not for everyone. Johannes is one of those who are seeking new paths') (I, 196). The discovery of these new paths is threatened equally by the socialism of Braun and the conservatism of Johannes' parents; Anna, however, introduces a ray of optimism:

Auf der einen Seite beherrschte uns eine schwüle Angst, auf der andern ein finsterer Fanatismus. Die übertriebene Spannung scheint nun ausgeglichen. So etwas wie ein frischer Luftstrom, sagen wir aus dem zwanzigsten Jahrhundert, ist hereingeschlagen. . . . Zum Beispiel, Leute wie Braun wirken doch auf uns nur noch wie Eulen bei Tageslicht (I, 237).

On the one side we were dominated by an oppressive anxiety, on the other by grim fanaticism. The extreme tension now seems to be resolved. A kind of fresh breeze, let's call it a breeze from the twentieth century, is blowing. . . . People like Braun, for instance, now seem to us like owls in the daylight.

The positive end towards which Johannes and Anna are aspiring is not very precisely defined; they are not themselves yet in a position to define it precisely; but we are given a number of hints about its quality. This fresh breeze will bring with it a renewed interest in art. A common interest in music is one of the things which brings Johannes and Anna together. Significantly, Anna has recently taken up music again after having given it up for six years; whereas Braun is moving in the opposite direction, to take the view that in the present social situation art is a luxury which mankind cannot afford: 'Es gibt vielleicht Dinge zu verrichten, die augenblicklich wichtiger sind als sämtliche Malereien und Schreibereien der Welt' (I, 201). (This, incidentally, was one objection made by the Social Democrats to the foundation of the *Volksbühnen*.) In Act II Anna gives a summary of a story by Garschin, *Die Künstler*, which leads to a violent disagreement between Johannes and Braun. Johannes takes the view that a work of art does more good for mankind than the active attempt to alleviate human misery. It immediately becomes clear that Johannes sees his own work in this way; although produced in isolation, it is a thing of great social value. Its importance is a justification for the compromises he makes; these are a means of saving energy and preserving the emotional and mental equilibrium which is necessary for artistic creation; as Anna says, 'Die Konflikte bringen die Menschen um ihre Kraft' (I, 205). This is, of course, a politically irresponsible view, and it is one of the sadder facts of Hauptmann's life that he still held it in 1932.[14]

Johannes' book is also his only justification for his treatment of Käthe. Her intellectual limitations mean that she cannot give him the support and encouragement he needs in his work, and her practical demands are a distraction. Marie Weil, in Hirschfeld's *Die Mütter* is a tougher character, who can do more to alleviate the practical burdens, but she cannot give any positive encouragement to the musical talents of Robert Frey; Wagner is lost on her. Anna, by contrast, is always the understanding, never the demanding, partner (for this reason emancipation is never allowed to become an issue in this play; it would raise the question of Anna's rights). The justification for Anna's continued presence is that she can assist Johannes in the process of self-fulfilment, and so enrich his work. Hauptmann is here faced with the perennial problem of the *Künstlerdrama*; he has to make us believe in the value of the work in question; Johannes' statement that the fourth chapter has twelve pages of footnotes is scarcely enough to do that.

A similar special-plea is a feature of Carl Hauptmann's play *Marianne*. The heroine of this play, a young pastor's wife, is encouraged to revolt against the life-denying pietism of her husband and her family by the arrival of the progressive artist, Fritz. They are two young people bound together by a love of nature and the countryside and a passionate hatred of urban civilization. They value personal integrity more highly than consideration for others, and they share a pantheistic love of Life, which resembles the quasi-mysticism of Schlaf's *Frühling* (1896) and the effusions of Wille and Bölsche in their Friedrichshagen period: 'Natürlich möchte ein jeder gern so ein klein oder groß Wunder in sich! Ja—was will man eigentlich sonst?—das Unfaßbare fühlbar machen' ('Of course everyone would like to experience a miracle, great or small! Indeed—what else does one really want?—but to make what is inconceivable tangible').[15] It becomes clear from *Marianne* that Carl Hauptmann holds the view that man has an inherent need for some kind of religious experience, and that this is not likely to be explained away by scientific positivism or milieu-theory. Like Johannes Vockerat he respects belief (but not dogma), and to a consistent radical must appear conservative; above all he rejects a 'naturalism' which would presume to explain man in social terms:

Der Naturalismus hat recht, sofern er das Milieu ergriff. Aber nicht, weil er damit ins [sic] Menschen als Naturwesen, sondern nur als Sozialwesen Einblick gewährt. Der Naturalismus ist die Kunst des Menschen als Sozialwesen. Aber wenn er damit die Naturwesen erklären will, so irrt er. Die

Naturalism was right in turning to milieu. But only in that it thereby provided insight into man as a social being, not as a natural being. Naturalism is the art of man as a social being. But if it thinks it can explain the natural being, then it is wrong. The deepest secrets of our passions are rooted in another nature

tiefsten Verborgenheiten unserer Lei-
denschaften wurzeln in einer anderen
Natur, und das Milieu, das sie bilden
half, ist längst versunken.[16]

and the milieu which helped to form it
disappeared long ago.

Irrationalist vitalism provides an explicit programme for Carl Hauptmann's
play of 1894, and makes for a dull tendentious drama. Anna Mahr's 'fresh breeze
from the twentieth century' blows from the same direction; one obvious symptom
of this is Johannes' anti-urbanism: 'Ich hasse die Stadt. Mein Ideal ist ein weiter
Park mit einer hohen Mauer ringsherum. Da kann man so ganz ungestört seinen
Zielen leben' (I, 189). In view of their origins it is scarcely surprising that there
should be this affinity between the two plays, for the character of Johannes is, to
some extent, based on Gerhart Hauptmann's elder brother; and it has been
shown that Johannes Vockerat shares, in some detail, the theories and attitudes
of Carl Hauptmann.[17] Johannes' work corresponds to Carl's planned *Grund-
linien einer allgemeinen Biomechanik*: and Carl's polemic against the psychologist,
Wilhelm Wundt, has its counterpart in Johannes' attack on the biologist, Emil
Du Bois Reymond, who had, in fact been attacked very vehemently in 1890 by
Julius Langbehn in *Rembrandt als Erzieher*.[18] There are other respects in which
the hero of the play might be considered a 'Langbehnist': his hostility to Braun's
egalitarianism, his hostility to formal education—'Auf meine Schulbildung spucke
ich' (I, 203)—and the high value he places on art. It is true that Johannes appears
to be some sort of scientist (Haeckel was one of his teachers) and that Langbehn
was hostile to the dominance of science; but Langbehn opposed science because
it demands increasing specialization; the way Braun describes Johannes' work in
Act I as 'philosophisch-kritisch-psycho-physiologisch' suggests that it ought to
be comprehensive enough not to be condemned for specialization.[19]

I would not wish to suggest that *Einsame Menschen* was directly influenced by
Langbehn's book, any more than I wished to suggest in my earlier discussion of
the political development of the Naturalists that the views of Bruno Wille were
a direct result of Langbehn's influence. It is, however, important to recognize
that this play was written in a climate of increasing receptivity to anti-rationalist,
individualist ideas, but that, unlike *Marianne*, it preserves a certain scepticism
about the attitudinizing which such a climate can produce in a basically weak
character.

In Anna's eyes, of course, Johannes is a strong character, bold enough to insist
on his own individuality, and attempting to secure some kind of grasp on the
world, without reducing it by seeing it in terms of some systematic ideology.
Johannes is unable to realize his aspirations; Anna thus compares him with a
revolutionary hero, who dies for his people: 'Zum Tode gequält durch Gefangen-

schaft, bist du jung gestorben. Im Kampfe für dein Volk hast du deinen ehrlichen Kopf niedergelegt' (I, 240). But in the final act of the play Anna's comparison is shown to be an egregious one. When the time for Anna's departure comes—that is after his final confrontation with his father—Johannes proves to be anything but the man he was proclaimed to be: 'Geben Sie mir einen Anhalt. Geben Sie mir etwas, woran ich mich aufrichten kann. Einen Anhalt. Ich breche zusammen. Eine Stütze. Alles in mir bricht zusammen, Fräulein' ('Give me some support. Give me something to hold on to. A prop. I am on the point of collapse. Help me. Everything within me is folding up') (I, 252). Anna recognizes Johannes' need for an ideal which will make life purposeful and—anticipating the end of *Kollege Crampton*—offers him an illusion: 'Die Ahnung eines neuen, freien Zustandes, einer fernen Glückseligkeit gleichsam, die in uns gewesen ist, die wollen wir bewahren. Was wir einmal gefühlt haben, soll von nun an nicht mehr verlorengehen' ('The prophetic insight which we had into a new state of liberty, a distant state of bliss, let us preserve that. What we once felt shall not be lost, now or in the future') (I, 253). It is difficult to say how far Anna is aware that what she is offering is an illusion—she has in any case nothing else to offer—but, as far as Johannes is concerned, the illusion is of very short duration. His own response to Anna's departure shows him that he has been deceiving himself about the nature of the bond between them; in reality it was not new, and it was not free, but very old, very impulsive, and very passionate. Knowledge proves destructive; Johannes commits suicide.

So Hauptmann ends a trilogy of plays united by their concern for the position of the idealist in a changing world. At his moment of crisis Alfred Loth felt that he was faced with three possible alternatives:

Es gibt drei Möglichkeiten! Entweder ich heirate sie, und dann . . . nein, dieser Ausweg existiert nicht. Oder— die bewußte Kugel. Naja, dann hätte man wenigstens Ruhe. Aber nein! So weit sind wir noch nicht, so was kann man sich einstweilen noch nicht leisten —also leben! kämpfen!—weiter, immer weiter (I, 94–95).

There are three possibilities! Either I marry her, and then . . . No, that cannot be done. Or—a bullet through the head. That would at least bring peace. But no! It's not that bad, that's a luxury we can't yet afford—so live! fight!—forward, ever forward.

Confident—to the point of insensitivity—in his own ideals, Loth opted for the third possibility; Wilhelm Scholz, lacking all confidence, but trusting, despite himself, in the power of love, chose the first; Johannes Vockerat, a man disillusioned by the discrepancy between reality and the ideal he cherishes, takes the second.

Notes to Chapter VII

¹ Cf. H. Stuart Hughes, *Consciousness and Society. The reorientation of European social thought. 1890–1930*, London, 1959, chapter 2, 'The decade of the 1890s', pp. 33–66.

² See above, chapter 4.

³ Gerhart Hauptmann, *Die Kunst des Dramas*, pp. 98–102. Cf. also F. W. J. Heuser, 'Biographisches und Autobiographisches in "Einsame Menschen" ', *Gerhart Hauptmann*, pp. 247–58; and Karl Musiol, 'Carl Hauptmann und Josepha Kodis', *Deutsche Vierteljahrsschrift*, XXXIV (1960), pp. 257–63.

⁴ *Jahrhundertwende*, p. 39; p. 45.

⁵ *Das Werden des neuen Dramas*, Berlin, 1898, II, 69 ff., 299 ff.

⁶ In the first performance the play was shortened by the omission of the fourth act. An obvious comment on this came in the *Magazin für die Literatur des In- und Auslandes*, LX (1891), pp. 204–5, in the shape of a parody entitled 'Der höhere Zustand', which consisted of a first and a fifth act, and the explanation: 'Der zweite, dritte und vierte Akt können mit Bewilligung des Dichters von der Regie gestrichen werden. Die Handlung fährt mit Beginn des fünften Aktes dort fort, wo wir sie soeben verlassen haben'. Nevertheless even the omission of the fourth act will significantly flatten the characterization of both Johannes and Anna.

⁷ Georg Hirschfeld, *Die Mütter*, Berlin, 1896, p. 43.

⁸ Miller the Musician behaves in a similar way towards his daughter in Schiller's *Kabale und Liebe*. Luise is, of course, less sceptical than Johannes Vockerat. *Kabale und Liebe* was, incidentally, the Naturalists' favourite play from the standard repertoire. Brahm chose it to open his first season at the *Deutsches Theater*, and it figures prominently in the programmes of the *Volksbühnen*.

⁹ Jenny C. Hortenbach, *Freiheitsstreben und Destruktivität. Frauen in den Dramen August Strindbergs und Gerhart Hauptmanns*, Oslo-Bergen-Tromsö, 1965, pp. 91–106. *The Father* had been presented by the *Freie Bühne* on 12 October 1890.

¹⁰ Hauptmann's characterization of Frau Käthe corresponds quite remarkably to Dr Benjamin Spock's description of 'The Blue Feeling' (*Baby and Child Care*, revised edition, 1957, §15); Johannes' behaviour is the opposite of what Spock advises in the section entitled 'The Father's Part' (§18–20).

¹¹ *Freie Bühne*, II (1891), p. 200.

¹² For Tolstoy's views see 'Zweites Nachwort zur "Kreutzersonate" ', *Freie Bühne*, I (1890), pp. 1009 ff.; and 'Von den Beziehungen der Geschlechter zu einander', ibid., pp. 1192 ff. For the views current among the Friedrichshagen circle of writers see: Julius Hart, 'Freie Liebe', *Freie Bühne*, II (1891), pp. 369 ff., 396 ff., 445 ff., and 468 ff.; Bruno Wille, 'Moralische Stickluft', *Freie Bühne*, IV (1893), pp. 816 ff. While I agree with Guthke (*Gerhart Hauptmann*, p. 71) that Johannes' views on the relationship between the sexes are treated ironically, I do not agree that this makes *Einsame Menschen* part of a critique of Naturalism, for Johannes' views are not representative of the Naturalist movement.

¹³ The extent of the contrast between Hauptmann and his contemporary, Wedekind, can be gauged if one compares Hauptmann's treatment of Johannes with Wedekind's treatment of Ernst Scholz in *Der Marquis von Keith*, to whom Keith remarks: 'Wem wie du von Jugend auf jeder Schritt zu einem seelischen Konflikt auswächst, der beherrscht seine Zeit und regiert die Welt, wenn wir andern längst von den Würmern gefressen

sind!', *Ges. Werke*, IV, 50. In the sketches for a drama, 'Der Niggerjud', Wedekind identifies himself with Keith and Hauptmann with Scholz; see Heuser, 'Hauptmann und Wedekind', p. 245.

¹⁴ Chapiro, *Gespräche mit Gerhart Hauptmann*, p. 40.

¹⁵ Carl Hauptmann, *Marianne*, Berlin, 1894, p. 60.

¹⁶ Carl Hauptmann, *Leben mit Freunden. Ges. Briefe*, Berlin, 1928, p. 45.

¹⁷ Heuser, 'Biographisches und Autobiographisches in "Einsame Menschen"', p. 251.

¹⁸ Ed. cit., pp. 94–95.

¹⁹ Langbehn writes (p. 63): 'Die künstlerische Weltanschauung ist . . . nur scheinbar eine subjektive, in Wirklichkeit aber die einzig objektive; da die Welt ein in sich zusammenhängendes und geschlossenes Ganzes bildet . . . so ist nur diejenige Weltanschauung eine objektive, welche den einzelnen Organen dieses Ganzen, innerhalb desselben und in stetem Hinblick auf dasselbe, ihren richtigen Platz anweist: der Spezialist kann nicht objektiv sein'. Cf. Hauptmann's jotting of 1890, quoted by Voigt, 'Gerhart Hauptmann's naturalistische Anfänge', *Hauptmann Studien*, p. 55; 'Verhältnis des Spezialisten, Gelehrten zum Philosophen ist dasselbe wie das des Holzschen Naturnachahmers zum Dichter. Wie am Philosophen ganz und gar nichts unpersönlich ist, so auch am Dichter nicht.'

VIII

Die Weber

Hauptmann began the first plans of *Die Weber* at the same time as *Vor Sonnen-aufgang* when he was in Zurich in 1888. But it was not until 1890 and 1891, when he made two trips into the *Eulengebirge*, that he first began working seriously on this, his fourth play. The dialect version, *De Waber*, was completed by the end of 1891, and the more familiar, 'dem Hochdeutschen angenäherte Fassung' prepared from it by March 1892. In the meanwhile Hauptmann had completed *Kollege Crampton* with remarkable speed, and had seen it performed at the *Deutsches Theater* on 16 January 1892. He was now an established dramatist and could also have expected a public première for *Die Weber*, but a protracted dispute with the authorities necessitated the resurrection of the *Freie Bühne*, and the play was given its first performance on 26 February 1893.

Hauptmann deeply resented the ban on his play. The label of Socialist was becoming increasingly unfashionable among the Naturalists, and Hauptmann insisted that his drama was 'wohl sozial, aber nicht sozialistisch'.[1] In his efforts to secure the lifting of the ban Hauptmann's advocate, Richard Grelling, himself the author of a minor social drama, *Gleiches Recht* (1892), went even further than this. He claimed that the author of *Die Weber* was on the side of law and order, for he had allowed the authorities to triumph through the intervention of few soldiers, that the play could not be a danger in contemporary circumstances since the *Arbeiterschutz-Gesetzgebung* was sufficient to prevent the recurrence of such poverty,[2] and for good measure he pointed out that a performance of the play could do little harm, since three-quarters of the audience in the public theatres came from the upper-classes, and that censorship could do nothing to prevent the performance of the play before the working-class audiences of the *Volksbühnen*.[3]

On appeal the ban was lifted, and *Die Weber* was given its first public performance at the *Deutsches Theater* on 25 September 1894. But the resistance of the conservatives was not over. The Kaiser cancelled his box at the theatre, and local authorities all over Germany sought to prevent further performances of the play until after the turn of the century. Until the very end of Hauptmann's life it remained a source of great bitterness to him that he had once been identified with the forces of disorder; in 1942 he wrote:

Man hat mich wie einen Verbrecher behandelt, wie einen Lumpenhund! Wir	I was treated like a criminal, like a common rogue! Under Wilhelm II this play

mußten mit diesem Stück, das unter
Wilhelm dem Zweiten jahrelang nicht
aufgeführt werden durfte, vor die Ver-
waltungs- und Oberverwaltungsge-
richte ziehen. Im Preußisch enLandtag
wurde ich beschimpft. Ein adliger Herr
sagte wörtlich: Der Kerl—damit meinte
er mich—der Kerl gehört hinter Schloß
und Riegel![4]

was banned year after year, and we had
to take it before the courts. I was
abused in the Prussian Assembly. A
member of the nobility said, literally:
That fellow—and he meant me—ought
to be behind bars!

Understandably *Die Weber* was given a warmer welcome by the political left
than any other Naturalist drama. The Social Democrat leaders, Wilhelm Lieb-
knecht and Singer, were in evidence at the première; and the play was subsequently performed three times by Bruno Wille's *Neue Freie Volksbühne*, and
seven by Mehring's *Freie Volksbühne*. Wille states that the reception of the play
was enthusiastic: 'From my experiences I can only say that *Die Weber* . . . made
a more powerful impact on the working class than any other social drama I have
known'.[5] I say this is understandable without thereby wishing to challenge
Hauptmann's own view that this play is not a piece of socialist propaganda. For
all its grimness *Die Weber* is a play which has certain positive, even optimistic,
features which are lacking from the great majority of Naturalist dramas: it shows
a community of people struggling against the utmost oppression to maintain a
basic human dignity, people whose souls can bear suffering and yet not stifle.

A contemporary social drama, Max Halbe's *Eisgang* (1892), displays the
resigned pessimism which is more typical of the Naturalists. In a few scenes—
which Franz Mehring admired[6]—the social movement among the working
classes is briefly presented, but, as in *Einsame Menschen*, the tone and mood of
the play derive more from the predicament of the hero, Hugo Tetzlaff, a young
intellectual no longer convinced that his family has an inalienable right to the
estates it has inherited for generations, but not yet ready to throw in his lot with
the working classes. Tortured by the indecision and impotence of the *Übergangsmensch*, and the hereditary weakness of a decadent family, he drowns in
spring, as the frozen river cracks and the ice is carried downstream; the *Eisgang*
of the play's title is thus a symbolic destruction of the past, without very much
suggestion of promise for the future.

Hauptmann's *Die Weber* differs from *Eisgang* and other Naturalist social
dramas in a further significant respect: it is a genuine working-class drama. For
once a Naturalist dramatist goes beyond the fairly narrow limits of most of the
works we have so far discussed, which tend to treat social or ethical problems
from a bourgeois-intellectual standpoint and in a bourgeois setting. Langmann's
Bartel Turaser (1897), although it is set in a proletarian milieu, works from

middle-class assumptions, asking the question whether the poor can afford to conform to the traditional moral code, rather than asking direct questions about the justification of this code. Plays such as *Vor Sonnenaufgang*, *Winterschlaf*, Fulda's *Das verlorene Paradies* (1890), or Sudermann's *Die Ehre* (1889), do touch on the problems of the working classes in a changing society, but they all relate such problems to the socially-conscious middle-class intellectual. The same is true of the Naturalist novelists, Hans Land and Felix Hollaender. This bias arises from a basic disagreement between the Naturalists and the socialist movement about what constitutes the characteristic reality of this age. For the young Naturalist writers it *was* no doubt the *prise de conscience* by the intellectuals, and the consequences this can have for them. *Die Weber* concentrates on a spontaneous revolt within a working-class community, but even here we have an episode devoted to the young *Kandidat*, Weinhold, who is dismissed by his employer for taking the weavers' part.

A comparison with Hauptmann's other mass-drama emphasizes the individuality of *Die Weber* even further. Despite the careful painting of the historical canvas, the background detail of the Peasants' War, *Florian Geyer* (1896) remains primarily the story of the agonies of a leader. Geyer is a selfless hero who abandons all the privileges of the aristocrat to take up the task of serving his country, by bringing 'German disharmony' to an end. But of those he has come to serve only a select handful, Löffelholz, Tellermann, Besenmeyer, the prostitute, Marei, recognize their potential saviour. Without a leader the peasants are unable to weld themselves into a unified community, and remain a number of disparate factions. In Geyer's absence the rival leaders order a foolhardy attack on a strongly fortified position, which leads directly to their defeat and the martyrdom of Geyer—for which one leader disclaims responsibility with the words of Pontius Pilate: 'Ich wasche meine Hände in Unschuld' (I, 659). In a strange mixture of nationalism and Christianity, which recalls the ideas of Lagarde, Florian Geyer is presented as *Messiah* and *Führer*. Geyer does not, however, measure up to the claims which are made—by other characters—for his strength and powers of leadership. He is too indecisive and inactive a character to fill satisfactorily the role of *Führer*. He is too scrupulous to seize the leadership when he has the chance. When the play was first performed in 1896 its reception was disastrous; it is difficult to say with any certainty why this was so, but it is interesting that in the *successful* revival of the play a few years later the leading role was given to Rudolf Rittner, who had played Schäferhans in the earlier production. Rittner—as the famous portrait by Lovis Corinth seems to confirm—set out to compensate for the inconsistencies in the role, by carefully emphasizing Geyer's vitality:

Stellen Sie sich vor, unter einem Hundert Menschen ist Florian Geyer der Held, der Mann—jedenfalls reden so die Leute von ihm. Und nun hat Florian Geyer, sehr im Gegensatz zu seinem Ruhm, mehr Passives als Aktives in seinem Wesen . . . sollte der Zuschauer dasselbe von Florian Geyer glauben, wie seine Bauernschar auf der Bühne, so blieb mir gar nichts übrig, als alle die Stellen in der Rolle herauszuarbeiten, in denen er herrschend, entschlußkräftig, kühn und zur Tat bereit erscheint. Um der inneren Wahrheit willen.[7]

Imagine, out of a hundred characters Florian Geyer is *the* man—or at least that's what people say. But Florian Geyer, despite his reputation, is more passive than active . . . if the audience was to have the same opinion of Florian Geyer as his peasant followers on stage, then I had no alternative but to lay special emphasis on those parts of the role in which he appeared commanding, decisive, bold, and ready to act. For the sake of consistency.

If we read the play without the guidance of Rittner, our attention will not be concentrated on the hero's task, and why he should have failed—this becomes rather obvious—but on his progress as an individual through suffering and betrayal to an ultimate transcendence over his unworthy enemies and followers. Nowhere is the other-worldly superiority of Geyer more evident than in the death-scene, which must have been strongly influenced by Hebbel's *Agnes Bernauer*. Like Agnes, Geyer faces his pursuers with the words of Christ: 'Wen suchet ihr' (John, 18, iv), and like Agnes he commands the spontaneous respect of his enemies, holding all but the most criminal at bay. He falls to the crossbow of the villainous Schäferhans, who is promptly denounced as a 'Bluthund'; and we are explicitly reminded of the messianic pattern of his experiences as Lorenz von Hutten claims Geyer's sword, and reads the inscription: 'Nulla crux—nulla corona' (I, 710).

Nevertheless these symbolic intrusions are in certain respects at odds with the facts of the play. The mass of the peasants and their leaders are presented as an obstacle to the realization of the hero's ideals, and so our sympathy is elicited for his gradual hardening into an aristocratic attitude, and his vehement denunciations of the peasants: 'Kehricht seid ihr Kot, von der Landstraße, elendes Gerümpel, das Gott besser hätt hinterm Ofen lassen liegen, nit das Seil wert, daran euch der Henker müßt ufziehen' ('You are trash, muck from the street, a miserable rabble. God would have done better to leave you lying in a dark corner. You're not worth the rope with which you should be hanged') (I, 667–8). Geyer's denunciations are the response of a rejected leader; they are the result of disappointment and weakness, not strength; in the context of the play they are given considerable justification; but this indulgence of anger remains incompatible with the symbolic equation of Florian Geyer and Christ.

The remoteness of the historical material of *Florian Geyer* permitted Haupt-mann to adapt it and create a play which is very typical of the attitudes of its time, a play which, like *Einsame Menschen,* justifies withdrawal from social commitment. Despite Hauptmann's greater familiarity with the conditions of the Silesian weaving industry, *Die Weber* is a much less personal work. In this play the power of the facts with which Hauptmann was working seems to have had a disciplinary effect, as they did perhaps on two other plays, *Das Friedensfest* and *Rose Bernd,* for which Hauptmann was provided with a ready-made and moving story. The actual subject of the play, an account of the spontaneous outbreak of the weavers' revolt of 1844, was thoroughly documented in the historical accounts of Wilhelm Wolff and Alfred Zimmermann.[8] Both accounts provide a story strong enough and dramatic enough not to need radical changes. As a dramatist Hauptmann's achievement was to recognize this, and to respect the inherent structure of the story, while making those changes necessary to make the material stageworthy. There is every reason to believe that the consequent restraint, call it Naturalist or not, is responsible for the quality of *Die Weber.* When free of this restraint Hauptmann was capable of writing about these same weavers with appalling condescension:

Das Innere dieser halbzerfallenen Berg-hütten, in deren Mitte das rhyth-mische Wuchten des Webstuhls, das Schnalzen und Scheppern des Schiff-chens tönte, war gleichsam beim ersten Anblick anziehend. Der Webstuhl ist nun einmal ein Ding, an dem zu sitzen die Göttin Kirke nicht verschmäht. Und der musikalische Klang ihrer Arbeit über die Insel Ogygia verknüpft sich mir mit jedem Webstuhle.[9]

The interior of these half-derelict moun-tain cottages, within which could be heard the rhythmic pulsating of the loom, the click-clack of the shuttle, was, at first sight, somehow attractive. The loom is indeed a thing at which the god-dess Circe did not disdain to sit. And the music of her work on the island of Ogygia is associated in my mind with every loom.

In the fifth act of *Die Weber* news of the revolt reaches the old weaver, Hilse, who responds incredulously:

Du kenntest mir meinswegen sagen: Vater Hilse, morgen mußt du sterben. Das kann schonn meeglich sein, werd' ich sprechen, warum denn ni?—Du kennt'st mir sagen: Vater Hilse, morgen besucht dich d'r Keenig von Preußen. Aber daß Weber, Menschen wie ich und mei Sohn, und sollten solche Sachen vorgehabt—nimmermehr! Nie und nim-mer wer ich das glooben (I, 453).

As far as I'm concerned you could tell me: Father Hilse, tomorrow you're go-ing to die. That may well be, I'd say, why not?—You could say: Father Hilse, tomorrow the King of Prussia's coming to see you. But that weavers, men like me and my son, should have had things like that in their minds—never! I will never ever believe it.

The play itself provides the answer to Hilse's incredulity. It resembles the analytical dramas of Naturalism in that it too provides a full explanation of a striking and improbable event, in this case the outburst of a revolutionary spirit among the weavers, after years of oppression and patient suffering. Here Naturalism does not—any more than it did in *Die Familie Selicke*—mean a lack of purpose or structure.

Once again the essential 'gesture' of the drama is captured in a striking opening-scene, as the weavers, *Heimarbeiter*, present their finished work, as they wait—symbol of dependence and inability to control their own lives—for the inspection of their work and payment. The weavers' spirits are low, they are obviously in poor health, over-worked, and underpaid; the treatment they receive from the chief-clerk, Pfeiffer, and the cashier, Neumann, is harsh. Resistance to this treatment is shown only by a redoubtable young weaver from Langenbielau, Bäcker, who receives his full payment;[10] but Bäcker's behaviour is symptomatic of an undercurrent of discontent among the weavers, for, as we soon learn, he has been engaged with others in a demonstration against the employers the previous evening; the storm, suggested in the stage direction, and in the passing comment of the 'first Weaver', is about to break. This threat is intensified by the second episode in this act, the collapse of the hungry child, which brings Dreißiger into the centre of the stage, and gives him an opportunity to justify himself. He explains his difficulties, and offers, magnanimously it would seem, to take on more workers; but when Pfeiffer announces the terms it becomes clear that he is taking advantage of a pool of unemployment to depress wages still further. The curtain falls to the discontented murmurings of the assembled weavers; Hauptmann has skilfully taken us to the point in the story described by the contributor to the *Vossische Zeitung* of 22 June 1844: 'Unleugbar herrschte in Peterswaldau schon seit längerer Zeit unter einem großen Teil der Arbeiter eine starke Gährung, ein Geist der Unzufriedenheit, der nur eines zufälligen Anstoßes bedurfte, um in lichten Flammen auszubrechen' ('Undeniably there had long been in Peterswaldau a marked restiveness among a large section of the workers, a spirit of discontent, which only needed a chance spark to break out openly in flames').

This chance impulse is provided in Act II, in which the same pattern of a quiet beginning and steadily rising tension is repeated. The act begins by showing a different aspect of the weavers' life, the home of the Baumert family, where we witness the same mixture of despair and resignation among the wives of the weavers. The function of Moritz Jäger corresponds to that of Bäcker in Act I. A period of military service has broadened his horizons, taken him to the city, and opened his eyes to the misery of the conditions under which the weavers live. Even more important, life in the army has kept him fit; he is dressed in a complete outfit of clean, smart clothes, whereas the weavers are clad in rags; like Bäcker, he is physically distinguished, he is red-cheeked, he stands straight, and has to bend to come through the door, whereas the weavers are pale and stoop naturally, so that they seem to fit the low, oppressive houses in which they live. Jäger, then, is physically up to leadership, and as an ex-soldier he has a primitive idea of the power of a mass of people. Apart from genuine outrage at the way his family and friends have to live, he also has personal reasons for agitating. He had once been regarded as a layabout and a ne'er-do-well; the threat, 'You just wait till you do your National Service' had become depressingly familiar to him: 'Na nu nehmt amal an: wie oft habt ihr m'r nich de Helle heißgemacht. Dir wern se Moritz lehrn, hiß's immer, wart ock, wenn de wirscht zum Militä kommen. Na nu seht ersch, mir is gar gutt gegangen' (I, 365). Moritz has indeed made good; he has money, a watch, and a polished accent: 'Das feine Sprechen hab' ich mer aso angewehnt, daß iich's gar nimeh loo'n kann' ('I've gotten so used to talkin' proper, I can't get shut of it') (I, 361). He acts, in part at least, out of a desire for recognition, and recognition is easily won. To the weavers he seems to have accomplished the impossible; he has broken out of the enclosed weaving community, and he brings them the promise of release.

The most important symbol of this promise is the song which he has brought from the world outside. *Das Blutgericht* provides the weavers with a simple articulate assessment of their woes such as they had not previously known. As Moritz Jäger reads it to them they come to feel for the first time that they understand their situation: 'Jedes Wort . . . jedes Wort . . . da is all's aso richtig wie in d'r Bibel' (I, 377). With this feeling resignation and impotence give way to violence and hatred, passivity to activity: 'Und das muß anderscher wern, sprech' ich, jetzt uf der Stelle. Mir leiden's nimehr! Mir leiden's nimehr, mag kommen was will' ('And all that must change, I say, now this minute. We won't put up with it any more! We won't put up with it any more, come what may') (I, 379). The song is also used most effectively by Hauptmann to indicate, within the limits of the dramatic form, the gradual formation of a mob out of the various individual weavers: in Act I, the song is mentioned, by Bäcker; in Act II it is introduced to some of the weavers by Moritz Jäger; in the third act a group of weavers leave the inn singing the song; and in the fourth act it is heard off-stage, issuing from the large crowd assembled outside Dreißiger's house. This is a fine example of Hauptmann's faithful, but skilful adaptation of his source; Zimmermann describes the effect of the song as follows:

> for a long time discontent showed itself only in abuse and threats. Then suddenly a song cropped up, which expressed all the general grievances so clearly that it was on

everyone's lips in a flash, the weavers' song. The *Vossische Zeitung* wrote: 'It is an explicit manifesto of all the complaints and grievances which until then were only circulating covertly and slowly. . . . The song sped like a call to arms from house to house; it fell like a lighted fuse among the seething tempers'. (p. 351).

Act III follows the pattern established by the two previous acts. The scene changes again, to the village inn, and the action begins with a relatively calm discussion, in which the exploitation and oppression of the weavers by the clergy, the village carpenter, the land-owning nobility, and the farmers is relentlessly revealed, until the weavers march off, the rebellious, threatening mob which invades Dreißiger's house at the end of the fourth act.

The release of this anarchic, animal fury, which amazes some of the weavers themselves, is explained quite fully and quite rationally. The participation of certain individuals, Moritz Jäger, Wittig the smith, is given a quite detailed personal motivation, but underneath the personal reasons, and common to all the weavers, is the ceaseless pressure of social circumstances. The statement of the 'first weaver' in Act I: 'A Weber is ock' ne Sache' (I, 329), calls to mind Marx's condemnation of the 'over-valuation of the material world (*Sachenwelt*) and the devaluation of the human world'. The confusion of means and ends, whereby what should be made for use is made for its commercial value (the weavers make cloth, but are clad in rags) also recalls Marx's criticism of nineteenth-century bourgeois society; and in the discussion in Act III Hauptmann uses Marx's own example, the theft of wood.[11]

The revolt itself does not, of course, arise from any clear Marxist insight on the part of the weavers. Moritz Jäger is not a *Bote aus der Fremde* like Ibsen's Lona Hessel, who argues from a carefully thought-out position, he simply helps release the pent-up energies and hatreds of the weavers. The revolt is a despairing outcry or, as old Baumert puts it, a chance to get a breath of fresh air. The weavers do not seriously expect it to bring about any permanent improvement in their conditions. Bäcker and Baumert, two of the most sympathetic and sensible weavers, do not dispute Hilse's assertion that they will end up in prison; they do not care; and this is not just empty bravado, for they have no reason to care: 'Im Zuchthause is immer noch besser wie d'rheeme. Da is ma versorgt; da braucht ma nich darben' (I, 475). These weavers are not closely related to the class-conscious proletariat of Hauptmann's own day. Like Halbe's *Eisgang*, the play is not even set in the city, but in its author's native province, among the country workers—engaged in cottage-industry—whom he knew most intimately. Moreover Hauptmann's verism, that is to say his fidelity to his sources and his avoidance of anachronism, has excluded any argument for or against organized socialism. There is not in *Die Weber*, as there is in Ernst Toller's *Die Maschinen-*

stürmer (1922), a single far-sighted figure to whom the future can be said to belong. Hauptmann's is both a better play and a more effective piece of social criticism for this reason. Where the hero, Jimmy Cobbett, is involved, *Die Maschinenstürmer* has a strong thematic resemblance to *Florian Geyer*—only the hero is compared to Lord Byron *and* Christ—but the play is more effective where it makes a direct appeal for human pity through its portrayal of the suffering and deprivation of the weavers. It is for this particular aspect of his play that Toller is most indebted to Hauptmann, and it is here that Hauptmann is not to be surpassed. The care and affection with which Hauptmann has depicted all his weavers, and which only rarely borders on sentimentality (the starving child of Act I) is a powerful testimony to Hauptmann's social concern, and constitutes a fierce social attack.

There is every justification for regarding *Die Weber* as a tendentious work. In making the revolt understandable Hauptmann has gone a long way towards making it forgiveable. At the same time there is little doubt of his indictment of the employers. Dreißiger is allowed to plead the weak competitive position of the Silesian weaving industry, but, although this is regarded as a fact by the historians, it carries little weight in the drama, because Dreißiger is manifestly concerned only to exploit the situation as best he can. Zimmermann's account singles out the firm of Zwanziger for its reputation for particular harshness (p. 350), but the play goes further than this; the effect of showing just the one firm is to make it a representative of the whole class.

The direction of the play's attack is not substantially altered, as Theodor Fontane argued, by the fifth act. It is true that this act provides the first signs of resistance from among the weavers themselves, but it also introduces another powerful supporter of the revolt in the person of Luise Hilse, an outraged mother, who is the equal of Bäcker, Wittig, and Jäger in terms of fury and energy. Moreover the resistance of Hilse is overcome; his son, Gottlieb, disobeys him and joins the rebels, and the revolt spreads from Peterswaldau to Langenbielau. There is also a certain ambiguity about Hilse's resistance, which requires explanation, for he does not disown the weavers, but prays for their safety: 'Nu, lieber Herrgott im Himmel! schitze die armen Weber schitz meine armen Brieder!' (I, 477). Hilse's solidarity with his fellow-weavers in their hostility to their employers is not seriously in doubt, and his clash with them is primarily a clash of personality. Hilse's attitude differs from that of his fellow-weavers because of those differences in character which cannot be fully explained in Marxist terms by environment. Hilse, with his pronounced streak of Silesian pietism, is an example of a man with a strong psychological need for religion; and throughout his life his social situation has reinforced this need. Now an old man, near to death, with little to hope for in this world, he naturally clings more strongly than the other weavers to the beliefs which have sustained him, to his 'certainty' of happiness in the world to come. His attitude approaches panic when this seems threatened; hence his unreasoning severity towards the child, Mielchen, who has brought into his home a silver spoon which does not rightly belong there: 'Mach, daß wir den Satansleffel vom Halse kriegen' ('Get that devilish spoon out of here') (I, 455). For a man like Hilse it is too much to ask whether he has not been duped by an alliance of Church and bourgeoisie; but his attitude to the revolt is a clear reflection of the teaching of the local pastor, Kittelhaus. In Hilse's eyes the revolt is the work of the devil ('Satansarbeit'), the words of Luise are godless ('gottlose Reden'), Bäcker and his followers are emissaries of Satan: 'Wo bringt euch d'r Teiwel her mit Stangen und Äxten?' (I, 467); he thus accepts the equation between the prevalent social order and the laws of God, which Kittelhaus made in Act IV, in saying of the angry weavers: 'Sie treten Gottes Gesetz mit Füßen' (I, 419). The discrepancy between the miserable surroundings in which Hilse lives, and the *gratitude* he expresses for the goodness of heaven in his prayer at the opening of Act V, strengthens the impression that he has been fobbed off with the promise of an afterlife which will compensate for the misery which is now his lot, that his religion is 'die phantastische Verwirklichung des menschlichen Wesens, weil das menschliche Wesen keine wahre Wirklichkeit besitzt . . . der Ausdruck des wirklichen Elends and die Protestation gegen das wirkliche Elend'.[12] Superficially Hilse is distinguished from his fellow-weavers by his firm adherence to his religious beliefs, but a consideration of the quality of these beliefs makes his solidarity with them much clearer. His 'Christianity' is as much a religion of vengeance as of forgiveness:

Fer was hätt' ich denn hier gesessen— und Schemel getreten uf Mord vierzig und mehr Jahr? und hätte ruhig zugesehn, wie der dort drieben in Hoffart und Schwelgerei lebt und Gold macht aus mein'n Hunger und Kummer. Fer was denn? Weil ich 'ne Hoffnung hab'. Ich hab was in aller der Not. *Durchs Fenster weisend*: Du hast hier deine Parte—ich drieben in jener Welt: das hab' ich gedacht. Und ich lass' mich vierteeln— ich hab 'ne Gewißheet. Es ist uns verheißen. Gericht wird gehalten; aber nich mir sein Richter, sondern: mein is die Rache, spricht der Herr, unser Gott (I, 463).	Why should I have been sitting here— treading this loom like mad for forty years or more? quietly watching him over yonder, living in vanity and luxury, and making a packet out of my hunger and misery. Why? Because I have hope. I've got something, despite all this misery. *Pointing out of the window*: You're getting your share here—I'll get mine in the next world: that's what I've been thinking. I'm ready to stake my life on it—I'm certain. We've been promised. The day of judgement will come; but we are not the judges; vengeance is mine, saith the Lord, our God.

This attitude, which can hardly have been picked up directly from Pastor Kittelhaus, is just as much a cry of hatred as the inarticulate fury of the other weavers, or their revolutionary song, *Das Blutgericht*; it is indeed possible that Hilse's speech was in fact suggested to Hauptmann by two verses of the original *Blutgericht*, which Hauptmann did not include in the play:

O euer Geld und euer Gut,	O all your goods will melt away
Das wird dereinst vergehen	And all your riches too,
Wie Butter an der Sonne Glut,	Like butter in the sun's fierce ray,
Wie wirds um euch dann stehen?	And where will that leave you?
Wenn ihr dereinst nach dieser Zeit	After your life of ease is done,
Nach eurem Freudenleben	After your riotous days,
Dort, dort in jener Ewigkeit	When you, before your God alone,
Sollt Rechenschaft abgeben.[13]	Must justify your ways.

Hilse is the one example of a weaver who has an alternative to *Das Blutgericht*, a satisfying and thoroughly coherent assessment of his own situation; his life has purpose and shape. Whether this assessment has any higher validity, is in dramatic terms, irrelevant; his convictions determine his actions and mean that he is not open to the seductions of Moritz Jäger. Hilse's Old-Testament Christianity is a protest and an expression of suffering similar in intensity to the protest of the outraged mother, Luise Hilse; and even though this protest has about it a certain life-denying character, it is in no way to be likened to the unsympathetic inwardness of Rose Bernd's father. It remains a thing of value, for is it not also evidence of that indomitable spirit to which this play is a tribute, and which makes it a work of admiration as much as a work of pity?

There is about Hilse's attitude a defiant heroism, which contributes to the positive quality of the play—a quality which would have been lost completely if Hauptmann had finished the account, by going on to show how the revolt was crushed and the weavers imprisoned. And before interpreting *Die Weber* as a grimly pessimistic work, we should bear in mind that it was open to the author to make his pessimism much more explicit, without in any way abandoning the historical accuracy which informs this play. Even so, there is a finality about Hilse's death; it rounds the play off with an excellent curtain, in the conventional sense; and in view of the dominant position which he occupies in this final act, a certain authority does accrue to him and to his utterances. If this is indeed an attempt to make us take Hilse's words at face value, or to suggest that his sufferings have endowed him with a superior insight beyond the reach of his fellow-weavers, then it is an attempt which comes too late in the play. The suspicious rationalist in Hauptmann has done his job too well for us to be able to take this view of his conclusion.

A much more pronounced ambiguity informs the whole of the short play *Hanneles Himmelfahrt* (1893). The attention to causal details, and the consequent undermining of the authority of the religious insight is, if anything, even more scrupulous than in *Die Weber*. The play falls into three parts, showing the objective world of the young Hannele Mattern's present situation, the nightmare world from which she has tried to escape by suicide, and her dream of heavenly bliss. All three worlds are inextricably intertwined, for Hannele's vision of heaven is determined by a strange mixture of earthly hatreds and compensations: a desire for vengeance on a cruel step-father, a childlike urge for power, attention and significance, a yearning for maternal affection, and an innate religious humility and piety.[14] The sexual element is particularly strong; the emphasis on physical torment at the hands of the step-father recalls the masochistic fantasies of Wendla Bergmann in Wedekind's *Frühlings Erwachen*; while the 'stranger', who is played by the same actor as the teacher, Gottwald, is both the figure of Christ, and at the same time the masculine ideal of a young girl whose sexual impulses are just awakening, and who has taken literally the Christian metaphor of the 'bride of heaven'.

In her review of the play, Lou Andreas-Salomé stressed the subjective nature of Hannele's dreams: 'we encounter here a child of this earth, and her earthly longings'.[15] If we are prepared to adopt this standpoint, then the 'sentimentality' of the play is no longer a fault, but part of its overall consistency; the critic Siegfried Jacobsohn describes Hannele's vision, as it was presented in Rittner's production of 1913, in the following words:

> a heaven . . . which a snob would describe as kitsch, because he forgets that this heaven is not constructed according to his taste, but according to the fairy-tale taste of a young village-girl . . . By sound and image, by changing from earthly to supernatural lighting, he distinguishes between Hannele's dream and reality.[16]

Hauptmann views the religion of Hannele with the irony and the scepticism which he applied (if only intermittently) to the attitudes of Frau Buchner, Johannes Vockerat, and Hilse—although in *Hanneles Himmelfahrt* the use of verse tends to objectivize the vision to a far greater extent—but the individual need for religion and the fact and consequence of its existence are allowed. By 1893 the Naturalists had begun to develop a considerable interest in religious manifestations, and a greater tolerance towards religious needs.[17] Religion, as it is treated in *Hanneles Himmelfahrt*, and to a lesser extent, *Die Weber*, offers the dramatist an opportunity to extend his range of expression without entirely abandoning the deeply engrained premises of Naturalism. *Hanneles Himmelfahrt* shows how, by the use of the 'play-within-a-play', the Naturalist drama can be opened up to include the completely subjective vision. Taken together these two plays show Hauptmann developing a style which permits that free activity of the artistic imagination demanded by the now dominant 'individualists' among his Naturalist contemporaries.

Notes to Chapter VIII

[1] In a letter of 1 August 1893, quoted by C. H. Moore, 'A hearing on "Germinal" and "Die Weber" ', *Germanic Review*, XXXIII (1958), p. 32.

[2] The bad harvest of 1890 had caused further trouble among the Silesian weavers, so it is possible that Grelling's words were meant ironically.

[3] During the period of the Third Reich Hauptmann was invited—and refused—to co-operate on a film version of *Die Weber*, which would have included a conclusion, showing how well things were in the contemporary weaving industry; C. F. W. Behl, *Zwiesprache mit Gerhart Hauptmann*, München, 1949, pp. 154–5.

[4] Quoted from K. L. Tank, *Gerhart Hauptmann*, p. 28.

[5] 'Erinnerungen an Gerhart Hauptmann', *Mit Gerhart Hauptmann*, ed. Heynen, p. 108.

[6] Mehring, 'Eisgang', *Ges. Schriften*, XI, 135.

[7] Quoted from H.-A. Schultze, *Der Schauspieler Rudolph Rittner*, p. 148.

[8] Wilhelm Wolff, 'Das Elend und der Aufruhr in Schlesien', *Deutsches Bürgerbuch für 1845*, ed. H. Püttmann, Darmstadt, 1845 (this is the Wilhelm Wolff to whom Marx dedicated the first volume of *Das Kapital*); A. Zimmermann, *Blüthe und Verfall des Leinengewerbes in Schlesien*.

[9] *Breslauer Neueste Nachrichten*, 25 November 1938.

[10] Hauptmann follows his sources very closely here. Pfeiffer's assertion: 'Das is a Bielauer Weber. Die sind überall d'rbei, wo's 'n Unfug zu machen gibt', reflects the report in the *Vossische Zeitung*, 10 June 1844: 'Die Langenbielauer Arbeiter sind wegen ihrer Energie und Halsstarrigkeit bekannt'. It is more comfortable for Dreißiger to attribute the revolt to agitators (individuals) than to conditions; cf. above pp. 12–13.

[11] Karl Marx, 'Debatten über das Holzdiebstahlgesetz', *Marx-Engels Gesamtausgabe*, Frankfurt a.M., 1927, Ser. 1, I, 266 ff.

[12] Karl Marx, 'Zur Kritik der Hegelschen Rechtsphilosophie', *Gesamtausgabe*, Ser. 1, I, 607.

[13] Quoted from *Die Weber. Dichtung und Wirklichkeit*, p. 117. For a discussion of Hilse's religion see H. M. Wolff, 'Der alte Hilse', Guthke and Wolff, 'Das Leid im Werke Gerhart Hauptmanns', pp. 69 ff.

[14] Cf. H. M. Wolff, 'Hannele', Guthke and Wolff, op. cit., pp. 74–82.

[15] 'Hannele', *Freie Bühne*, IV (1893), p. 1346.

[16] Quoted from H.-A. Schultze, *Der Schauspieler Rudolph Rittner*, p. 87.

[17] Cf. H. Hart, 'M. von Egidy', *Freie Bühne*, III (1892), p. 1288; Bruno Wille, 'Der Naturprediger Johannes Guttzeit', *Freie Bühne*, II (1891), p. 376. Guttzeit was the man who had inspired Hauptmann's short story *Der Apostel* (1890).

IX
The Naturalist comedy

Comedy was not a field in which the Naturalists—either German or European—were particularly productive, nor was it one in which they particularly excelled. Gerhart Hauptmann did not begin his first comedy, *Kollege Crampton* (1892), until after the completion of *Die Weber*, by which time Naturalism was widely reckoned to be in decline. This is not entirely coincidental, for the veristic doctrine itself, and certain characteristics of the Naturalist movement as it developed in Germany, are peculiarly hostile to the adoption of a comic view. The purpose of this chapter is to show how the relaxation of the earlier aggression, and an increasing tendency to indulgence or sentimentality, allowed the movement to embrace a form which had not hitherto received a great deal of attention—except in the form of satirical social criticism—from the earnest young writers of this generation. The results of this, even in the best Naturalist comedy, *Der Biberpelz* (1893), testify to a continuing unease in handling the genre: like many more famous antecedents in the field, the German Naturalists exploited the comic possibilities in the behaviour of the blind, automaton-like monomane (von Wehrhahn in *Der Biberpelz*, Gehrke in Holz's and Ernst's *Sozialaristokraten*) but their comic monomanes pale into relative insignificance beside the great *sympathetic* monomanes of Naturalist literature, such as the bigotted old Hilse of *Die Weber*, the self-flagellating Fuhrmann Henschel, or the pathetic Henriette John of *Die Ratten*. There is about the German Naturalist comedy a certain lack of incisiveness which derives, I will suggest, both from an inherent conservatism and from the inhibitions arising from specifically Naturalist convictions; but it is the inherent conservatism, of which I have already spoken on a number of occasions, which prompts the Naturalists to stop short of the ruthless disdain and the radical consequentiality of the greatest exponents of the comic genre.

It was a contemporary of the German Naturalists, Henri Bergson, who saw in the monomane the richest source of comedy: 'A comic person is one who automatically follows his own path, without bothering about contact with others. The purpose of laughter is to correct his distraction and awaken him from his dream.'[1] Defined in this way comedy is a genre with an extrinsic purpose, and is thus limited to what we normally tend to describe as satirical comedy. Such comedy might also tend to be conservative, in that it can readily be used to defend the *status quo* from the threat of fragmentation when the individual is tempted to pursue his own isolated course.[2] One of the clearest examples of this is the use of comedy to ridicule the avant-garde in literature or art; as, for instance, in Molière's *Les Femmes Savantes*, or, to take an example from German Naturalism, in Act III, scenes i–v of Otto Ernst's *Jugend von Heute* (1899), where a rather motley collection of individuals holds a poetry-reading (ten lines of one of the poems consist of *Gedankenstriche*).

In comedy of this kind, however—and Bergson's definition does not take sufficient account of this—a point can well be reached where the moral or social purpose of the writer seems to have become subordinate to the simple desire to make the spectator laugh. 'Really it is all tragedy', says a character in Ivy Compton-Burnett's *Mother and Son*, 'comedy is a wicked way of looking at it, when it is not our own'. This 'wicked way of looking at it' is, perhaps, an important ingredient of great comedy. Modern criticism of Molière, recognizing this, has ceased to place such exclusive emphasis on the social criticism in his work, and has directed our attention rather to his career as a man of the theatre, who earned his living by making people laugh.[3] To this kind of writer the *'faux dévot'* (Tartuffe) and the provincial *imitators* of the 'précieuses' can offer more promising material than the real thing; and the work of such a writer might be more strongly informed with gratitude to the purveyor of comic situations than with any desire to correct his characters' relationship to society. Such detachment is more nearly achieved in the chilly black comedy of Ibsen's *Hedda Gabler* (if one overlooks the rather ineffectual comfort offered by Thea Elvsted) or in the radical nihilism of Schnitzler's *Reigen*, than in the comedies of the German Naturalists.

The social-critical stance of the Naturalists and their desire to engage literature in the problems of the age, made them favourably disposed to purposeful satirical comedy from the outset; but the theoretical dislike for tendentiousness, as exemplified in the early critical writings of the Hart brothers, for instance, gave rise to certain reservations. In the earlier dramas of Gerhart Hauptmann (satirical) comedy is restricted to a few brief episodes; and in the movement as a whole tragi-comedy, in the widest sense of the term, is felt to be the most congenial genre.[4] Where the dramatist does indulge in a satirical attack the theoretical limits are often stretched, and, particularly among the lesser dramatists, naturalistic characterization readily gives way to caricature. *Hilfsprediger* Boretius in Max Halbe's early play, *Freie Liebe* (1889), the heroine's father and fiancé in Hartleben's *Hanna Jagert* (1893), and the heroine's fiancé (again) in Hirschfeld's *Pauline* (1899), are all caricatured in the course of a satirical attack designed to safeguard certain social values. This strictly functional use of comedy might suggest that the respective dramatists are less than certain about the merits of their cases; and this is not at all surprising, in view of the rapidity with which the Naturalist position is modified in this decade. These three plays do, in fact, provide a rather good barometer of this unsettled period. The earliest, *Freie Liebe*, is ethically 'progressive', defending the right of Ernst Winter and his young friend, Elise, to enjoy life and live together without being married; the second, which dates from the period immediately after the breach with socialism, is less decisive; it defends the right of Hanna to lead her own individual life, but concedes that she has a certain debt of gratitude to the Socialist and the altruist who were responsible for her liberation from the constraints and conventions of the past, and whom she now deserts; Hirschfeld's play, the latest, is quite unashamedly and unambiguously conservative, advocating the acceptance of the social situation and an underprivileged position in it, provided that decent, humane people are at the top.

Satirical attacks, which tend to be episodic, and tend to become increasingly conservative in character, are further inhibited by the Naturalist doctrine of absolute determinism. Where this operates, it generates a feeling of oppression by uncontrollable external forces, and precludes any possibility of genuine independence or superiority; no one can be free enough to be detached. Just as the belief in relentless laws of causality excludes guilt, and inhibits tragedy, so also it excludes ridicule and prevents satirical comedy. The 'moral laxity' which Gustav von Aschenbach so abhorred, the 'tout comprendre, c'est tout pardonner' of Naturalist theory, is a double-edged weapon. Old Thienwiebel in *Papa Hamlet* is a perfect example of the character who is potentially comic because of his *idée fixe*, and Holz and Schlaf do go a long way towards exploiting this potentiality; but they clearly experience the obligation of the Naturalist to make his fantasies plausible, and so they give these fantasies a psychological explanation, relating them (as compensatory delusions) to Thienwiebel's present milieu, and his past experiences and ambitions as an actor. The central figure in this work is therefore at once comic and pathetic. The same is true, though to a lesser extent, of the comic episodes in Hartleben's tragedy, *Rosenmontag* (1900). This play, which was one of the great popular successes of the Naturalist movement, and was given 205 performances at Brahm's *Deutsches Theater*, belongs in the tradition of the *bürgerliches Trauerspiel*. Its hero is a young officer, Hans Rudorff, who is in love with a working-class girl. The schemer's role is shared by Rudorff's twin cousins, Peter and Paul von Ramberg; this doubling of the role is a stock device, which achieves comic effects without caricature. The interference of the Rambergs breaks up the affair, and leads to Rudorff's suicide, but their motives are honest and they themselves are well-meaning in a way that Schiller's Wurm and Lessing's Marinelli are not. The traditions of a family with a long military tradition, and the stultifying influence of barrack-room life are illuminated in realistic scenes which provide the best moments of the play. Here again explanation amounts to a kind of justification; and the Rambergs appear pathetic in their superficial and naïve confidence that their scheming will one day earn them their cousin's gratitude.

Ludwig Anzengruber was a dramatist who was close enough to the German Naturalists to earn their admiration, and his plays were very popular among the *Volksbühnen*, but he wrote within the tradition of a country richly endowed with comedy, Austria, and at a time when the doctrines of Naturalism had not been formulated. He also preserved a basic belief in individual freedom and human independence. These are clearly factors which enabled him to create in his best comedy, *Die Kreuzelschreiber*, a work which is superior to anything the German Naturalists wrote in this genre. The theme of Anzengruber's play is basically a serious one; interclerical rivalry leads to irresponsible meddling in family-life, and turns wives against their husbands: the priest of one village secures the support of the men for a document proclaiming adherence to the traditions of the Catholic faith and expressing hostility to so-called Lutheran innovations, whereupon the priest of the neighbouring village appeals to the women to make their husbands recant and go on a pilgrimage to Rome in penance for their sins. There is no doubt whatever that Anzengruber's play is a play with a purpose; as always, his attack on the Roman Catholic Church is in earnest, and, typically, he wrings every last drop of emotion from the plight of an old peasant, Brenninger, who kills himself in despair over the futile and unnecessary quarrel with his wife.

Nevertheless there is more to Anzengruber's very amusing play than its overt polemic purpose. The viewpoint of the most important character in the play, Steinklopferhans, is one of detachment, not one of anger, and it is a viewpoint we are encouraged to share. The various events we witness are thus all part of one great comedy in which we are not involved. The message of Steinklopferhans is that man, even at his basest and most exposed can always glory in a certain inviolability: 'Es kann dir nix geschehen!'.[5] Steinklopferhans has experienced the ultimate in misery and isolation, but even in these depths the restorative power of nature is not eliminated, and he has recovered to assert with confidence that the world is a happy place: 'Die Welt is a lustige Welt.'[6]

Secure in his ultimate truth, he can stand aside from the action of the play as spectator and commentator. He can look on and laugh when the respectably married Anton is suddenly and surprisingly confronted with his former sweetheart; when the prosperous Großbauer von Grundldorf enters the village inn and so easily obtains the signatures of the (mostly illiterate) men for his document; when Josepha, the wife of Anton, successfully follows the example of Lysistrata, and persuades her husband to go to Rome as a penance; or when Josepha pathetically tries to run the farm in her husband's absence. In each case Steinklopferhans is ready with the laconic commentary of the superior, far-sighted observer: 'Ich steh da am Posten! . . . Und melde gehorsamst, daß der Hauptmann der Kreuzelschreiber . . . dort beim Fenster h'neinretiriert ist!—No, dafür sein morgen d' Weiber obenauf!!' ('I stand at my post! . . . And I have to report that the captain of the cross-signers . . . has retreated through that window!— Well, tomorrow it's the women who will be on top!!').[7]

He intervenes in the action to help Anton clear up the confusion, but, characteristically, he does so in a way which prolongs the amusement of the detached observer. True to his principle, 'Solang Gspaß war, hom ich über eng lachen mögen' ('As long as there was a joke, I've enjoyed laughing at you.')[8] he organizes the men for the pilgrimage, asks their wives to provide financial support, and enrolls a band of devout, young, single women, which includes Anton's former sweetheart, to accompany the pilgrimage as 'Bußschwestern'. In this final scene the comedian Anzengruber is revealed at his most radical, and the moral purpose behind his play is almost forgotten. Once Anton is back in his customary masculine position of ascendancy he exploits his advantage to the full, sparing his wife no discomfort, until she turns the tables again, by threatening to find herself a man to console her. Equilibrium is restored, and the pilgrimage is called off, whereupon one of the men, Altlechner, who cannot stand his wife, hastily makes a break for Rome. In *Georges Dandin* Molière pursued his comic purpose with even more rigour, but the German Naturalists never do.

This kind of detachment is most closely approached in certain episodes of Hauptmann's *Der Biberpelz*. The shrewd Frau Wolff perceives the robot-like predictability of the Prussian official, von Wehrhahn, who is so concerned with his defence of 'die höchsten Güter der Nation' against socialism that he overlooks all manner of real crimes, and she turns her knowledge of von Wehrhahn's blindness to her own advantage. Beginning with the relatively trivial crime of poaching, she then steals wood from her daughter's employer, Krüger, and finally his beaver-coat; in the sequel, the tragi-comic *Der rote Hahn* (1901), Frau Wolff (now Frau Fielitz) has progressed to arson and fraud. The action of the two plays is therefore repetitive; indeed, the plays depend for their comic effects on repetition, which is emphasized by the regularity of the scene-changes between Frau Wolff's house, where the *coups* are prepared, and the court-room, where the crimes are investigated. Both plays depend very much on comedy of situation of a fairly basic kind: the outwitting of the slow and foolish by the quick and nimble. The best examples of this are the two most famous examples, the endings of the first and third acts of *Der Biberpelz*; in the former Mitteldorf, an employee of the court, unwittingly assists Frau Wolff and her husband as they set out to steal Krüger's wood, while in the latter Krüger brandishes a piece of his own wood, which he has found outside Frau Wolff's house and which he does not recognize, vowing that he will catch the thief.

Hirschfeld's *Pauline* stands in much the same relationship to *Der Biberpelz* as his *Die Mütter* does to *Einsame Menschen*. It shares the same cyclic structure, showing a sequence of events in which the heroine outwits her numerous suitors by playing off one against another.

Both plays therefore have a structural resemblance to Molière's *Les Fourberies de Scapin*, a farce consisting of a sequence of episodes in which the central character outwits a series of dupes. In farce the central character derives his value from what he does, from the skill, the style, the pace with which he outwits others; the only value which he can be said to embody is the value of comedy itself. In the Naturalist drama, where the portrayal of character tends to be more important than action, the momentum which is essential to farce cannot be developed, and, at the same time, what the character *does* can be distinguished from what the character *is*. In Hirschfeld's play Pauline's employer says of her: 'bei all ihrer Unverschämtheit ist das Mädel anständig geblieben, so keusch und nett wie keine andre' ('for all her cheek, the girl has remained decent, as modest and pleasant as anybody');[9] that is to say Pauline's vitality, her love of freedom, her philosophy of enjoyment without involvement, are all seen as a threat to her basic humanity; she preserves her value *despite* those of her qualities which provide the comic episodes in the play. The same is true of Frau Wolff in Hauptmann's *Der Biberpelz*. Her redeeming qualities are her elemental maternal energy, her good sense, and her basic decency; Hauptmann is most careful to distinguish her transgressions from those of the police-informer, Motes, and his wife. In her basic convictions she conforms to the most important values; in *Der Biberpelz* she commits no crimes which seriously harm others, and one cannot believe she would. However, the ambitions she cherishes for her daughter, Adelheid, recall the foolishness of the mother in many a *bürgerliches Trauerspiel*, and indicate that her dishonesty is a sign of incipient corruption by a society in which material success is the most important yardstick of achievement. The rather mild foolishness of Frau Wolff's ambitions becomes intensified into the blindness of Frau Fielitz in *Der rote Hahn*, where she undiscriminatingly admires her vain and parasitic son-in-law, Schmarowski: 'das is a proweeckter Kerl! An dem is kee 'nausgeschmissenes Geld! Da is keene Angst: der wird sein' Weg machen' ('that man's got his wits about him! He's a good bet! You mark my words, he'll get on') (II, 23). The destruction of Frau Wolff's humanity as she becomes increasingly dominated by a frantic desire to get on at all costs is the aspect of the two plays which Brecht chose to emphasize when he adapted them for performance on a single evening. With this end in view, he encouraged his leading actress to exploit to the full the repetitive structure of the two plays: 'Sie muß voll den günstigen Umstand ausnützen, daß die beiden Stücke ähnliche Situationen enthalten; nur so kann die Entwicklung der Wolffen sichtbar gemacht werden.'[10] But when the two plays are considered as a pair, the later, and weaker, play casts its tragi-comic shadow over the whole. The undermining of the former Frau Wolff's vitality and the weakening of her hold on life as her personal anxiety increases, inevitably colour the way in which we view her earlier misdemeanours. *Der Biberpelz* can remain a comedy only if we view it in isolation.

Even when it is viewed in isolation one can sense a certain timidity on the author's part which has prevented a full unfolding of comic effects. The very end of the play, without doubt one of its best moments, provides a good example of this timidity:

WEHRHAHN. Und so wahr es ist, wenn ich hier sage: die Wolffen ist eine ehrliche Haut, so sag ich Ihnen mit gleicher Bestimmtheit: Ihr Doktor Fleischer, von dem wir sprechen, das ist ein lebensgefährlicher Kerl!
FRAU WOLFF. Da weeß ich nu nich . . . (I, 542).

WEHRHAHN. If, as I can truly say, Frau Wolff is an honest woman, then I can say with equal certainty: that Dr Fleischer, of whom we have been speaking, is a very dangerous fellow!
FRAU WOLFF. I wouldn't know about that . . .

The comic effect of these lines is two-fold; in the first instance they show the predictable von Wehrhahn giving vent yet again to his obsession, and secondly they exploit the dramatic irony which naturally arises from von Wehrhahn's blindness. Here, then, is a satirical attack on von Wehrhahn and the society he represents, but an attack whose force is blunted because von Wehrhahn is not totally wrong in his judgement. Indeed, the whole tendency of the play has been to show that Frau Wolff really is 'eine ehrliche Haut', despite her weaknesses; and the most natural response for an actress in the part to secure from her audience, as Brecht points out, is unthinking approval.[11] If this were not so, if Frau Wolff were clearly and consistently an amoral character, the social criticism of the play would be fiercer, and the conclusion crueller to von Wehrhahn; above all it would be more comic.

Brecht's appreciation of the role of Frau Wolff distantly recalls some outspokenly hostile comments which Karl Kraus once made about German comedy in general, and Hauptmann's *Die Jungfern von Bischofsberg* in particular. He condemns a kind of humour 'which humourless people would like to see defined as a metaphysical smile at all the weaknesses of mankind, and which, it is true, is more peaceful and reassuring, but no more praiseworthy than all attempts to bore them to death'.[12] The humour which Kraus is attacking is not harsh and aggressive, but complacent, indulgent, and tolerant. It is the humour which enables us to come to terms with the world in which we live, and which enables us to smile on the activity of Frau Wolff, while still disapproving of the sentiments implied in her statement to her husband that you just have to get on, and no one will ask questions: 'Wenn de erscht reich bist . . . und kannst in der Eklipage sitzen, da fragt dich kee Mensch nich, wo de's her hast' (I, 501). It is the kind of humour to which Hauptmann was referring in the words: 'Humor ist eine der Formen, durch die der Mensch sein Geschick wo nicht überwindet, wenigstens trägt',[13] and which is enshrined in his first comedy, *Kollege Crampton*.

Like *Papa Hamlet* and Holz's and Jerschke's tragi-comedy, *Traumulus* (1904), it treats the problem of an individual in an illusory relationship to reality. In the two works on which Holz collaborated—and, indeed, in Hauptmann's own *Schluck und Jau* (1900)—there is a much greater awareness of the fragility and the dangers of illusion. *Kollege Crampton*, however, is almost a plea for the understanding and tolerance of the eccentricities and weaknesses of a creative artist; here, as in *Einsame Menschen*, *Michael Kramer*, and *Die versunkene Glocke*, the artist's wife fails significantly to support him.

Since its first performance, when its success was attributed largely to the contribution of the actor, Georg Engels, in the title-role, *Kollege Crampton* has been regarded as a character-drama. Its episodic action is designed to reveal the protagonist's lack of a will strong enough to resist external circumstances, and his consequent tendency to escape, with the assistance of a vivid imagination and a liberal dose of alcohol, into the easier world of self-delusion. It did not pass unnoticed that Hauptmann's views on alcohol had changed radically since *Vor Sonnenaufgang*. Hartleben wrote a 'sixth act' for Hauptmann's play in which Crampton's pupil and benefactor, Max Straehler, returns from the theatre where he has seen the earlier play, and announces that he cannot now marry Crampton's daughter, Gertrud, because he fears she may have inherited her father's alcoholism.[14]

Kollege Crampton can end happily because Hauptmann sees to it that external circumstances do not resist the imaginative desires of his hero. The wealthy Max helps Crampton along by providing him with an ideal studio and a commission, so that he is completely sheltered from harsh reality; Max's brother enters into the spirit of the game by allowing Professor Crampton to persuade himself that he is to pay rent for the studio. The effect of all this bounty is a sudden urge of resolve by the hitherto inactive Crampton: 'Jetzt müssen wir schuften, Max, wie zwei Kulis!' (I, 318). There is no Relling, as there is in *The Wild Duck*, to pour cold water on the illusion, but it is, to say the least, doubtful whether this final resolve holds out any real promise; particularly since Crampton spreads the burden of responsibility by his use of the first-person plural. There is no very strong evidence in the play that Crampton's gifts are not simply part of the illusion, particularly if one holds the view that the ability to create *something* is an integral part of creative ability.[15] There is little reason to believe that Crampton's talent will unfold more productively in his new-found, feather-bedded isolation, and the 'humour' of this play does not require that it should. The point about this kind of humour—and this is what makes it rather feeble—is that it involves an indulgent, patronizing tolerance, such as is extended to the waywardness of a child; and it is a certain childlike innocence which is presented as Crampton's most endearing feature.

In *Kollege Crampton*, as in *Der Biberpelz*, a more radical approach would surely have produced better comedy. What little amusement there is in the conclusion of *Kollege Crampton* derives from the automatic, predictable quality of Crampton's behaviour; from the suspicion, which might have been the certainty, that he will continue to behave as before, to drink, to idle away his time unproductively, and to delude himself that he is a potentially great man, hindered by a hostile and jealous environment.

If, as has been suggested, the satirical attack on the monomane—comedy as Bergson defines it—has an inherent conservative tendency, then how much truer is it that the tolerant 'humour' which replaces it, entirely in *Kollege Crampton*, partially in *Der Biberpelz*, tends towards the preservation of the existing social order, by smiling on the weakness of those who come to terms with it. This kind of humour emerges in the later stages of Naturalism, along with an increase in tolerance to other means by which the individual can come to terms with a hostile world, for instance the religious compensations of Hilse and Hannele. Both developments take place after the period of greatest political commitment is over.

Notes to Chapter IX

[1] *Le Rire. Essai sur la signification du comique* (1912), Paris, 1920, p. 137.

[2] Cf. René König, *Die naturalistische Ästhetik in Frankreich*, pp. 190–1.

[3] Cf. René Bray, *Molière. Homme de Théâtre*, Paris, 1954. It was a performance of *L'Avare* which prompted Hauptmann to write *Kollege Crampton*, and in the same year he was at work on a play entitled *Der eingebildete Kranke*, which was never completed.

⁴ K. S. Guthke, *Geschichte und Poetik der deutschen Tragikomödie*, Göttingen, 1961, p. 218.

⁵ *Sämtliche Werke*, IV, 73.

⁶ Ibid., p. 70.

⁷ Ibid., p. 65.

⁸ Ibid., p. 70.

⁹ Georg Hirschfeld, *Pauline*, Berlin, 1899, p. 23.

¹⁰ Bertolt Brecht, *Schriften zum Theater*, Frankfurt a.M., 1964, VI, 302. Cf. *Theaterarbeit. 6 Aufführungen des Berliner Ensembles*, Dresden, 1952, pp. 171–226. For some comments on the possible influence of *Der Biberpelz* on *Mutter Courage*, see H. W. Reichert, 'Hauptmann's Frau Wolff and Brecht's Mother Courage', *German Quarterly*, XXXIV (1961), pp. 439–48.

¹¹ *Schriften zum Theater*, VI, 302.

¹² 'Von Humor and Lyrik' (1921), *Die Sprache*, München, 1954, p. 206.

¹³ 'Über dramatische Kunst' (1914), *Die Kunst des Dramas*, p. 139.

¹⁴ 'Kollege Crampton, VIer Akt', *Freie Bühne*, III (1892), p. 218. Hartleben had been anticipated by a brief note in *Kladderadatsch*, 1890, p. 60: 'Neues aus der Familie Selicke: Neues Unglück, der Landpfarrer Wendt hat abgeschrieben und die Verlobung aufgehoben. Grund: dringender Verdacht, daß die Trunksucht des Alten auf Toni sich vererben könnte.'

¹⁵ Guthke (*Tragikomödie*, p. 256) confidently attributes to Crampton a 'zweifellos vorhandene große Begabung'; he forgets Grillparzer's words: 'was nicht ausgeführt wird, ist leer; was nicht ausgeführt werden kann, ist verrückt'.

X

Some later dramas

By 1898 Gerhart Hauptmann was Germany's most respected dramatist, although the works of Sudermann were more popular with the general public. He had behind him one undisputed and well-deserved success in *Die Weber*, perhaps the finest of all his works, but his other popular successes, *Der Biberpelz*, *Hanneles Himmelfahrt*, and *Die versunkene Glocke*, were much slighter works. The very real merits of the austere *Das Friedensfest* had not been fully appreciated, and his most ambitious play, *Florian Geyer*, had, to Hauptmann's great disappointment, met with a cool response from public and critics alike. It is to the works of the next ten or so years, which include *Und Pippa tanzt!* (1906) and the novel, *Der Narr in Christo Emanuel Quint* (1910), as well as the later Naturalist dramas, that Hauptmann owes his enduring reputation. These dramas, the four most important of which I shall examine in this chapter, were widely regarded as marking a return by Hauptmann to his earlier Naturalist style, although they were, of course, written when Naturalism had long ceased to exist as a closely-knit literary movement, and when Hauptmann himself was no longer writing exclusively in the Naturalist vein. The purpose of this chapter is to assess the importance of the Naturalist experiment for Gerhart Hauptmann; to consider how much of the original scientific-rationalist impulse remains, and in what way this is responsible for the excellence or the shortcomings of these later works.

These plays do provide something of a bridge between the earliest works and Hauptmann's later, more strenuously 'poetic' works; and they begin to show clearly Hauptmann's preoccupation with the theme of human suffering. Accordingly, these works, more than any others, have been taken by critics as a key to the understanding of the *œuvre* of Gerhart Hauptmann. Again and again it is to these works that critics have turned for the clearest—and in the case of *Rose Bernd* probably the finest—examples of Hauptmann's achievement in giving dramatic shape to the painful oppression of the trapped and the pursued; again and again the student of Hauptmann will encounter such quotations as Henschel's fatalistic lament: 'ane Schlinge ward mir gelegt, und in die Schlinge da trat ich halt nein' (I, 993); Rose Bernd's despairing outcry: 'Hernach bin ich von Schlinge zu Schlinge getreten, daß ich gar ni bin mehr zur Besinnung gekomm' (II, 256); Frau John's dull protest at the excrutiating pressure she must always endure: 'Angst! Sorge! Da wißt ihr nischt von' (II, 773).

In order to present a total picture of Hauptmann's philosophy, or to support a particular interpretation of his plays, a number of critics have also looked outside his dramas, and considered other of his comments on the problem of suffering, such as the following, from the short essay *Von den Möglichkeiten des Theaters* (1930):

Der Kampf von Menschen untereinander wird auch im Drama höheren Stiles dargestellt. Über allem jedoch zeigt es den Kampf mit der unsichtbaren Macht, die wir mit dem Namen 'Schicksal' getauft haben. Auf seiner Bühne ist am Ende nicht mehr der Mensch des Menschen Feind. Vielmehr erkennt er sich selbst und erkennt den andern und weiß unter der Hellsicht des Schmerzes meistens, daß sie beide schuldig-schuldlos sind. Sich ihm ergeben ist hier die einzige Form, sich über das Schicksal zu erheben (VI, 813).

The conflict of man against man is also presented in the drama of high style. But it shows primarily the conflict with that invisible power which we call 'Fate'. On this stage man is no longer the enemy of man. Rather he recognizes himself and others for what they are, and generally, in the lucidity occasioned by pain, recognizes that they are both at the same time innocent and guilty. To yield before it is here the only way of overcoming Fate.

There are obvious dangers in approaching Hauptmann's work in this way. However interesting and informative Hauptmann's occasional essays and speeches may be—and his greatest admirers would not claim that they are consistently either—they can only ever be of secondary importance in the interpretation of his dramas. Speculation about the intentions of any author is not often a very rewarding pursuit; and this is especially true where an author of plays like *Vor Sonnenaufgang* and *Einsame Menschen* is concerned. It would, I believe, be mistaken to read Hauptmann's plays in the light of his supposed intentions, and to see in them a pattern of suffering and transcendence, leading to a lucid understanding of the tragic constitution of the universe. In the four plays which I intend to discuss there is still a sufficient residue of the relativism of the Naturalists to call in question the validity of any claims to absolute knowledge. And to insist that all the rich realistic details of these plays are only there as symbols of a deeper level of reality, is to falsify Hauptmann's achievements as a dramatist.

Michael Kramer (1900) is the play which might be said to embody a philosophy of suffering in the most explicit form; it is therefore the least dramatic and, by any standards, the least naturalistic of these four works. It relates the story of Kramer's son, Arnold, who wastes his talent, disappoints his father's hopes, and suffers humiliation and persecution at the hands of a group of bourgeois philistines, until eventually he can bear no more, and commits suicide. Kramer's daughter, Michaline, and a former pupil, Lachmann, have lengthy roles, but no importance in the dramatic action; they never appear on stage at the same time as Arnold (except for one brief moment in the third act, when he rushes past them in his flight from the Bänsch restaurant), and they do not influence the action around him in any way. Their principal, and really rather too obvious, function is to establish, by direct characterization, the stature of Michael Kramer, and so the authority of what he says;[1] their secondary function is to complete the philosophical dialogue, by providing a receptive audience for Michael Kramer. This second function is frequently little more than a formality, for many of Kramer's speeches have that sententious, quotable style which one associates with speeches aimed directly at the audience. In the final act, at the climax of his philosophizing, Hauptmann is clearly straining against the limitations of Naturalist doctrine, and the conventions of Naturalist practice, for he very nearly allows Kramer a monologue: Lachmann, to whom Kramer's words are ostensibly being addressed, retires behind a curtain, taking a candle to set beside the corpse of Arnold, and leaving Kramer alone in view to make the apparently authoritative judgement: 'Wenn erst das Große ins Leben tritt, . . . dann ist alles Kleine wie weggefegt. Das Kleine trennt, das Große, das eint . . . Der Tod ist immer das Große . . . der Tod und die Liebe' ('When something great appears before us, . . . then everything petty is, as it were, swept away. That which is petty is divisive, that which is great unifies . . . Death is always great . . . Death and love').

Through his suffering and in his death Arnold is judged to have triumphed over his persecutors: 'Was sich herbeiläßt, uns niederzubeugen, ist herrlich und ungeheuer zugleich. Das fühlen wir dann, das sehen wir fast . . . da wird man aus Leiden—groß' ('That which deigns to crush us is both glorious and monstrous. We feel it, we almost see it . . . out of suffering we become—great') (I, 1168). But, as so often in the dramas of Hauptmann, there remains a discrepancy between the character's words and the objective evidence (i.e. the evidence of the drama) on which these words are based. Although there is no sign of an attempt to undermine Kramer's authority in the way we have seen the authority of other characters undermined, his statements do not carry a great deal of conviction. This is very largely because an attempt to make Arnold's triumph all-embracing has, in fact, trivialized it. For what exactly is Arnold's triumph? Among the characters who assemble in the final act to pay homage to the dead Arnold is Liese, the daughter of the restaurant-proprietor Bänsch, whom Arnold had favoured with so much attention. She, the representative of the philistine world which despised and destroyed Arnold, arrives on the scene just in time to hear Michael Kramer's words of praise for his son's genius: 'Ich sehe zu diesem Jungen hinauf, als wenn es mein ältester Ahnherr wäre!' (I, 1171), words which seem, in retrospect, to justify Arnold's boasts of Act III:

Reisen Sie mal nach München hin und fragen Sie 'rum bei den Professoren . . . ob die wohl vor mir verfluchten Respekt haben . . . Die haben Respekt und die wissen warum. Ich kann mehr, wie die Kerle alle zusammen. Im kleinen Finger. Zehntausendmal mehr. Mein eigner Vater mit inbegriffen (I, 1145).	Just go to Munich and ask the professors . . . if they damn' well respect me . . . They respect me, and they know why. I can do more than all of them put together. With my little finger. Ten thousand times more. My own father included.

But these were childish boasts, phrased childishly, with Liese's trivial criteria of worldly, and especially financial, success in mind. To contrive a scene which justifies these boasts is to create a triumph of a very insignificant order.

Nor is there, if we consider it in its context, very much substance to the proclamation of a greater triumph made by Arnold's father, for Hauptmann fails to convince us that what Kramer says has any validity outside his own imagination, and it is on this that the meaning of the play ultimately depends. As its title suggests, this play is essentially a character-drama, and it is concerned with the development of Michael Kramer himself, in the face of the great suffering caused him by his son.[2] Disappointed that his son has squandered a precious talent, Kramer has tried to guide him, only to find that he, too, has failed, and cannot approach his son as a father should. He is not the man to disown his son, and so Arnold's failures, suffering, and eventual death become the father's suffering. Through this experience he comes to change his attitude towards his son, and in the end he ceases to insist that Arnold had wasted his talent. He looks through his dead son's sketches with a tolerance he had not previously practised: 'Da sind seine Peiniger alle versammelt. Sehn Se, da sind sie, so wie er sie sah. Und hör'n Se, Augen hat er gehabt. Das ist der wahrhaftige böse Blick, aber's ist doch ein Blick!' ('There are all his persecutors assembled. There they are, you see, as he saw them. And listen, he had eyes. It's a truly evil point of view, but it's a point of view!') (I, 1168).

These sketches are the creation of an imagination distorted by pain and persecution, and Kramer accepts his son's subjective insight on these terms, as a thing of value; he does not suggest that Arnold's suffering has produced a transcendent lucidity. This may prompt us to recall a brief exchange between Michaline and Lachmann in Act III:

LACHMANN. Die Kraft zur Illusion . . . : das ist der beste Besitz in der Welt.	LACHMANN. The power of illusion. . .: that is the dearest possession in the world.

MICHALINE. Du meinst also eigent-   MICHALINE. You really mean imagi-
lich Phantasie; und ohne die kann ja ein   nation then; and no one can be an artist
Künstler nicht sein.   without it.
LACHMANN. Ja. Phantasie und den   LACHMANN. Yes. Imagination, and the
Glauben daran (I, 1152).   belief in it.

The conclusion of the play might well be considered in the light of these words. Michael Kramer's claims about his son's triumphant death might also be regarded as an illusion, the creation of an imagination distorted by a sense of failure, and involuntarily compensating. As a father's cry of regret, Kramer's final statements about Arnold have every justification in the structure of the drama, although another dramatist—Ibsen, Brecht, or even the younger Hauptmann— might have treated Michael Kramer less tenderly.

In explaining his change of attitude towards his son, Michael Kramer speaks the following words: 'Leid, Leid, Leid, Leid. Schmecken Sie, was in dem Worte liegt? Sehn Se, das ist mit den Worten so: sie werden auch nur zurzeiten lebendig, im Alltagsleben bleiben sie tot' ('Pain, pain, pain, pain. Just get a taste of what is in the word. You see, words are like that; they only occasionally come to life; in everyday life they remain dead.') (I, 1168). In the strictest sense (and external to the context), these words imply a rejection of Naturalism, which is, after all, the literature of the everyday. They demand the application of principles of concentration and careful selection of material which are contrary to much early German Naturalist theory, and to most critical preconceptions about this particular literary style. Such principles did, of course, have some influence on the composition of even the first Naturalist dramas—especially on the choice of subject: the situation of crisis—but they were not applied with the consistency with which they are applied in the four plays under discussion in this chapter. Here the dramatist's attention is focussed almost exclusively on those characters whose imaginative power or disposition makes them particularly open to intense mental anguish. This was not immediately appreciated by those of Hauptmann's contemporaries who had turned their backs on Naturalism, and some dismissed his renewed concern with inarticulate (or just lower-class) characters as a retrogressive step, which decisively limited the spiritual content of the drama. Among such critics was the erstwhile pioneer of Naturalism, Julius Hart, who wrote of *Fuhrmann Henschel*: 'we are groping about again in the dark and foggy atmosphere of the old "fate-drama", which was, of course, an essentially naturalist form, and suffered from the deficiency which is so evident in Gerhart Hauptmann's play, the narrowness and constriction of spiritual life.'[3] Such criticism, however, misses Hauptmann's crucial point: Henschel's inarticulateness implies a limitation on his intellect, but not on his imagination. Indeed, the contrast between Henschel and the rationalist Siebenhaar (like the contrast between the brothers Robert and Wilhelm Scholz in *Das Friedensfest*) shows intellect and imagination varying in inverse proportion. Henschel is totally exposed; he has no defence against his destructive imagination. As Hauptmann wrote elsewhere: 'Wer sich der Phantasie ergibt, muß sie beherrschen' (VI, 995).

The rigour with which the principles of selection and concentration are applied results in the much tauter dramatic structure of the later as compared to the earlier Naturalist dramas. The basic dramatic technique remains the same; as in *Vor Sonnenaufgang* and plays like it (*Jugend, Winterschlaf, Meister Oelze*), the dramatist takes an act of violence, and explains the events leading up to it. Now more experienced in the theatre, he tends to exclude anything which does not bear directly on the outcome. (In a revised version of *Meister Oelze*, published in 1909, Schlaf eliminated from the last act everything which delays the approaching death of the central figure.)[4] In this context it is interesting to note that Hauptmann was prompted to write *Rose Bernd* (1903), the tautest in structure of all his Naturalist dramas, by his experience as a juror at the trial of a village girl for infanticide.

Concentration, then, is achieved by the elimination of inessentials, resulting in a tendency towards 'closed' rather than 'open' form. In the earlier works characters did not develop, and a full story could only be told by the (often implausible) compression of a large number of events into a brief period of time; the causal process leading up to these events was revealed—with an implausible rapidity—through the intervention of an inquisitive stranger. The later plays resemble *Einsame Menschen* in that they stretch over a longer period of time. The action of *Rose Bernd* lasts four to five months, that of *Fuhrmann Henschel* (1898) over a year, and so a story can be told in its entirety. The act intervals represent a longer chronological break, and so contain more new events which are revealed in the course of the following act: the rape in *Rose Bernd*, the murder of Pauline Piperkarcka in *Die Ratten* (1911). Dramatic action is thus more consistently a reaction by the characters to events which have already taken place, but which the audience has not witnessed. The plays flow more evenly; there is no call for those hurried conclusions which the younger Hauptmann tended to impose when it seemed there was no more material left to uncover.

The principle of concentration is applied equally in the treatment of character and milieu; but here again the earlier dramatic technique has been refined rather than radically altered. The earliest Naturalist dramas were certainly rich in gratuitous background detail, but the dramatists were seldom guilty of the literal-mindedness of the theatre-director who played *Wallensteins Lager* in a snowstorm—because the history books said the events took place on 22 February.[5] The Christmas setting, which is common to *Die Familie Selicke* and *Das Friedensfest*, the lighting directions in *Einsame Menschen*, have a clearly symbolic function, and are not just gratuitous details. Schlaf's revision of *Meister Oelze* is again symptomatic. The later version omits the directions that Oelze should spit on the stage, but the tubercular coughing which announces his arrival remains, not as a simple shock effect, but as a means of arousing in the audience a feeling of disgust for Oelze which the conclusion of the play requires.

While the structure of *Fuhrmann Henschel* is still relatively slack, and many episodes are not fully integrated—it is, for instance, difficult to see the significance of all the scenes involving Franziska Wermelskirch—*Rose Bernd* is full of functional detail: the ominous hum of Streckmann's threshing machine, the oppressive weather of Act III, which suggests the imminent breaking of a storm, and the whole progress of the drama from spring to autumn, from morning to evening, from a fruitful landscape to old Bernd's chilly middle-class parlour.[6] Like the title of *Die Ratten*, all this is evidence of a conscious intensification of the symbolic, and a re-assertion of those elements of Poetic Realism inherited by the German Naturalists.

It is this symbolic aspect of Hauptmann's work which many of his admirers have chosen to emphasize at the expense of the more straightforward realistic elements. One can only conclude that for some the term 'Naturalism' is so firmly established as a term of abuse, that an esteemed author must be defended against it at all costs. In an interpretation of *Rose Bernd*, which is in many ways quite excellent, Hans-Joachim Schrimpf argues, reasonably enough, that Hauptmann has used the Naturalist manner in detailed description, milieu, biological and psychological motivation, but without thereby explaining the real causes of the catastrophe; these, he asserts, are to be sought in some incomprehensible fate:

> [sie] liegen in einem unbegreiflichen Schicksal, das über sein Opfer hereinbricht, indem es sich Elementarantriebe bedient, die sich wechselseitig ausschließen, aber doch zerstörerisch aufeinander zugeordnet sind. Die soziale Wirklichkeit, Herkunft, Milieu, äußere Verhältnisse sind dabei nur [sic] das Medium, durch das dieses Schicksal es-haft hindurchwandelt . . . und in dem es sich verwirklicht.[7]

The Naturalist theorist, Wilhelm Bölsche, saw man as a victim in a deterministic system whose mainsprings we do not fully understand;[8] because Hauptmann's plays reveal him as sharing this uncertainty they are to some extent open to speculative interpretations such as that advanced by Schrimpf. There is, however, little *positive* evidence in the plays to support such interpretations. Hauptmann does not make at all clear the precise nature of the destructive force which seems to operate against mankind, and, more important, he does not make it clear whether this force has any objective existence outside the imagination of the victim. In any case, whatever his intention, his achievement, and it is a very considerable achievement, has been to capture the suffering of the victim here and now. Hauptmann's understanding of the form this suffering takes, how it works, how it affects the victim and his fellow men, is more profound than his unclear implications about its first causes or its transcendent significance. This is the achievement of a dramatist rather than a philosopher; and it is an achievement, I would venture to suggest, which owes a great deal to Naturalist demands for observation and imitation as the first essentials in artistic creation.

In this respect *Fuhrmann Henschel*, *Rose Bernd*, and *Die Ratten* are better plays than the less dramatic *Michael Kramer*, in which a philosophy of suffering is more lucidly expounded. In all four plays, however, the meticulous attention to details of causation reveals a rational attempt to explain the catastrophe. We learn from Michaline Kramer that her mother was largely responsible for the alienation of her father and her brother: 'Um Arnolds Vertrauen hat Vater gebuhlt . . . Unsere Mutter steht Vater innerlich fern, aber wenn sie mit Arnold irgendwas hatte, da wurde sofort mit Vater gedroht. Auf diese Weise . . . Was hat sie bewirkt?' (I, 1166). This takes us right back to the problem of *Das Friedensfest*, the complicated family relationships which arise from an unhappy marriage; but we are given little of the insight into this social situation provided by the earlier play, and no opportunity to assess at first hand the real influence of this factor.

Heredity and environment do not have an absolutely dominant effect on the characters in any of these plays, but in the other three their function is much more closely defined. Economic factors, her humble social origins and her present position of dependence, do much to determine Hanne Schäl's relationship to Henschel. (She closely resembles Helene in Anzengruber's novel, *Der Sternsteinhof*, who starts out as a domestic servant with no means, and vigorously brushes aside all obstacles to become the owner of a farm.) Economic factors also play a part in Henschel's decision to marry Hanne, even if they do little more than assist him to rationalize his strong sexual attraction towards her. And hereditary weakness provides a perfectly logical explanation for the death of Henschel's sickly child, despite the suspicions of Hanne's enemies.

Rose Bernd's relationship to her seducer, Flamm, is also very strongly influenced by her inferior social status. The ambiguities of this relationship are captured very skilfully in the opening scenes of the play; despite Flamm's insistence that she should not address him in a formal way: 'Du sollst nich immer Herr Flamm sagen!' (II, 188), Rose is too unsure of herself to call him 'Christoph' very often, and occasionally she compromises, with 'Herr Christoph'.[9]

Old Bernd is materially dependent on his daughter and—therefore—his prospective son-in-law. His desire to have Rose marry soon, and to have her marry August, is very closely connected with the latter's recent purchase of the Lachmann house. Streckmann's loose-living is associated with his peripatetic occupation: 'Wo unsereens hinkommt mit d'r Dreschmaschine, uff all den Gietern eim Lande rum, da braucht eener o ni fer Nachrede sorg'n' (II, 197). Whilst it is the infirmity of his wife, and the loss of their son, Kurt (of Rose's age), which first directed Flamm's attentions to Rose.

The provincial, Silesian setting is an important aspect of *Fuhrmann Henschel* and *Rose Bernd*; but *Die Ratten* takes us back to the Berlin of *Der Biberpelz* and the Naturalist novel of the 1880s. Hauptmann returns to the city in order to condemn it as an environment hostile to the establishment of real contact between people.

The principal and overriding factor in the motivation of these plays is, as it was in the earlier works, the way people are fashioned, their dominant, inherent characteristics: the unfulfilled maternal instinct of Frau John, the sensuality of Rose Bernd, the sexual pride of Streckmann, the split personality of Henschel, which prompts him in his wife's illness to engage as a maid and, subsequently (like Bahnwärter Thiel) to marry, a woman whose whole nature is such as to bring about his disintegration between the two poles of his character. Causal explanations do not go beyond this point. No reason is offered to explain why characters should be so fashioned, or why circumstances should be so delicately balanced; and in these circumstances it is perfectly natural and rationally acceptable that an uncomprehending central figure should feel himself to be the exposed and helpless victim of a cruel external fate; it is not unreasonable that a character such as Henschel should conclude: 'Ich hab's woll gemerkt in mein'n Gedanken, daß das und war uf mich abgesehen' (I, 993). There is, therefore, a set of reasons behind such conclusions which is sufficient to undermine any claim they have to objective truth; and yet there is no clear attempt on the part of the author to distance himself from these conclusions; he does not adopt a superior, ironic standpoint. It appears from this that for Hauptmann, the dramatist, the greater significance lay not with the question of the validity or non-validity of an interpretation of the world, but with the simple fact of its existence, and its consequences for the action of his play.

If the interpretation of the world is really a pained outcry, an expression of the personal feeling of exposure, then the force with which it is communicated to an audience will depend very much on that audience's view of its justification, and therefore on the strength with which the author (or, *faute de mieux*, the actor) endows the central character. It is here that *Fuhrmann Henschel* comes out badly in comparison with *Rose Bernd*, for the primitive Silesian hero, who is presented so much more sympathetically than the limited rationalist, Siebenhaar, and the rootless proletarian, Hanne, has a tendency to persecute himself which trivializes his genuine suffering. Hanne's advice, 'Sie sollten nich nachgeben gar zu sehr!' (I, 917), touches directly on his weakness. His very first entry, which is always of immense importance in the theatre, resembles that of Johannes Vockerat in *Einsame Menschen*; it immediately establishes him as a character lacking in any sort of resistance to misfortune: 'Das weeß auch der liebe Himmel, was das muß sein: da wird mersch Weib krank! da fällt m'r a Ferd! 's is balde, als wärsch uf mich abgesehen!' ('God only knows what's the matter: first my wife gets ill! then one of my horses breaks down! It's almost as if someone's got it in for me!') (I, 883). He lacks that indomitable spirit which could assert itself even through the dull resignation of the weavers. And he cannot begin to aspire to the mythological stature of Job, which Alfred Kerr claimed for him.[10]

The desire to lend an emotional depth and an expressive intensity to the drama could (and eventually did) result in the stylized, rhetorical drama of the Expressionists. But so long as this desire is combined with a Naturalist insistence on rational causation and plausibility, the dramatist will find himself increasingly forced to select the unusual and even the abnormal. Hauptmann justifies such selection as follows: 'Das Bereich dessen, was man gesund und normal nennt, wird im Affekt verlassen. Ein Drama ohne Affekt ist undenkbar, daher es immer einigermaßen ins Pathologische übergreifen muß' ('The sphere of the healthy and normal is left in the height of passion. A drama without high passion is inconceivable, and so it must always reach out to some extent into the pathological') (VI, 1042). The weakness of Hauptmann's statement is one of the fundamental weaknesses of the Naturalist position; he does not here seem disposed to place a different valuation on the response to suffering of a neurotic and prematurely aged man (Henschel) and that of a strong, healthy woman in the prime of life (Rose Bernd). Nevertheless, the breakdown of a character who has shown the will to resist is bound to impress us as more moving, more nearly tragic, than the abject surrender of a person such as Henschel. Although it should be added that, on another occasion, Hauptmann seems to have shared this latter view: 'Ibsen sieht das Tragische meist nur in der sogenannten gescheiterten Existenz. Tragik bei voller Existenz ist die höhere' ('Ibsen generally sees tragedy in life's so-called failures. The tragedy of a fulfilled character is superior') (VI, 1043).

Because of the feebleness of Henschel, Hanne Schäl comes to demand much greater attention, despite her formal subordination in the play. Her strongest impulse is the one that is so deficient in him, the instinct of self-preservation. She ruthlessly strives to suppress all those qualities which might hinder her advance, even to the point of disowning her child. Her social climb is achieved at great cost in human terms, and it remains a precarious achievement. As long as she is struggling purposefully upwards her deeper anxieties are fully sublimated in frantic industry; but once she has arrived her security melts away. She cannot be at ease with her husband, and during his absences she is oppressed constantly by fear of his return. The desires of a hot-blooded young woman married to an older man find an outlet in her affair with the waiter, George, but the tension of expectation and the fear of discovery combine to prevent her from deriving any satisfaction from this affair; all she does derive is nervous irritation:

Derweil hab ich alleene gesessen und hab gewart't bis tief in die Nacht. Eemal —ich weeß nich was das muß gewest sein! A Vogel muß sein ans Fenster geschlagen—da dacht ich du wärscht's, und ging ich ans Fenster und macht es auf. Hernach da ward ich aso verbost, ich konnte die halbe Nacht nich einschlafen. *Sie schlägt mit der Faust schwach auf den Tisch.* Ich weeß nich, ich bin auch noch immer verbost (I, 943).	And I was sitting here alone waiting till late at night. Once—I don't know what it can have been! A bird must have bumped against the window—I thought it was you, and went and opened the window. And afterwards I was so irritable, I couldn't sleep for half the night. *She bangs on the table weakly with her fist.* I don't know, I'm always so irritable.

Her frequent outbursts of temper over trivial incidents cause us to wonder how long she can maintain her equilibrium, and they produce a certain sympathy for her, in the way evident weakness arouses sympathy even for Hoffmann in *Vor Sonnenaufgang* and Robert Scholz in *Das Friedensfest*. Despite their tough façade, here are three characters, who are not utterly depraved; will they, in fact, stop short of utter depravity? It is speculation about Hanne's subsequent fate, rather than about where Henschel's suffering has led him, which merits our attention as the final curtain falls on this open-ended play.

The same question arises in *Die Ratten*, through the figure of Bruno Mechelke. Here, however, the central character, Henriette John, is a rather stronger character than Henschel, and so Bruno, her younger brother, does not attract a disproportionate amount of attention. His brief appearance in Act IV, after he has murdered Pauline, and the challenging bravado of his reply when his sister suggests that the police might catch him, implies that he, too, is strenuously attempting to conceal an inner disquiet: 'Na jut, denn mache ick Bammelmann, und denn ham se uff Charité wieder ma wat zum Sezieren' ('All right, they'll string me up, and then they'll have something else to cut up at the hospital') (II, 813).

In contrast to Henschel, Rose Bernd is a character whose glory is her strength, vigour and energy; as her father boasts—to Streckmann of all people—'Das is a

Mädel! Die soll a sich warm halten' (II, 200). The play, a starkly pessimistic work, reveals the hunting-down of a magnificent creature, and her reduction to a state of abject despair. The causal process, as I have suggested, appears to begin in the individual make-up of the victim, in the sensuality of Rose, which causes her to become involved with Flamm. Flamm, for his part, is married to an invalid wife; and Rose's father is eager to match her with a physically unequal partner in August. The actual details of the plot are exceedingly complex, because much remains unspoken, and misunderstood by the various characters. The crucial point is that once Rose knows she is expecting Flamm's child she is in a vulnerable position, for she needs both to marry August, and to prevent Streckmann from gossiping about her association with Flamm. Streckmann, affronted in his sexual pride that Rose is attracted not to him, but to Flamm, will not be bought off with cash, and so Rose has no choice but to go to his cottage, as he suggests. Not knowing that Rose is pregnant, he does not realize that she only comes out of panic, and interprets her coming in the way one would expect a Streckmann to interpret it:

STRECKMANN. Du bist mir nachgelaufen dahie!
ROSE. Was . . .?
STRECKMANN. Bist in meine Wohnung gekomm'n und hast mir de Helle heeß gemacht.
ROSE. Und du . . .
STRECKMANN. Nu was denn?
ROSE. Und du? Und du?
STRECKMANN. A Kostverächter biin ich halt ni.
ROSE. Streckmann! . . . Ich biin zu dir gelaufa in Himmelsangst! Ich hoa dich um's Himmels wille gebattelt . . . du sullst m'r mit August'n a Weg freigahn. Ich biin uff a Knien gekruchen vor dir und du sagst itz, ich wär dir nachgelaufa? Asu is: du hust a Verbrecha geton!! Du hust an mir a Verbrecha beganga!! (II, 227).

STRECKMANN. You came running after me!
ROSE. What . . .?
STRECKMANN. You came to my house and made things hot for me.
ROSE. And what about you . . .
STRECKMANN. Well, what about me?
ROSE. And what about you? What did you do?
STRECKMANN. I never refuse anything tasty.
ROSE. Streckmann! . . . I came running to you in fear of my life. I begged you for God's sake . . . to leave me and August alone. I crawled on my knees to you, and you're saying I was running after you? Here's how it was: you committed a crime!! You committed a crime against me!!

The possibility that there might be some way out for Rose is not entirely excluded; the tragedy is that she is unable to see this. Certainly she can expect nothing from Flamm; the end of Act IV shows that sexual jealousy is no less a fault in him than in Streckmann; but he is not a strong character, and Frau Flamm is perfectly willing to help Rose. Act V shows that August, who has matured considerably in the course of the play, is also sympathetic, and he comes forward with a familiar proposal: 'Mer ziehn ei de Welt! A Onkel von mir is ei Brasilien drieben. Mir wern mitnander a Auskumm hoan!' ('We'll go abroad. I've got an uncle out in Brazil. We'll manage together') (II, 257). Moreover, Rose's father is not the obstacle which Meister Anton is in Hebbel's *Maria Magdalene*, for, although self-righteous and narrow-minded, he is somewhat feeble in the exercise of his authority, and, provided he can go to church he is content to let Rose get on with the work, even on a Sunday.[11]

What prevents Rose from taking, or even trying, either possibility of escape is the feeling of guilt which clouds her relationship with just those two characters who offer help; she does not expect, and so hardly seems to hear their offers. She lacks the hardness which enables Hanne Schäl to take from anybody; and is therefore thrown back on herself. Like Hauptmann's weavers, she does not calculate very far ahead; her lies are a primitive attempt at self-defence, by an unreflecting character, and they only get her more deeply ensnared:

> ROSE. 's is nischt zwischen uns gewest, a liegt!
> FLAMM. Sagt a, daß zwischen euch was gewest ist!?
> ROSE. Ich sag' weiter nischte, als daß a liegt! (II, 243)

> ROSE. There wasn't anything between us; he's a liar.
> FLAMM. Does he say there was something between you!?
> ROSE. I'm not saying anything, except that he's a liar.

The climax of the play comes when Rose gives up the struggle, when her lies give way to a shrill condemnation of the world in which she has suffered:

> Aus Lieg'n und Trieg'n besteht die Welt. . . . Da hoa ich wull ernt in de Sterne gesehn! Da hoa ich wull ernt geschrien und geruffa! Kee himmlischer Vater hat sich geriehrt. . . . Itze is halt was ieber uns alle gekomm—ma hat sich dagegen gewohrt und gewohrt (II, 256).

> The world is nothing but lies and deceit. . . . I looked up at the stars! And I cried and screamed. No father in heaven stirred. . . . Something has fallen upon us all—no matter how hard we struggled against it.

Now this is precisely what we would expect from Rose in her particular circumstances of pain and isolation, and we ought therefore to be rather hesitant about interpreting these words as a genuine tragic insight. To be dramatically convincing and humanly significant the words need be no more than a cry of protest. The last words of the play are spoken by August; he certainly does not accept the universal validity of Rose's pessimistic generalizations, nor does he, after the initial shock, dwell on the horror of her crime, but he cuts instinctively across

all moralizing to proclaim with compassion and admiration: 'Das Mädel . . .
was muß die gelitten han!' ('That girl . . . what she must have suffered!')
(II, 259).

This display of profound sympathy for the character who is by temperament
open to suffering is, as we have seen, a feature common to many of Hauptmann's
plays. But this openness to suffering is not admired for the tragic insights which
it might bring, rather for the human qualities which are complementary to it.
Characters like Paul John, old Bernd, and Hanne Schäl can close themselves up,
in an attempt to protect themselves, but the price they pay in human terms is
very high. Hauptmann admires in his open characters their idealism, their
preservation of traditional values of unselfishness, generosity, consideration for
others; in the domestic dramas this means especially family values. This is most
clearly evident in the case of Henriette John; but it is also true of Michael
Kramer, who bitterly regrets his failure as a father; while Henschel, in his
concern for Hanne's child, and Rose in her devotion to her father and to Frau
Flamm, are contrasted sharply with Hanne, who can deny her own child, and
old Bernd, who bigotedly turns his back on his despairing daughter.

Hauptmann was sufficiently in tune with the thought and attitudes of his day
to know that these old values are fragile, that they are often based on illusions,
and that to accept them is to expose oneself to suffering or ridicule, but he shrinks
from the alternative.

A brief consideration of Schlaf's play *Meister Oelze* will illustrate the transitional position of Naturalism in a rather different way. The play shows a bitter
trial of strength between Oelze and his step-sister, Pauline, in which the latter is
trying to extract the confession that Oelze murdered her father and cheated her
out of her inheritance. She has justice on her side, but is motivated by the same
impulse as her step-brother, the desire for property for herself and her family.
She works ruthlessly on the conscience of the sick Oelze, but he possesses a
primitive resilience which enables him to hold out to the end. It was this resilience which Schlaf chose to emphasize in a retrospective Nietzschean interpretation of the conclusion of the play as 'der Sieg eines selbst in der von Gewissens-
bissen aufs äußerste erschwerten Agonie unerschütterlich zähen und festen
Manneswillens'.[12] Another interpretation of the conclusion is, however, possible, for Oelze's victory is a pyrrhic victory; the struggle to preserve his property
costs him his life. However amoral he would like to be, he, like Hanne Schäl,
is not secure from the qualms of conscience. The unresolved conflict within and
between the two main characters ensures that *Meister Oelze* is more than just
another inferior celebration of the *Übermensch*, and makes it one of the better
works by the minor dramatists of German Naturalism.

Notes to Chapter X

¹ Although one might expect it to have been frowned upon by the theorists, direct characterization occurs quite frequently in the German Naturalist drama: in *Vor Sonnenaufgang* there is Loth's self-characterization, and there is his description of the drunken old Krause; in *Das Friedensfest* Robert provides direct characterizations of all the members of the Scholz family; in *Einsame Menschen* there is Anna's disparaging analysis of Braun; in *Die Familie Selicke*, Wendt's eulogy of Toni.

² A recent analysis decisively places Michael Kramer at the centre, and suggests that his two children, the sterile, but stable Michaline, and the gifted, but unstable Arnold, are to be seen as an externalization of his own inner conflict. See Helmut F. Pfanner, 'Deutungsprobleme in Gerhart Hauptmanns "Michael Kramer" ', *Monatshefte*, LXII (1970), pp. 45–54.

³ 'Hauptmanns jüngstes Bühnenwerk', *Das literarische Echo*, I (1898–9), p. 284.

⁴ See H. Praschek, 'Zum Zerfall des naturalistischen Stils', *Worte und Werte, Festschrift für Bruno Markwardt*, Berlin, 1961, pp. 315–21.

⁵ Joachim Weno, *Der Theaterstil des Naturalismus*, Phil. Diss., Berlin, 1951, p. 210.

⁶ H. J. Schrimpf, 'Rose Bernd', *Das deutsche Drama*, ed. Benno von Wiese, Wiesbaden, 1958, II, 178.

⁷ Ibid., p. 173. In a recent analysis Oskar Seidlin treats the two plays *Der Biberpelz* and *Der rote Hahn* in a similar way, seeing beneath the surface of the plays an archetypal struggle of man and woman; 'Urmythos irgendwo in Berlin', *Deutsche Vierteljahrsschrift*, XLII (1969), pp. 126–46. Seidlin does, however, point out the merits of the concrete descriptive detail and the vigorous social criticism which are to be found on the surface of the play (p. 130).

⁸ *Die naturwissenschaftlichen Grundlagen*, p. 3.

⁹ Cf. W. Butzlaff, 'Die Enthüllungstechnik in Hauptmanns "Rose Bernd" ', *Der Deutschunterricht*, XIII (1961), p. 63.

¹⁰ 'Fuhrmann Henschel', *Neue deutsche Rundschau*, IX (1898), p. 1315.

¹¹ Schrimpf, op. cit., gives a comparison of *Rose Bernd* with *Maria Magdalene* and Wagner's *Die Kindermörderin*. The question of influence is not of major importance, but it is interesting to note that Hebbel's play was in performance at the *Deutsches Theater* from 5 November 1901.

¹² 'Die Freie Bühne', *Der Greif*, I, ii, 48.

XI

The dramatic style of Naturalism

Diderot, Lessing, auch Goethe und Schiller in ihrer Jugend, wendeten sich in neuerer Zeit vornehmlich der Seite realer Natürlichkeit zu . . . Diese Art der Natürlichkeit aber kann bei einer Überfülle bloß realer Züge leicht wieder nach einer anderen Seite ins Trockene und Prosaische hineingeraten, insofern die Charaktere nicht die Substanz ihres Gemüts und ihrer Handlung entwickeln, sondern nur, was sie in der ganz unmittelbaren Lebendigkeit ihrer Individualität ohne höheres Bewußtsein über sich und ihre Verhältnisse empfinden, zur Äußerung bringen . . . Natürliche Menschen verhalten sich in ihren Unterredungen und Streitigkeiten überwiegend als bloß einzelne Personen, die, wenn sie ihrer unmittelbaren Besonderheiten nach geschildert sein sollen, nicht in ihrer substantiellen Gestalt aufzutreten im Stande sind. . . . Das echt Poetische wird . . . darin bestehen, das Charakteristische und Individuelle der unmittelbaren Realität in das reinigende Element der Allgemeinheit zu erheben, und beide Seiten sich mit einander vermitteln zu lassen.[1]

Diderot, Lessing, and also the young Goethe and Schiller, are among modern authors who espoused a predominantly naturalistic mode of expression . . . This kind of naturalism, however, can, because of an excess of merely realistic features, easily fall into the extreme of prosaic flatness, in that the characters are not allowed to develop the essential characteristics of their inner life and action, but express only what they experience directly as individuals, without any higher awareness of themselves or their situation . . . Real people, in their daily conversations and arguments, generally behave as merely single individuals; if they are to be depicted as such they cannot be seen in their substantive form. . . . True poetry . . . will raise the characteristic and individual features of actual reality into the purifying medium of universality and so reconcile the two sides with one another.

Hegel, writing long before the emergence of a Naturalist movement in Germany, or any other country, has provided a basis for much of the criticism of German Naturalism, and so his words provide a suitable starting point for this concluding chapter. The purpose of the chapter is to consider two separate aspects of this criticism; that is to consider the charge that the concentration by the German Naturalist dramatists on precise realistic detail has the effect of restricting the scope of their work, by lending it the appearance of the purely individual case-history; and, secondly, to consider the further objection, that the characters in a drama of this kind—and particularly the characters in Hauptmann's dramas—

lack that awareness of their own predicament which, according to the strictest Hegelians, is a necessary pre-condition of representative stature.

Such criticism has come from widely divergent sources. On the one hand, Wilhelm Dilthey is critical of the association of art and science in Naturalism.[2] Truth, he agrees, should be the object of literature, but the revelation of truth consists in finding a central point of vantage from which life can be comprehended in its totality. Thus the base and the ugly can only figure in art if they are shown in relation to the beautiful and the valuable. Memory is still the mother of the muses, but we come nearer to the artistic act when we cease to try and recall the single, particular impressions of one isolated moment, and use the memory creatively to produce images which represent objects in all their perceivable aspects, 'Vorstellungen, deren jede den Gegenstand in allen seinen von uns wahrgenommenen Lagen repräsentiert'.[3]

Representative significance, in a social-historical sense, was the principal criterion by which the Marxist critic, Franz Mehring judged the dramas of German Naturalism; he condemns *Einsame Menschen*, recognizing in its hero, Johannes Vockerat, no more than the 'Friedrichshagen type', but praises the characterization of Hoffmann (the bourgeois social-climber) in *Vor Sonnenaufgang*, and the old Heinickes (*Lumpenproletariat*) in Sudermann's *Die Ehre* (1889). At the same time he criticizes the amassing of detail which he regards as gratuitous, in *Vor Sonnenaufgang* and *Kollege Crampton*, citing the words of Engels: 'Der wirkliche Realismus geht nicht von den kleinen, zufälligen Eigenschaften der Menschen aus.'[4]

Now clearly the social realism which a critic such as Mehring would regard as the ideal kind of literature is not the kind of literature which would have appealed to Dilthey, but that need not concern us here. These dissimilar viewpoints converge in rejection of Naturalism; just as in both the early and the later, Marxist, criticism of Lukács, Naturalism is rejected with equal firmness. Holz's statement, 'Die Kunst hat die Tendenz, wieder die Natur zu sein', is seen in such criticism as a programmatic statement of the Naturalists' artistic intentions; the works of the Naturalists are seen as small, individual sections of life, shown in extensive totality, where the presence of detail in description, to the minutest degree, *localizes* the action, effectively excluding any symbolic intensification or raising to type, and making the Naturalist drama nothing more than the reportage which Wedekind satirizes in *Die junge Welt*.

Among the Marxist critics, Helmut Praschek supports his argument with an original and ingenious analysis of certain plays, which suggests that the German Naturalist dramatists deliberately reinforced the effect of particularization by the systematic exploitation of improbability. Coincidences such as Loth's meeting with two old friends, Hoffmann and Schimmelpfennig in *Vor Sonnenaufgang*, the Christmas reunion of the Scholz family in *Das Friedensfest*, the sudden and violent deaths at the conclusion of *Die Weber* and Halbe's *Jugend*, in short, all those occurrences which, however fully motivated, strike us as possible, but improbable—are held to emphasize the singularity and so the completely unrepresentative nature, of the 'slice of life' which has been dramatized.[5] A theoretical pendant to this practice could perhaps be found in the words of Bölsche who argued that closer observation could well lead a writer to make greater use of coincidence in his work: 'man kann . . . sagen, daß eine schärfere Beachtung des Zufalls in seiner tatsächlichen Erscheinung den Dichter eher darauf führen wird, ihm eine mehr, als eine weniger wichtige Rolle zuzuteilen.'[6]

The most cursory examination of the Naturalist dramas will reveal ample evidence for such an interpretation. Indeed, the extent of detail in stage-directions and cast-lists is the feature which strikes most readers most immediately. This applies particularly when—as they frequently are—dramatic characters are based on real-life characters; as, for instance, in the case of Professor Crampton, Robert Scholz, most of the characters in Holz's and Ernst's *Sozialaristokraten*, and the brothers Friedrich and Wilhelm Kern in Ernst von Wolzogen's *Das Lumpengesindel* (1892).[7] As far as the action of the plays is concerned, the diffuseness of the Naturalist drama is very often the direct result of a tendency to compile rather than condense: in *Die Familie Selicke* we witness five different kinds of reaction to the death of Linchen, instead of one typical expression of grief; in *Die Weber* we experience a whole range of possible reactions to the oppression exerted by the factory-owners, from the anger of an outraged mother of starving children, and the self-assertion of the braggart, to the ambiguous quiescence of the pietist, Hilse, and the complacent indifference of the traveller from the town; and Hauptmann's first three plays can be seen as a trilogy, constituting an exhaustive discussion of three possible solutions to one basic problem.[8] The effect of such a style is to undermine the economy normally associated with the dramatic form; instead of the concentrated presentation of the essential ('die intensive Wesenhaftigkeit'), which Lukács regards as dramatic, we are shown the more extensive picture of reality, which he describes as epic.[9]

The burden of criticism such as that to which I have been referring is that in a drama the detail of the Naturalist style is superfluous, except on its own misconceived terms, as a reflection of the planlessness of life. Even on these terms, however, much of this detail is still dispensable, for it is so minute as to be imperceptible: in *Die Familie Selicke* there is a stage direction which tells us that Walter returns to his room, and that the light shines through a chink in his door until, eventually, it is extinguished; other stage-directions are, quite simply, unrealizable: Act I of Halbe's *Freie Liebe* contains stage-directions indicating the time registered by a clock on the stage, but it is scarcely conceivable that the dialogue Halbe has provided could be stretched to fill the amount of time it ought to fill,[10] it is also unlikely that an actor could successfully follow all the impressionistic stage-directions of Hauptmann's early plays; and even given a performer such as Eleonora Duse, who could apparently flush or turn pale at will,[11] is it likely that such details could have been noticed by the average member of the audience, seated at some distance, in a theatre without spots or any moveable light-sources, and in which the upward shadows cast by the footlights tended to obscure the face?[12] Nor are such details always the result of great care and great thought on the part of the author; before the *Ausgabe letzter Hand* of 1942, Hauptmann's *Die Weber* included a direction that the one-armed Hilse should join his hands in prayer.

If we were to accept the view that the accumulation of detail does limit decisively the scope of the drama, then we must surely be inclined to conclude that all the German Naturalist dramas have no more than cultural-historical value to the modern reader; like old newsreels, they tell us what sort of clothes people used to wear, or how they used to furnish their houses. This is the view of Guthke, but he makes the one, predictable, exception—Hauptmann—for the wrong reason: namely that Hauptmann's plays are coherent entities, which expose a clear meaning ('gegliederte sinntragende Ganzheiten') in a way that the Naturalist milieu-drama, such as *Die Familie Selicke*, does not.[13] While one must agree that the work of Hauptmann does stand out from among that of his contemporaries, it is manifestly not because of his ability to set forth a clear meaning or message; for all their weaknesses, the plays of Sudermann are unquestionably 'sinntragende Ganzheiten'; even *Die Familie Selicke* is as clearly structured and as consistent as *Vor Sonnenaufgang*. The inferiority of the great majority of the Naturalist dramas, and the relative superiority of the works of Hauptmann, presents the critic with a problem, but this problem is not to be solved by accepting all the objections to Naturalism, and asserting that Hauptmann had nothing to do with the movement.

We need, in fact, to be wary of accepting as a basic premise that Naturalism was, or even could have been, totally successful in its supposed intention of presenting the particular, individual 'slice of life'. In his review of *Die Familie Selicke*, Theodor Fontane draws attention to the transformation which the artistic process inevitably brings about:

Es bleibt ein gewaltiger Unterschied zwischen dem Bilde, das das Leben stellt, und dem Bilde, das die Kunst	There remains an enormous difference between the picture which is given by life itself, and the picture given by the work

stellt; der Durchgangsprozeß, der sich vollzieht, schafft . . . eine rätselhafte Modelung, und an dieser Modelung haftet die künstlerische Wirkung, die Wirkung überhaupt.[14]

of art; whatever happens in between brings about a strange transformation, and this transformation is responsible for the artistic effect, indeed for any effect.

The theatre, as an art form, has a very strong tendency to mediate between the general and the particular. It is very difficult for any spectator to regard the theatre-set as no more than the actual environment of an individual case-history, for the dramatist, even the Naturalist dramatist, is prevented by considerations of time and space, visibility and audibility, from effectively giving a complete and accurate background; what detail he does provide must necessarily be selective, abstracted. Moreover the dramatist, especially in the 'theatre of illusion', lacks the opportunity, which the epic narrator has, of interrupting his story from time to time (in the manner of Sterne's narrator in *Tristram Shandy*, or Diderot's in *Jacques le Fataliste*) to insist on its singularity or documentary truth. Hauptmann's comments on *Vor Sonnenaufgang* suggest that, as far as this play is concerned, he might almost have welcomed such an opportunity. He argues, in effect, that his play is an 'open' drama, and that we do not see in it a complete characterization of Alfred Loth; all we see is one episode, which shows him in a less than flattering light:

> Nicht der ganze Alfred Loth mit all seinen Empfindungen, Gedanken, Eigenschaften, Fähigkeiten, sondern nur Alfred Loth unter gewissen im Drama vorhandenen Bedingungen ist geschildert.[15]

Yet, as one may well conclude from the fact that Hauptmann found it necessary to offer such an apologia for his character, the drama itself fails to make it sufficiently clear that it is only an episode; and it is the drama in which we, as spectators or critics, are interested. The conditions of the drama are the only conditions under which we know Loth; our knowledge of his behaviour under these conditions must provide the basis for any deductions we care to make about his possible behaviour in different circumstances.[16] At the very least, Loth's actions will be understood as characteristic of *him*; and to this extent the events of the play will at once be the basis of a generalization. When we find that emotions are expressed with a degree of intensity that is unusual in our everyday life, and when we perceive that the German Naturalist dramatist—like the French classicists—habitually chooses to present what can best be described in d'Aubignac's words as a 'jour illustre', then with what degree of conviction can we continue to assert that the events of the German Naturalist drama should be regarded as individual events of no more than average significance?

But just as we should be wary of assuming that the Naturalists *could* have successfully presented the particular and the individual as the particular and the individual, so should we also be wary of assuming that this was, in fact, their *intention*. Where the dramatist relies on stage-directions to convey information which is of importance to the understanding of the play, the demands of the theatre count for more than the demands for truth to life. Aware, no doubt, that facial expression was unlikely to convey a great deal in the theatre of the 1890s, Hauptmann endowed an unusually large number of his characters with a propensity for fainting at moments of crisis, in the way Kleist's characters do. In a play such as *Das Friedensfest*, in which the contrast between characters is of immense importance, the contrast in physical appearance (between, for instance, Frau Scholz and Frau Buchner) is of an exaggerated starkness. This same play also contains a number of examples of the use of mime to replace the monologue, which was abhorrent to Naturalist theory; it is hardly necessary to point out that mime, as an independent art form is about as realistic as opera or ballet.[17] Naturalism requires a change in acting style; it does not require that acting should cease to have a *style*.

The Naturalist drama, as it developed in Germany, is a much less simple and consistent phenomenon than is often supposed, and it requires from the critic a more pragmatic approach than it has often received. Too many critics have abstracted from the work of a limited number of writers, and from their own preconceptions about 'naturalism', a theory which they have treated as if it provided a consistent basis to the dramas of the period, and have failed to expose discrepancies between theory and practice. (Thus Helmut Praschek's thesis cleverly reconciles certain implausibilities with the theory which *he* has abstracted, but completely overlooks the fact that Schlenther, a critic whose work he does not consider, roundly condemns some of these very implausibilities.[18]) The majority of critics have also failed to give an accurate indication of the range of the theory itself. On a number of occasions I have referred to the views of the Hart brothers, and drawn attention to their moderate demands for *Ideal-realismus*, emphasizing the closeness of their views to those of the traditional idealist critics. In view of the convergence of idealists and Marxists in the demand for representative characters, it is not surprising that one can also find among the theoretical writings of the Naturalists statements which resemble Marxist demands; for instance, Bleibtreu's distinction between 'dichterischer Realismus' and 'Beobachtungsrealismus' is a re-statement of the views of Engels.[19] But among the Naturalist critics, it is the most distinguished, Otto Brahm, who comes closest to the Marxist position. This emerges most clearly in his interpretation of classical literature. Despite the bitter hostility which prevailed between him and Franz Mehring, there is a great deal of similarity between their respective interpretations of Schiller's *Kabale und Liebe*.

Mehring saw the classical period in German literature as an expression of the struggle of the middle-classes against feudalism, transferred to the literary arena, because the situation of the time inhibited direct political action. He admired in Schiller a more overtly political writer than Goethe, and emphasized in his writings on Schiller his humanist ideals, his hatred of tyranny, his stirring pathos, and his consistent struggle against 'die deutsche Misere'.[20] Mehring's admiration even extends to the aesthetic writings, which he sees as part of an attempt to educate the public towards a political reformation. Mehring shared Brahm's special admiration for the 'revolutionary' play *Kabale und Liebe*, which, he felt, showed, in typical form, the essential struggle of its age, and he recognized in Miller the Musician the classical embodiment of the German middle-classes. But besides relating the play to its social and economic background, Mehring shows its place in literary history; he points out its resemblance to *Emilia Galotti*, and its relation to the genre, *bürgerliches Trauerspiel*; he traces the genesis of the play itself, and shows Schiller's change in attitude to Lady Milford; and he gives a detailed analysis of the famous ensemble-scene in the house of Miller. Brahm places slightly more emphasis on the purely literary background, giving a more detailed comparison of the finished play with earlier drafts; but he too sees the play clearly in the context of its social background, which he interprets in the same way as Mehring; he sees in the ensemble-scene an episode of cultural history: the confrontation of the Swabian court with the Swabian middle-class, in the person of Miller. He even explains Luise's religious devotion, in a way which might be thought more typical of a Marxist, as a compensation for the misery she must undergo in her social situation: 'das gedrückte, zum Handeln und zum Hoffen gleich verlorene Empfinden, das in der Vorstellung eines Jenseits über das Elend dieser Welt sich fortträumt.'[21]

Brahm and Mehring can be seen to agree in principle in admiring the art of Schiller as an example of social realism, and they agree in the details of their interpretation, because they recognize the political conflict of bourgeoisie and aristocracy as the characteristic reality of Schiller's age. The Naturalists and the Marxists do not, however, agree about what constitutes the characteristic reality of their own age, and so major disagreements—to which we have already had occasion to refer—emerge in the criticism of contemporary works. The Naturalist works which Mehring singles out for praise are social dramas, such as *Die Weber*, *Der Biberpelz*, Halbe's *Eisgang*, and Ibsen's social dramas from *Pillars of Society* onwards; and Mehring's interpretations squarely emphasize the social dimension of these works, but criticize them where they pessimistically overlook the promise of social re-organization held out by the rising working class movement. Brahm lacked Mehring's confidence in the Social Democrat movement of his day, but this is perhaps not quite the same as saying—as Mehring did—that he was totally deficient in any understanding of history.[22] As his work on Schiller shows, Brahm was fully awake to the social implications of German classical literature, and therefore did not need Mehring to remind him that, 'in ihren großen Tagen hat sich die bürgerliche Ästhetik nie auf dem Phantom der "reinen Kunst" ertappen lassen, die durch keine Berührung mit den sozialen Kämpfen ihrer Zeit befleckt werden dürfe'.[23] In fact Brahm, who was at the centre of the German Naturalist movement from its beginning to its end, was enough of an idealist—Mehring would have said a conservative—to see in Ibsen's dramas an absolute dichotomy of individual and society, but also enough of a realist to admire its treatment most in the social dramas after *A Doll's House*, and thereby to incur the hostility of the more consistently idealist Hart brothers.[24]

Between Heinrich Hart and Otto Brahm German Naturalist theory covers a wide range; and even Brahm has been accused fairly strongly of a tendency to idealize social problems into timeless, existential problems—that is a tendency to abstraction rather than to the concrete particularization which is generally associated with Naturalism. This suggests quite forcefully that it is erroneous to argue that the demands of the German Naturalist theorists permit of no symbolic intensification, or that they permit the details of description to have no more significance than they would have in normal everyday life. This was not so for the Poetic Realists; it was not so in the theatrical productions of the Meiningen Court Theatre; nor can it be said that Zola and Ibsen used description in this specifically non-symbolic, veristic way; and in view of the cumulative influence of all these, it would be most surprising to find that the German Naturalists did. In fact, in our examination of Naturalist dramas we have already seen that much of that detail, which appears at first sight to figure only as part of an exhaustive catalogue of chance background, is revealed, on closer examination, to have a symbolic function, to create and intensify an atmosphere appropriate to the dramatic situation, or to extend the reference of a story by prompting comparisons and analogies.

There is, however, a great deal of inconsistency here, and this inconsistency, arising from a mixture of symbolism and verism, is one of the major faults in the German Naturalist drama. In Flaischlen's *Martin Lehnhardt* (1894) the hero's acquisition of a gun seems to anticipate a despairing suicide, or at least a tragic and significant accident, like the shooting of Annchen in *Jugend*, but it has no significance at all; it is a false trail laid by the dramatist—as if to say that in his drama, as in life, not all tensions are resolved in the way the traditional theatre leads us to expect. But Flaischlen is not consistent; the accidental breaking of a statuette of Christ does have the symbolic significance which is implied. The veristic principle is therefore called in question; those elements which are not woven purposefully into the structure of the play, begin to look like token offerings to a purely theoretical conviction.

In the later years of Naturalism there are signs of an awareness of this shortcoming, and the unintegrated detail is much reduced. In *Rose Bernd* the principle of dramatic concentration is, as we noticed, completely dominant. By the careful selection of significant episodes a story is told from beginning to end, following a clear pattern, and strongly supported by an equally clear pattern of symbols. Symbolism is also much more easily accommodated with Ibsen's concentrated dramatic style; but at its weakest, Ibsen's choice and handling of the symbol can be as clumsy, and its effect nearly as tedious, as in his German followers.

This inconsistency in the style of the German Naturalists is rooted, I believe, in a basic uncertainty, which I have found reflected in a number of fields. It appears most strongly in the work of Hauptmann, and it is necessary to emphasize this, because, while many literary historians have been prepared to see the minor Naturalists written off as experimenters in the blind-alley of the individual and the particular, there has been a marked tendency among the German admirers of Hauptmann to detach him from his contemporaries, and see in his works symbolic, metaphysical statements, which penetrate beneath the level of social reality to some fundamental essence. Analogies have thus been drawn between the work of Hauptmann, and that of Böhme, Schopenhauer, and Hebbel.[25]

Mitleid, the compassionate expression of solidarity with suffering humanity, is more typical of the German Naturalists than the expression of faith in sociopolitical remedies; moreover suffering is presented as something constant, which extends across social barriers without becoming different in kind; this might be felt to suggest that social criticism is never more than superficial. In Hauptmann there is even a tendency to regard the capacity for suffering as a significant measure of human worth. But, as I have argued in the previous chapter, Hauptmann's plays do not give an unambiguous answer to the question, what is the purpose of suffering? Is suffering simply a meaningless, but inescapable factor in existence, carrying no promise of redemption, as in the dramas of Büchner; or, arising from the divine, from the very spring of life itself, does it provide the privilege of contact with a deeper reality, a higher, more lucid perception, a 'Hellsicht des Schmerzes'? If the latter, then why should Hauptmann have so meticulously rooted the suffering of his characters in their social and psychological situation? It is because of this scrupulous attention to causal detail that Hauptmann's Naturalist plays are so ambiguous; he once said of *Hanneles Himmelfahrt*: 'Erdenpein schuf die Himmelseligkeit'—but as transcendence or compensation?

A useful analogy can, I think, be drawn between the inconsistencies of the German Naturalist movement, and the basic contradiction which Dilthey found in the philosophy of Hegel; namely the contradiction between the stated theoretical conviction of the *relativity* of any historical reality, and the implicit claim, raised by the Hegelian system itself, to *absolute* metaphysical completeness.[26] Scientific, theoretical Naturalism does not posit an ideally ordered world, in which man occupies a central position, from which speculative activity can give him a complete, absolute spiritual comprehension of that world. The reality of the Naturalists consists, in theory, of the discovered facts of the positive sciences; in such a world there can be no teleological certainty; all is governed by a relentless mechanical causality, which even controls man's spiritual activity. Causality stands in relation to freedom as the relative does to the absolute; a view caused by a given set of circumstances cannot aspire to absolute validity, but can only be expected to be valid as a function of those circumstances. But under this theoretical acceptance of rational, scientific relativism, there still lurks a continued need for absolute, metaphysical certainties, derived through religious or artistic insight.

It was this *theoretical* conviction which demanded a revolution in the drama: the development of an anti-heroic milieu-drama, in which man more or less disappears in his environment.[27] The characters in such a drama would tend to be victims, unfree and incapable of responsibility, therefore incapable of incurring the idealists' tragic guilt, or developing 'die Substanz ihres Gemüts'.[28] Interpersonal conflicts, expressed fully and completely in dialogue form, must give way where an active role is allowed to extra-personal forces, whose overall purpose the dramatist himself does not feel able to explain adequately, and which therefore resist containment in the rounded, complete, symbolic framework of the traditional drama.[29] If the audience is to understand that the dramatic clash is not brought about by an active exercise of will, an *epic* manner is required: through a profusion of stage-directions an implied narrator can tell us that his characters are a direct product of a certain set of circumstances, which have their own independent existence in the empirical world. The drama must be a sequence of tableaux, which reveal milieu and character, but without relating to any pre-ordained purpose, such as a plot structure; it must therefore contain no complete, rounded action, but be 'open' at both beginning and end.[30]

The clearest and most constructive exposé of a theory of epic drama on these lines occurs in a rather obscure review of *Vor Sonnenaufgang*, which appeared shortly after the first performance of Hauptmann's play in 1889.[31] The reviewer, who uses the pseudonym Kaberlin, praises especially the first three acts of the play for the absence of any active conflict of wills, and the consequent lack of theatrical tension, which, he argues, is redressed by a feeling of excited participation arising from the spectator's freedom to associate for himself ideas and images, to link cause and effect, in a way the individual characters within the drama cannot. Anticipating Brecht, Kaberlin requires dramatic presentation to be more passive, the spectator to be more active. Not surprisingly, he is highly critical of the conclusion of *Vor Sonnenaufgang*; anticipating Brechtian dramaturgy again, he condemns the re-emergence of a conventional theatrical tension, to which the mood of social sympathy becomes subordinated; as an alternative ending to the play, he suggests that Loth might have married Helene, in the knowledge that he would have been unhappy. As in his subsequent review of *Papa Hamlet*, he shows a preference for an 'open' ending, which would permit the basic mood of social sympathy to continue in its effect after the curtain had fallen: 'Die jungen Realisten glauben noch immer mit einem traurigen, ganz unvermittelten Schluß, die Wirkung steigern zu können, vergessen aber, daß eine plötzliche Verdichtung der Handlung nach einer breiten Darstellung die Einheit der Grundstimmung stört'.[32]

The kind of drama outlined by Kaberlin is *epic* in that subject and object are clearly present and separable, as two distinct viewpoints; the spectator has a horizon wider than that of the characters in the drama, for he is able to perceive the forces which determine the action. But the characters in such a drama, who are so far beneath us, and who are 'ohne höheres Bewußtsein über sich selbst und ihre Verhältnisse',[33] cannot, according to the strictest Hegelians, figure as our representatives in a tragic scheme.[34] In Kaberlin's epic drama, however, identification takes place on a different level: not between audience and character, but between the audience and the implied narrator; the spectator becomes *Mitdichter*. Limited characters are necessary in order that there should be a *drama* at all, for in the context of the determinist beliefs of the Naturalists, knowledge and action are incompatible; knowledge of the superiority of external forces will cripple the will to react against them; awareness in the Naturalist drama must therefore take the form of passive, undramatic contemplation. In its optimistic form this will appear as wonder at the grandiose, planless majesty of life, such as is expressed in the *novels* of Zola; in its more common, negative form it will appear as despair and resignation, the *lyric* moments for which Lukács praised those dramatically weak plays, *Florian Geyer* and *Michael Kramer*.[35] Only the Marxists have an answer; for while they still adhere to the determinist belief, they insist that their awareness is not incompatible with social action. Brecht, in his adaptation of *Der Biberpelz* and *Der rote Hahn*, introduces a new character, Rauert, with a Marxist awareness, who is therefore a 'representative' Socialist revolutionary.

The dichotomy knowledge—action is as important for the Naturalists as it was for their near-contemporaries Thomas Mann and Hugo von Hofmannsthal. The latter's comments on the characters in Ibsen's dramas show his understanding of this affinity:

Alle diese Menschen leben ein schatten-haftes Leben; sie erleben keine Taten und Dinge, fast ausschließlich Gedanken, Stimmungen und Verstimmungen. Sie wollen wenig, sie tun fast nichts. Sie denken übers Denken, fühlen sich fühlen und treiben Autopsychologie, das Reden und Reflektieren ist ihr eigentlicher Beruf.[36]	All these people live a shadowy life; they do not experience deeds and objects, but almost exclusively thoughts, moods, and depressions. They barely exercise their wills; they do almost nothing. They think about thinking, they feel themselves feeling, and they are constantly analysing themselves; their real vocation is talking and reflecting.

In consequence of this dichotomy the characters in the Naturalist drama fall into two basic categories, anticipated in Büchner's two tragedies, *Dantons Tod* and *Woyzeck*. A bourgeois, intellectual strain, re-inforced by the influence of Ibsen, biases the earlier works towards the Danton-type, the intelligent, withdrawn, inactive character, exemplified by Robert Scholz (although in *Das Friedensfest* the unintelligent Buchners are necessary to precipitate the action); while the later works, *Rose Bernd* and *Die Ratten*, are more concerned with the less intelligent, but active character.[37]

Where a character's knowledge still permits action, consistency with the determinist view means that this knowledge must be false or insufficient. Awareness of this kind, I have suggested, is not important as insight, but as expression, the response to a stimulus, a cry of pain; what is said is not identical with what is true, or even with what the speaker really means. The epic manner enables the dramatist to make some sort of intervention, and reveal the causality which makes the awareness only a relative awareness. This can also be true of that resigned, passive awareness, which more nearly corresponds to the theoretical views of the Naturalists themselves; we frequently encounter characters who express what sounds very like the determinist case, and yet who do not have the authority of the conventional *raisonneur*. If, in *Das Friedensfest*, Robert Scholz is presented as substantially correct in many of his insights, it is quite clear that this is coincidental, and that his opinions are just as much emotional expressions as those of other characters. The result of this is what Schlaf called the 'intimate drama'; knowledge, opinion, argument, do not arouse interest as such, but only in so far as they reveal a more primitive struggle; in the words of Maeterlinck, the purpose of the drama is: 'de faire entendre par dessous les dialogues ordinaires de la raison et des sentiments, le dialogue plus solennel et ininterrompu de l'être et de sa destinée'.[38]

Such a drama requires that intelligence and irony which *is* present in Hauptmann's work,[39] but which has often been overlooked, because it is not consistently present, and because it is balanced by the diametrically opposite tendency: the continued desire, despite all theoretical convictions, to express through his characters a view of life which is not merely relative or predominantly social; to continue to use the drama as a closed, symbolic, even metaphysical form. This ambiguity is among the most important characteristics of the German Naturalist drama: to refer for the last time to two crucial examples: in *Die Weber* and *Hanneles Himmelfahrt* it seems that the author recognized, as a Naturalist, the existence of individuals with a need for religion, which, because of a combination of historical and psychological circumstances, directs them to the Christian religion; and that then, in a thoroughly inconsistent way, he sought to re-establish the absolute validity of their Christian faith. More than any of his contemporaries, and increasingly in his later plays, Hauptmann continues to elevate various individual views, despite their dubious origins, because, we must conclude, he is so deeply impressed by intensity of expression, that he is not disposed to differentiate between the pathological and the mystical.

In a later drama, *Der weiße Heiland* (1920) we can find the lines:

Worte sind verwirrte Sprache.
Schrei ist Klarheit! Schrei ist Wahrheit!
Wahre Lust und wahre Pein!
Wutgeheul und Lustgestöhne
Pressen Götter aus den Seelen.   (II, 1297)

The balance has clearly changed, and it is a change we cannot look back on with much joy; the valuation of the ecstatic and the irrational here seems unconditional —but by the standards of Naturalistic theory the words are still ambiguous. Circumstances *force* the emergence of the 'divine'; 'truth' is not attained by the free activity of the independent spirit, but it is realized under intense pressure; there is a causality which might be held to limit or condition the 'truth' proclaimed, and so even these words can be said to contain evidence of both the impulses which go to make up the style of the German Naturalists as it actually was. This can best be defined in a formula which itself attempts to reconcile opposites: an essay at scientific, analytical understanding, which does not exclude the aim of metaphysical comprehension.

Conclusion

Closely knit artistic movements are not given to longevity. German Naturalism is no exception. The two full seasons of the *Freie Bühne*, 1889–90 and 1890–1, represent the creative peak; but at the same time they signify the beginning of the end, in that Brahm's policies provoked hostility among both the Berlin and the Munich Naturalists. As soon as it became a creative rather than a theoretical-critical movement, German Naturalism was bound to fall apart, for the theorizing which took place in the preceding decade was so extensive, and, in many instances, so contradictory, that no conceivable creative literary movement could have met its demands. Yet even though the practice does not exactly accord with the theory, if we attempt to view both as a whole, it is possible to recognize a certain family likeness. Seen as a whole, German Naturalist theory does not *propose* an extreme and revolutionary kind of literature; and, seen as a whole, the German Naturalist movement does not *provide* an extreme and revolutionary kind of literature. Rather, it combines, often in a perplexing way, such features as the traditionally German distaste for social and political reality, a pronounced nationalism, a distrust of the rational, on the one hand, with a commitment to precise, scientific observation and mimesis, on the other. German Naturalism compromises between inward, German conservatism and outward-looking, European radicalism.

Any development is in the conservative direction. The Naturalists' progressive political aspirations are not sufficiently deep-rooted to overcome one setback; and it takes little (Julius Langbehn!) to capture the enthusiasm of some of them for out-and-out reaction. The same is true of the creative work. Their critical satire is muted, and their comedies are tolerant and feeble; their dramas tend increasingly to compromise in the face of the demands of the traditional theatre, and they tend to revert to the closed, symbolic form of the classical drama. Nevertheless, the German Naturalists asserted the will to experiment, and the will to re-organize the theatre in such a way as to accommodate their experiments. It is here that the Expressionists take over.

Notes to Chapter XI

   [1] G. W. F. Hegel, 'Vorlesungen über die Ästhetik', *Sämtliche Werke* (Jubiläumsausgabe), Stuttgart, 1954, XIV, 496 f.

   [2] Wilhelm Dilthey, 'Die drei Epochen der modernen Ästhetik und ihre heutige Aufgabe' (1892), *Ges. Schriften*, Leipzig–Berlin, 1914, VI, ii, 242–87.

   [3] 'Goethe und die dichterische Phantasie', *Das Erlebnis und die Dichtung* (1877), Leipzig–Berlin, 1922, p. 182.

   [4] Mehring's comments on the various plays are to be found in *Ges. Schriften*, XI, 190, 191, 199, 245.

5 H. Praschek, *Das Verhältnis von Kunsttheorie und Kunstschaffen*, p. 30.

6 *Die naturwissenschaftlichen Grundlagen*, pp. 85–86.

7 Like the brothers Hassenpflug in Hauptmann's novel, *Der Narr in Christo Emanuel Quint*, the Kerns were modelled on Heinrich and Julius Hart. Actors, as well as authors, used this kind of esoteric detail in the impersonations. Rittner is said to have based his interpretation of the role of Hans in *Jugend* on the play's author, Halbe; and Kainz is said to have impersonated Conrad Alberti when playing Bäcker in *Die Weber*.

8 Cf. above, p. 116.

9 *Die Theorie des Romans*, Berlin, 1920, p. 31. See also 'Grundlagen der Unterscheidung von Epik und Dramatik', *Aufbau*, XI (1955), pp. 978–91. Much of the detail in the Naturalist drama is 'epic' in the sense that it was intended for the reading public. Most of the plays of the Naturalist period, including Hauptmann's first four plays, were published before they were performed. See Max Dessoir, 'Eine Erinnerung', *Gerhart Hauptmann und sein Werk*, ed. Ludwig Marcuse, Berlin-Leipzig, 1922, p. 19.

10 On p. 21 (*Ges. Werke*, I) it is three o'clock; by p. 31 the hands of the clock must reach five. See Praschek, op. cit., p. 45.

11 See Hugo von Hofmannsthal, 'Eleonora Duse', *Ges. Werke*, Prosa, I, 71.

12 Cf. Strindberg's complaints about the theatre of the period in the preface to *Miss Julie*.

13 *Gerhart Hauptmann*, pp. 60–61.

14 'Causerien über das Theater', *Ges. Werke*, Ser. 2, VIII, 303–4.

15 *Die Kunst des Dramas*, pp. 94–5.

16 Those who doubt the value of all such deductions might read A. D. Nuttall's 'The Argument about Shakespeare's Characters', *Critical Quarterly*, VII (1965), pp. 107–19.

17 Cf. Gert Mattenklott, *Melancholie in der Dramatik des Sturm und Drang*, Stuttgart, 1968, pp. 139–40. Mattenklott writes of Lenz's *Soldaten*: 'Auch hier verbürgt Sprachlosigkeit noch nicht die reine, individuelle Mitteilung. Denn wie kein anderes Phänomen des Ausdrucks beruht die Pantomime—auf Physisches beschränkt—auf Konvention'.

18 Paul Schlenther, *Gerhart Hauptmann*, Berlin, 1898, p. 78. See also Max Halbe, *Scholle und Schicksal*, pp. 427–8.

19 See above, p. 158.

20 'Schiller; ein Lebensbild für deutsche Arbeiter' (1905), *Ges. Schriften*, X, 91–241; 'Kabale und Liebe' (1909), ibid., pp. 252–8.

21 *Schiller*, Berlin, 1888–92, I, 295–323.

22 'Und Pippa tanzt' (1906), *Ges. Schriften*, XI, 339.

23 'Ibsens Klein Eyolf' (1895), *Ges. Schriften*, XII, 92.

24 Cf. above, p. 35. The Harts themselves provided Mehring with a sitting target; see his review of *Die Weber*, *Ges. Schriften*, XI, 277.

25 For examples of such interpretations see: Thomas Mann, *Gerhart Hauptmann*, Gütersloh, 1953; Guthke and Wolff, 'Das Leid im Werke Gerhart Hauptmanns'; Guthke, 'Hebbel, Hauptmann und die Dialektik in der Idee', *Hebbel Jahrbuch 1961*, Heide in Holst., 1962, pp. 71–77; H. J. Schrimpf, 'Struktur und Metaphysik des sozialen Schauspiels bei Gerhart Hauptmann', *Literatur und Gesellschaft vom 19ten ins 20ste Jahrhundert. Festgabe für Benno von Wiese*, Bonn, 1963, pp. 274–308.

26 'Die Jugendgeschichte Hegels', *Ges. Schriften*, IV, 219. See also Karl Löwith, *Von Hegel zu Nietzsche*, Stuttgart, 1953³, p. 138.

[27] Schlaf, 'Vom intimen Drama', *Neuland*, I (1896–7), p. 35.

[28] Cf. above, p. 157.

[29] Here, as elsewhere, Naturalist drama stands at the opposite pole to Greek tragedy, which offers a purposeful—even a tendentious—explanation of an otherwise incomprehensible myth: 'Die Umbildung der Sage nämlich geschieht nicht auf der Suche nach tragischen Konstellationen, sondern in der Ausprägung einer Tendenz', Walter Benjamin, *Ursprung des deutschen Trauerspiels* (1928), Frankfurt, a.M., 1969, p. 108.

[30] Cf. Szondi, *Theorie des modernen Dramas*, pp. 52–61; Schrimpf, 'Struktur und Metaphysik', pp. 285–95.

[31] Kaberlin, 'Eine Fortentwicklung des deutschen Dramas', *Das Magazin für die Literatur des In- und Auslandes*, LVIII (1889), pp. 696–700. For a slightly fuller discussion of this, see: John Osborne, 'Naturalism and the dramaturgy of the open drama', *German Life and Letters*, XXIII (1969–70), pp. 119–28.

[32] 'Neurealistische Novellen', *Das Magazin etc.*, LVIII, 713.

[33] Cf. above, p. 157.

[34] Cf. G. Lukács, 'Hauptmanns Weg', *Die Schaubühne*, VII (1911), p. 253: 'seine tragischen Helden wirken wie gehetzte Tiere: tief ergreifend in ihrer dumpfen Verzweiflung, können sie doch nicht symbolische Gestaltungen unserer Verstrickung und unseres Gehetztseins werden'.

[35] Ibid.

[36] 'Die Menschen in Ibsens Dramen', *Ges. Werke*, Prosa I, p. 88.

[37] As Szondi points out, the Naturalists tended to find their active characters among the lower classes: 'Das neue Drama fand [in den unteren Schichten] . . . Menschen, deren Willenskraft ungebrochen war; die sich für eine Tat, zu der ihre Leidenschaft sie trieb, mit ihrem ganzen Wesen einsetzen konnten' (*Theorie des modernen Dramas*, p. 71). Cf. Fontane's comments on the activity of the working classes, quoted above, p. 59.

[38] *Le trésor des humbles*, Paris, 1896, p. 181.

[39] Schrimpf, 'Struktur und Metaphysik', p. 197.

Appendix I

Plays presented by the Freie Bühne

1889
29. ix. Ibsen—*Gespenster*
28. x. Hauptmann—*Vor Sonnenaufgang*
17. xi. H. and J. de Goncourt—*Henriette Maréchal*
15. xii. Björnson—*Ein Handschuh*

1890
26. i. Tolstoi—*Die Macht der Finsternis*
2. iii. Anzengruber—*Das vierte Gebot*
7. iv. Holz and Schlaf—*Die Familie Selicke*, Alexander Kjelland, *Auf dem Heimwege*
4. v. Fitger—*Von Gottes Gnaden*
1. vi. Hauptmann—*Das Friedensfest*
12. x. Strindberg—*Der Vater*
30. xi. Hartleben—*Angele*, Marie von Ebner-Eschenbach—*Ohne Liebe*

1891
11. i. Hauptmann—*Einsame Menschen*
15. ii. Henri Becque—*Die Raben*
15. iii. Anzengruber—*Der Doppelselbstmord*
3. v. Zola—*Thérèse Raquin*

1892
3. iv. Strindberg—*Fräulein Julie*

1893
26. ii. Hauptmann—*Die Weber*
30. iii. Ernst Rosmer—*Dämmerung*

1895
12. v. Hirschfeld—*Die Mütter*

1897
11. iv. Emil Marriot—*Gretes Glück*, Ebner-Eschenbach—*Am Ende*

1898
15. v. Ernst Hardt—*Tote Zeit*, Hofmannsthal—*Die Frau am Fenster*

1899
12. xi. Eduard von Keyserling—*Ein Frühlingsopfer*

1901
19. v. Ernst Rosmer—*Mutter Maria*

Appendix II

Plays presented by the Volksbühnen, 1890–5

Die Freie Volksbühne, 1890–2 (Bruno Wille):

1890
Ibsen—*Stützen der Gesellschaft*
Hauptmann—*Vor Sonnenaufgang*
Ibsen—*Der Volksfeind*
Heinrich Hart—*Tul und Nahila* (a reading)

1891
Schiller—*Kabale und Liebe*
Sudermann—*Die Ehre*
Pissemski—*Der Leibeigene*
Fulda—*Das verlorene Paradies*
Reuter—*Kein Hüsung*
Schiller—*Die Räuber*
Anzengruber—*Der Doppelselbstmord*
Ibsen—*Bund der Jugend*
Hebbel—*Maria Magdalena*
Gogol—*Der Revisor*

1892
Halbe—*Eisgang*
Anzengruber—*Der Pfarrer von Kirchfeld*
Zola—*Thérèse Raquin*
Fulda—*Die Sklavin*
Ibsen—*Gespenster*
Ludwig—*Der Erbförster*
Ibsen—*Nora*

1892–5 (Franz Mehring):

(a) Plays from the repertoire of the *Lessingtheater*:
Anzengruber—*Das vierte Gebot, Der Meineidbauer, Die Kreuzelschreiber*
Sudermann—*Die Ehre, Heimat, Sodoms Ende*
Lessing—*Nathan der Weise, Emilia Galotti*

Grillparzer—*Der Traum ein Leben*
Kleist—*Der zerbrochene Krug*
Augier—*Die arme Löwin*
Blumenthal and Kadelburg—*Großstadtluft*
Björnson—*Fallissement*
Ibsen—*Stützen der Gesellschaft*

(b) Plays of the society's own choice:

H. Faber—*Der freie Wille*
Goethe—*Egmont*
Calderon—*Der Richter von Zalamea*
Schiller—*Kabale und Liebe*
Molière—*Der Geizige*
Verga—*Sizilianische Bauernehre*
P. Bader—*Andere Zeiten*
Hauptmann—*Die Weber*
Mellesville and Duveyrier—*Michel Perrin*
Edgreen and Leffler—*Wie man wohltut*
Held—*Ein Fest auf der Bastille*
Hauptmann—*Der Biberpelz*
Heyse—*Ehrenschulden*
Westenberger and Croissant—*Hildegard Scholl*
Reuter, *Kein Hüsung*
Augier, *Der Pelikan*

Die Neue Freie Volksbühne, 1893–5 (Bruno Wille):

Goethe—*Faust I*
Wolzogen—*Das Lumpengesindel*
Anzengruber—*Der G'wissenswurm*
Reuter—*Kein Hüsung*
Tolstoi—*Die Macht der Finsternis*
F. Lange—*Der Nächste*
Anzengruber—*Der Meineidbauer*
Molière—*Tartüff*
Hartleben—*Die Erziehung zur Ehe*

Hauptmann—*Die Weber*
Ostrowski—*Gewitter*
Halbe—*Jugend*
Anzengruber—*Die Kreuzelschreiber*
Ibsen—*Der Volksfeind*
Lessing—*Emilia Galotti*
Erckmann-Chatrian—*Der Rautzan*
Guinon and Dénier—*Die Dummen*
Freytag—*Die Journalisten*

Anzengruber—*Das vierte Gebot*
Hauptmann—*Einsame Menschen*
Becque—*Die Raben*
O. Vischer—*Schlimme Saat*
Benedix—*Die zärtlichen Verwandten*
Meyer-Förster—*Unsichtbare Ketten*
L'Arronge—*Mein Leopold*
A. Agrell—*Einsam*
Schiller—*Don Karlos*

Select bibliography

Includes those works on which I have drawn directly, plus a few others, which I have found to be of particular interest. For further material I refer readers to an indispensable guide for the serious student of the German Naturalist Drama: Sigfrid Hoefert, *Das Drama des Naturalismus*, Stuttgart, 1969.

(a) Primary sources:

Alberti, Conrad, *Brot ! Ein soziales Schauspiel in fünf Akten*, Leipzig, 1888.
Anzengruber, Ludwig, *Sämtliche Werke*, ed. R. Latzke und O. Rommel, Wien–Leipzig, 1920–8, 15 Bde.
Arent, Wilhelm (ed.), *Moderne Dichtercharaktere*, Leipzig, 1885.
Bahr, Hermann, *Die neuen Menschen*, Zürich, 1887.
Bleibtreu, Karl, *Dramatische Werke*, Leipzig, 1889, 3 Bde.
Dehmel, Richard, *Der Mitmensch* (1895), Berlin, 1909.
Dreyer, Max, *Winterschlaf* (1894), Stuttgart–Leipzig, 1904.
Ernst, Otto, *Jugend von Heute. Eine deutsche Komödie in vier Akten* (1899), Hamburg, 1900.
Ernst, Paul, *Lumpenbagasch—Im Chambre Separée. Zwei Schauspiele von Paul Ernst*, Berlin—Paris, n.d. (1898).
Flaischlen, Cäsar, *Toni Stürmer* (1891), Berlin, 1897.
—*Martin Lehnhardt* (1894), Berlin, 1910.
Fulda, Ludwig, *Das verlorene Paradies*, Stuttgart, 1892.
—*Die Kameraden*, Stuttgart, 1895.
Halbe, Max, *Gesammelte Werke*, München, 1917–23, 7 Bde.
Hardt, Ernst, *Tote Zeit*, Berlin, 1898.
Hart, Heinrich, *Gesammelte Werke*, ed. Julius Hart, Berlin, 1907, 4 Bde.
Hartleben, Otto Erich, *Ausgewählte Werke*, Berlin, 1909, 3 Bde.
Hauptmann, Carl, *Marianne*, Berlin, 1894.
Hauptmann, Gerhart, *Sämtliche Werke* (Centenar-Ausgabe), ed. H.-E. Haß, Frankfurt a.M.—Berlin, 1962– , 10 Bde.
Held, Franz, *Ein Fest auf der Bastille*, Berlin, 1889.
Hirschfeld, Georg, *Die Mütter*, Berlin, 1895.
—*Pauline*, Berlin, 1899.
Holmsen, Bjarne P., (see Holz, and Schlaf).
Holz, Arno, *Das Werk*, ed. H. W. Fischer, Berlin, 1924–5, 10 Bde.
Holz and Jerschke, Oskar, *Traumulus*, München, 1905.
Holz and Schlaf, Johannes, *Papa Hamlet*, Leipzig, 1889.
—*Die Familie Selicke*, Berlin, 1890.
—*Neue Gleise*, Berlin, 1892.
Ibsen, Henrik, *The Oxford Ibsen*, ed. J. W. McFarlane, London, 1961– .

Langmann, Philipp, *Bartel Turaser*, Leipzig, 1897.
Rittner, Rudolph, *Narrenglanz*, Berlin, 1906.
Rosmer, Ernst (= Else Bernstein), *Dämmerung, Freie Bühne*, IV, (1893).
Schlaf, Johannes, *Meister Oelze* Berlin, 1892.
—*Meister Oelze*, München–Leipzig, 1909².
—*Die Feindlichen*, Minden, 1899.
Sudermann, Hermann, *Dramatische Werke*, Stuttgart, 1923, 6 Bde.
Wedekind, Frank, *Gesammelte Werke*, ed. A. Kutscher und J. Friedenthal, München, 1920–1, 9 Bde.
Weigand, Wilhelm, *Der Vater*, München, 1894.
Wolzogen, Ernst von, *Das Lumpengesindel*, Berlin, 1892.
Zola, Emile, *Les Œuvres complètes*, ed. M. le Blond, Paris, 1927–9, 50 vols.

(b) Literary periodicals of the Naturalist period:

Das Magazin für die Literatur des In- und Auslandes, Berlin, 1832–1915.
Die Gegenwart, Berlin, 1872–1930.
Deutsche Rundschau, Berlin, 1874– .
Kritische Waffengänge, Leipzig, 1882–4.
Die Gesellschaft, München, 1885–1902.
Berliner Monatshefte, Minden–Leipzig, 1885.
Der Kunstwart, München, 1887–1932.
Kritisches Jahrbuch, Hamburg, 1889–90.
Deutschland, Glogau, 1889–90.
Freie Bühne für modernes Leben (*Die neue Rundschau*), Berlin, 1890– .

(c) Criticism, theory, and background:

Alexander, N. E., *Studien zum Stilwandel im dramatischen Werk Gerhart Hauptmanns*, Stuttgart, 1964.
Bab, Julius, 'Gerhart Hauptmann als Regisseur', *Gerhart-Hauptmann-Jahrbuch*, N.F. I (1948), pp. 147–53.
Bahr, Hermann, *Zur Überwindung des Naturalismus*, ed. G. Wunberg, Stuttgart, 1968.
Batley, E. M., 'Functional Idealism in Gerhart Hauptmann's "Einsame Menschen" ', *German Life and Letters*, XXIII (1969–70), pp. 243–54.
Behl, C. F. W., *Zwiesprache mit Gerhart Hauptmann*, München, 1948.
—*Gerhart Hauptmann. Überblick über sein Leben und Werk*, Würzburg, 1956.
—and Voigt, F. A., *Chronik von Gerhart Hauptmanns Leben und Schaffen*, München, 1957.
Berg, Leo, *Der Naturalismus*, München, 1892.
—*Der Übermensch in der modernen Literatur*, Paris–Leipzig–München, 1897.
Berger, P., *Gerhart Hauptmanns Ratten. Interpretation eines Dramas*, Winterthur, 1961.
Bergson, Henri, *Le Rire. Essai sur la signification du comique* (1912), Paris, 1920.
Bleibtreu, Karl, *Revolution der Literatur*, Leipzig, 1886.
Böckmann, P., 'Der Naturalismus Gerhart Hauptmanns' *Gestaltprobleme der Dichtung. Festschrift für Günther Müller*, Bonn, 1957, pp. 239–58.
Bölsche, Wilhelm, *Die naturwissenschaftlichen Grundlagen der Poesie*, Leipzig, 1887.
—*Hinter der Weltstadt*, Leipzig, 1901.

Boulby, Mark, 'Optimism and Pessimism in German Naturalist writers,' Ph.D. Diss., Leeds, 1951, 2 vols.

Brahm, Otto, *Heinrich von Kleist*, Berlin, 1884.

—'Henrik Ibsen', *Deutsche Rundschau*, XLIX (1886), pp. 193–220.

—*Schiller*, Berlin, 1888–92, 2 Bde.

—*Kritische Schriften*, ed. P. Schlenther, Berlin, 1913–15, 2 Bde.

—*Briefe und Erinnerungen*, ed. G. Hirschfeld, Berlin, 1924.

—*Theater–Dramatiker–Schauspieler*, ed. H. Fetting, Berlin, 1961.

Brandes, Georg, 'Emil Zola', *Deutsche Rundschau*, LIV (1888), pp. 27–45.

Brecht, Bert., *Theaterarbeit. 6 Aufführungen des Berliner Ensembles*, ed. Berliner Ensemble, Helene Weigel, Dresden, 1952.

—*Schriften zum Theater*, ed. S. Unseld, Frankfurt a.M., 1964, Bd VI.

Brinkmann, Richard, *Wirklichkeit und Illusion*, Tübingen, 1957.

Bronnen, Arnolt, *Vatermord*, Berlin, 1925.

Bulthaupt, Heinrich, *Dramaturgie des Schauspiels*, IV, Ibsen—Hauptmann, Oldenburg-Leipzig, 1901.

Butzlaff, W., 'Die Enthüllungstechnik in Hauptmanns "Rose Bernd",' *Der Deutschunterricht*, XIII (1961), H.4, pp. 59–70.

Chapiro, Josef, *Gespräche mit Hauptmann*, Berlin, 1932.

Conrad, Michael Georg, *Von Emil Zola bis Gerhart Hauptmann*, Leipzig, 1902.

Demetz, Peter, *Marx, Engels und die Dichter*, Stuttgart, 1959.

Demler, Leopold, *Arno Holz. Kunst und Natur*, Wien, 1938.

Dilthey, Wilhelm, 'Die drei Epochen der modernen Ästhetik und ihre heutige Aufgabe' (1892), *Gesammelte Schriften*, Leipzig-Berlin, 1914, VI, ii, 242–87.

Döblin, Alfred, 'Der Geist des naturalistischen Zeitalters' *Die neue Rundschau*, XXXV (1924), pp. 1275–93.

Doucet, F., *L'esthétique de Zola et son application à la critique*, Paris, 1930.

Emrich, Wilhelm, *Protest und Verheißung*, Frankfurt a.M., 1960.

Flaischlen, Cäsar, *Otto Erich Hartleben*, Berlin, 1896.

Fontane, Theodor, *Gesammelte Werke*, Berlin, 1904–10.

Garten, H. F., *Gerhart Hauptmann*, Cambridge, 1954.

George, D. E. R., *Henrik Ibsen in Deutschland. Rezeption und Revision*, Göttingen, 1968.

Glaß, Emil, *Die Psychologie und Weltanschauung in Gerhart Hauptmanns 'Fuhrmann Henschel'*, Phil. Diss., Erlangen, 1933.

Gooch, G. P., *History and Historians in the 19th Century*, London, 1920.

Grimm, Reinhold, 'Pyramide und Karussell', *Strukturen*, Göttingen, 1963, pp. 8–43.

Grothe, W., 'Die neue Rundschau des Verlags S. Fischer', *Börsenblatt für den deutschen Buchhandel*, XVII (1962), pp. 2171–266.

Grube, Max, *Geschichte der Meininger*, Stuttgart, 1926.

Guthke, K. S., 'Probleme neuerer Hauptmannforschung', *Göttingsche Gelehrte Anzeigen*, CCXIV (1960), pp. 84–107.

—*Geschichte und Poetik der deutschen Tragikomödie*, Göttingen, 1961.

—*Gerhart Hauptmann: Weltbild im Werk*, Göttingen, 1961.

—'Hebbel, Hauptmann und die Dialektik in der Idee', *Hebbel Jahrbuch* (1961), Heide in Holst., 1962, pp. 71–77.

—'Gerhart Hauptmanns Menschenbild in der "Familienkatastrophe" Das Friedensfest', *Germanisch-Romanische Monatsschrift*, XII (1962), pp. 39–50.

—and H. M. Wolff, 'Das Leid im Werke Gerhart Hauptmanns', *University of California Publications in Modern Philology*, XLIX, Berkeley, 1958.

Halbe, Max, *Scholle und Schicksal*, München, 1933.

—*Jahrhundertwende*, Danzig, 1935.

Hamann, Richard and Hermand, Jost, *Deutsche Kunst und Kultur von der Gründerzeit bis zum Expressionismus*, I, *Gründerzeit*, Berlin, 1965; II, *Naturalismus*, Berlin, 1959.

Hanstein, Adalbert von, *Das jüngste Deutschland* (1901), Leipzig, 1905.

Hartleben, Otto Erich, *Briefe an Freunde*, Berlin, 1912.

Haß, Hans-Egon, 'Zur Kunstanschauung Gerhart Hauptmanns', *Jahrhundertfeier für Gerhart Hauptmann, 15–21 November, 1962*, Köln, 1962.

Hauptmann, Carl, *Leben mit Freunden. Gesammelte Briefe*, Berlin, 1928.

Hauptmann, Gerhart, *Die Weber*, ed. M. Boulby, London, 1962.

—*Die Weber, Dichtung und Wirklichkeit*, ed. H. Schwab-Felisch, Frankfurt a.M.-Berlin, 1963.

—*Die Kunst des Dramas*, zusammengestellt von Martin Machatzke, Frankfurt, a.M.-Berlin, 1963.

—'Das zweite Vierteljahrhundert', *Die großen Beichten*, Frankfurt a.M., 1966.

Henze, H., *Otto Brahm und das Deutsche Theater in Berlin*, Berlin, 1930.

Hermand, Jost, 'Zur Literatur der Gründerzeit', *Deutsche Vierteljahrsschrift*, XLI (1967), pp. 202–31; now also in: Hermand, *Von Mainz bis Weimar, 1793–1919: Studien zur deutschen Literatur*, Stuttgart, 1969, pp. 211–49.

Heuser, F. W. J., *Gerhart Hauptmann*, Tübingen, 1961.

Heynen, Walter (ed.), *Mit Gerhart Hauptmann*, Berlin, 1922.

Hoefert, Sigfrid, 'Emile Zola dans la critique d'Otto Brahm', *Les cahiers naturalistes*, XXX (1965), pp. 145–52.

Hofmannsthal, Hugo von, *Gesammelte Werke*, Prosa I and II, Frankfurt a.M.-Berlin, 1956.

Holz, Arno, *Briefe. Eine Auswahl*, ed. Anita Holz und Max Wagner, München, 1949.

Hortenbach, Jenny C., *Freiheitsstreben und Destruktivität. Frauen in den Dramen August Strindbergs und Gerhart Hauptmanns*, Oslo–Bergen–Tromsö, 1965.

Hughes, Henry Stuart, *Consciousness and Society. The re-orientation of European social thought. 1890–1930*, London, 1959.

Kaiser, Gerhard, 'Die Tragikomödien Gerhart Hauptmanns, *Festschrift für Klaus Ziegler*, Tübingen, 1968, pp. 269–89.

Kayser, Wolfgang, 'Zur Dramaturgie des naturalistischen Schauspiels' *Die Vortragsreise*, Bern, 1958, pp. 214–29.

Kerr, Alfred, *Die Welt im Drama*, Berlin, 1917.

Klotz, Volker, *Offene und geschlossene Form im Drama*, München, 1960.

König, René, *Die naturalistische Ästhetik in Frankreich und ihre Auflösung*, Borna–Leipzig, 1931.

Kollwitz, Käthe, *Aus meinem Leben*, München, 1957.

Kraus, Karl, 'Von Humor und Lyrik' (1921), *Die Sprache*, ed. H. W. Fischer, München, 1954, pp. 201–13,

Lamprecht, Karl, *Alte und neue Richtungen in der Geschichtswissenschaft*, Berlin, 1896.

—*Deutsche Geschichte*. 1er Ergänzungsband, Berlin, 1902.

Landauer, Gustav, 'Gerhart Hauptmann', *Die neue Zeit*, X (1891–2), pp. 612–21.

Langbehn, A. J., *Rembrandt als Erzieher*, Leipzig, 1890.[2]

Lindau, Paul, *Dramaturgische Blätter*, Stuttgart–Leipzig, 1877.

Lindau, Paul, *Nur Erinnerungen*, Stuttgart–Berlin, 1917–19.

Löwith, Karl, *Von Hegel zu Nietzsche*, Stuttgart, 1953.[3]

Lukàcs, Georg, 'Das Problem des untragischen Dramas', *Die Schaubühne*, VII (1911), pp. 231–4.

—'Hauptmanns Weg', ibid., pp. 253–5.

—*Die Theorie des Romans*, Berlin, 1920.

—*Deutsche Literatur im Zeitalter des Imperialismus*, Berlin, 1947.

—'Grundlagen der Scheidung von Epik und Dramatik', *Aufbau*, XI (1955), pp. 978–91.

Maeterlinck, Maurice, *Le trésor des Humbles*, Paris, 1896.

Mann, Heinrich, *Im Schlaraffenland*, Leipzig, n.d. (1917).

Mann, Thomas, *Gerhart Hauptmann*, Gütersloh, 1953.

Marcuse, Ludwig (ed.), *Gerhart Hauptmann und sein Werk*, Berlin–Leipzig, 1922.

Martersteig, Max, *Das deutsche Theater im 19ten Jahrhundert*, Leipzig, 1924.[2]

Martini, Fritz, 'Soziale Thematik und Formwandlungen des Dramas', *Der Deutschunterricht*, V (1953), pp. 73–100.

—*Das Wagnis der Sprache*, Stuttgart, 1954.

—*Deutsche Literatur im bürgerlichen Realismus*, Stuttgart, 1962.

Matthews, J. H., *Les deux Zola ; science et personnalité dans l'expression*, Paris, 1957.

May, Kurt, 'Die Weber', *Das deutsche Drama*, ed. Benno von Wiese, Wiesbaden, 1958, II, 157–65.

Mayer, Hans, 'Gerhart Hauptmann und die Mitte', *Von Lessing bis Thomas Mann*, Pfullingen, 1959.

McFarlane, J. W., 'Hauptmann, Ibsen and the concept of Naturalism', *Hauptmann. Centenary Lectures*, ed. K. G. Knight and F. Norman, London, 1964, pp. 31–60.

McInnes, Edward, 'The domestic dramas of Gerhart Hauptmann. Tragedy or Sentimental Pathos ?', *German Life and Letters*, XX (1966–7), pp. 53–60.

Mehring, Franz, *Gesammelte Schriften*, ed. Höhle, Koch, Schleifstein, Berlin, 1960–3, 12 Bde.

Mendelssohn, Peter de, 'Die Geschichte der "Neuen Rundschau"', *Die neue Rundschau*, LXXX (1969), pp. 597–615.

Meyer, R. M., *Die deutsche Literatur des 19ten Jahrhunderts. Das 19te Jahrhundert in Deutschlands Entwicklung*, ed. P. Schlenther, Bd 3, Berlin, 1900.

Moore, C. H., 'A Hearing on "Germinal" and "Die Weber"', *Germanic Review*, XXXIII (1958), pp. 30–40.

Münchow, Ursula, *Deutscher Naturalismus*, Berlin, 1968.

Musiol, Karl, 'Carl Hauptmann und Josepha Kodis', *Deutsche Vierteljahrsschrift*, XXXVI (1960), pp. 257–63.

Nestriepke, Siegfried, *Geschichte der Volksbühne Berlins, I, 1890–1914*, Berlin, 1930.

Nordau, Max, *Die konventionellen Lügen der Kulturmenschheit*, Leipzig, 1883.

Nuttall, A. D., 'The argument about Shakespeare's characters', *Critical Quarterly*, VII (1965), pp. 107–19.

Osborne, John, 'Naturalism and the dramaturgy of the open drama', *German Life and Letters*, XXIII (1969–70), pp. 119–28.

Pfanner, Helmut F., 'Deutungsprobleme in Gerhart Hauptmanns "Michael Kramer"', *Monatshefte*, LXII (1970), pp. 45–54.

Praschek, Helmut, *Das Verhältnis von Kunsttheorie und Kunstschaffen im Bereich der deutschen naturalistischen Dramatik*, Phil. Diss., Greifswald, 1957.

—'Zum Zerfall des naturalistischen Stils', *Worte und Werte. Festschrift für Bruno Markwardt*, Berlin, 1961, pp. 315–21.

Rasch, Wolfdietrich, 'Zur dramatischen Dichtung des jungen Gerhart Hauptmanns' *Festschrift für F. R. Schröder*, Heidelberg, 1959, pp. 241–53.

Reichart, W. A., 'Grundbegriffe im dramatischen Schaffen Gerhart Hauptmanns', *PMLA*, LXXXII (1967), pp. 142–51.

Reichert, H. W., 'Hauptmann's Frau Wolff and Brecht's Mother Courage', *German Quarterly*, XXXIV (1961), pp. 439–48.

Ritter, Gerhard A., 'Die Arbeiterbewegung im wilhelminischen Reich', *Studien zur europäischen Geschichte aus dem Friedrich-Meinecke Institut der Freien Universität Berlin*, III, Berlin, 1959.

Röhl, J. C. G., *Germany without Bismarck: the crisis of government in the 2nd Reich*, London, 1967.

Root, Winthrop H., *German Criticism of Zola*, New York, 1931.

Ruprecht, Erich, *Literarische Manifeste des Naturalismus. 1880–1892*, Stuttgart, 1962.

Schickling, Dieter, *Interpretationen und Studien zur Entwicklung und geistesgeschichtlichen Stellung des Werkes von Arno Holz*, Phil. Diss., Tübingen, 1965.

Schlaf, Johannes, *Maurice Maeterlinck*, Berlin, 1906.

—'Die Freie Bühne und die Entstehung des naturalistischen Dramas' *Der Greif*, I (1913–14), i, 403–13, 480–89, ii, 38–48.

Schlawe, Fritz, *Literarische Zeitschriften, 1885–1910*, Stuttgart, 1961.

Schlenther, Paul, *Wozu der Lärm? Genesis der Freien Bühne*, Berlin, 1889.

—*Gerhart Hauptmann*, Berlin, 1898.

—*Theater im 19ten Jahrhundert*, ed. H. Knudsen, Berlin, 1930.

Schley, Gernot, *Die Freie Bühne in Berlin*, Berlin, 1967.

Schmoller, Gustav, 'Die Entwicklung und die Krisis der deutschen Weberei im 19ten Jahrhundert', *Deutsche Zeit- und Streitfragen*, II, Berlin, 1873.

Schrimpf, H. J., 'Rose Bernd', *Das deutsche Drama*, ed. Benno von Wiese, Wiesbaden, 1958, II, 166–85.

—'Struktur und Metaphysik des sozialen Schauspiels bei Gerhart Hauptmann', *Literatur und Gesellschaft vom 19ten ins 20ste Jahrhundert. Festgabe für Benno von Wiese*, Bonn, 1963, pp. 274–308.

—'Das unerreichte Soziale: die Komödien Gerhart Hauptmanns "Der Biberpelz" und "Der rote Hahn"', *Das deutsche Lustspiel*, ed. Hans Steffen, Göttingen, 1969, II, 26–60.

Schroeder, P., 'Arno Holz's "Die Kunst" and the problem of "Isms"', *Modern Language Notes*, LXVI (1951), pp. 217–24.

Schultze, H.-A., *Der Schauspieler Rudolf Rittner (1869–1943), ein Wegbereiter Gerhart Hauptmanns auf dem Theater*, Phil. Diss., Berlin, 1961.

Seidlin, Oskar, 'Otto Brahm', *German Quarterly*, XXXVI, (1963), pp. 131–40.

—'Urmythos irgendwo in Berlin', *Deutsche Vierteljahrsschrift*, XLIII (1969), pp. 126–46.

Sengle, Friedrich, 'Wunschbild Land und Schreckbild Stadt', *Studium generale*, XVI (1963), pp. 619–30.

Shaw, Leroy R., 'Witness of Deceit: Gerhart Hauptmann as critic of Society', *University of California Publications in Modern Philology*, L, Berkely, 1958.

Shepherd, W. A. G., *Social Conscience and Messianic Vision. A study in the problems of Gerhart Hauptmann's individualism*, Ph.D. Diss., Edinburgh, 1962.

Sinden, Margaret, *Gerhart Hauptmann. The Prose Plays*, Toronto–London, 1957.

—'Marianne and Einsame Menschen', *Monatshefte*, LIV (1962), pp. 311–17.

Soergel, Albert, *Dichtung und Dichter der Zeit*, I, Leipzig, 1911.

—and Hohoff, Curt, *Dichtung und Dichter der Zeit*, I (Neubearbeitung), Düsseldorf, 1961.

Sokel, W. H., 'Dialogführung und Dialog im expressionistischen Drama', *Aspekte des Expressionismus*, ed. W. Paulsen, Heidelberg, 1968.

Sorge, Reinhard Johannes, *Der Bettler, Eine dramatische Sendung*, Berlin, 1912.

Spitteler, Carl, 'Die Familie Selicke', *Gesammelte Werke*, Zürich, 1950, IX, 331–9.

Steiger, Edgar, *Das Werden des neuen Dramas*, Berlin, 1898, 2 Bde.

Stern, Fritz, *The Politics of Cultural Despair*, Berkeley–Los Angeles, 1961.

Stern, J. P., *Re-interpretations. Seven studies in nineteenth-century German literature*, London, 1964.

Schwerte, Hans, 'Deutsche Literatur im wilhelminischen Zeitalter', *Wirkendes Wort*, XIV (1964), pp. 254–70.

Stanislavsky, Constantin, *My Life in Art*, London, 1962.

Szondi, Peter, *Theorie des modernen Dramas*, Frankfurt a.M., 1959.

Tank, Kurt Lothar, *Gerhart Hauptmann in Selbstzeugnissen und Bilddokumenten*, Hamburg, 1959.

Toller, Ernst, *Die Maschinenstürmer*, Leipzig, 1922.

Trilling, Lionel, 'The morality of inertia', *A Gathering of Fugitives*, London, 1957, pp. 31–40.

Turner, D., 'Die Familie Selicke and the drama of Naturalism', *Periods in German Literature, Texts and Contexts*, II, ed. J. M. Ritchie, London, 1969, pp. 193–219.

Voigt, F. A., *Hauptmann Studien*, Breslau, 1936.

—'Grundfragen der Gerhart-Hauptmann-Forschung', *Germanisch-Romanische Monatsschrift*, XXVII (1949), pp. 271–86.

Volkelt, Johannes, *Ästhetische Zeitfragen*, München, 1895.

Wais, Kurt, 'Zur Auswirkung des französischen naturalistischen Romans in Deutschland', *An den Grenzen der Nationalliteraturen*, Berlin, 1958, pp. 215–36.

Weber, Max, *Schriften zur theoretischen Soziologie*, Frankfurt a.M., 1947.

Weno, Joachim, 'Der Theaterstil des Naturalismus,' Phil. Diss., Berlin, 1951.

Wiese, Benno von, 'Wirklichkeit und Drama in Gerhart Hauptmanns Tragikomödie "Die Ratten"', *Jahrbuch der deutschen Schiller- Gesellschaft*, VI (1962), pp. 311–25.

Wille, Bruno, *Philosophie der Befreiung durch das reine Mittel*, Berlin, 1894.

Wolff, Wilhelm, 'Das Elend und der Aufruhr in Schlesien', *Deutsches Bürgerbuch für 1845*, ed. H. Püttmann, Darmstadt, 1845.

Wölfflin, Heinrich, *Kunstgeschichtliche Grundbegriffe*, München, 1915.

Wunberg, G., 'Utopie und fin de siècle', *Deutsche Vierteljahrsschrift*, XLIII (1969), pp. 685–706.

Zander, Rosmarie, *Der junge Gerhart Hauptmann und Henrik Ibsen*, Limburg, 1947.

Zeller, Bernhard (ed.), *Gerhart Hauptmann. Leben und Werk. Gedächtnisausstellung des deutschen Literaturarchivs zum 100sten Geburtstag des Dichters im Schiller National-museum Marbach a.N., Katalog*, Stuttgart, 1962.

Ziegelschmidt, A., 'Gerhart Hauptmanns Ikarier', *Germanic Review*, XIII (1938), pp. 32–39.

Zimmermann, Alfred, *Blüthe und Verfall des Leinengewerbes in Schlesien*, Breslau, 1885.

Index